Beck-Wirtschaftsberater

Leadership in Professional Conversation

dtv

Beck-Wirtschaftsberater

Leadership in Professional Conversation

Translation of “Professionelle Gesprächsführung”

By Christian-Rainer Weisbach
and Petra Sonne-Neubacher

Deutscher Taschenbuch Verlag

Im Internet:

dtv.de

beck.de

Originalausgabe
Deutscher Taschenbuch Verlag GmbH & Co. KG,
Friedrichstraße 1a, 80801 München

Druck und Bindung: Druckerei C. H. Beck, Nördlingen
(Adresse der Druckerei: Wilhelmstraße 9, 80801 München)
Satz: Fotosatz Otto Gutfreund GmbH, Darmstadt
Umschlaggestaltung: Agentur 42 (Fuhr & Partner), Mainz
ISBN 3 423 50879 5 (dtv)
ISBN 3 406 52494 X (C. H. Beck)

Prologue

This book is about how you can achieve your goals by means of professional communication.

You will learn how to positively influence both private and business relationships by **leading** conversations. For this, you may understand language as a tool, which offers a wide range of opportunities. And you will soon find how powerful an instrument it can be.

One prerequisite for long-lasting success is to treat your dialogue partner with respect and regard and to offer him the chance to gain equal benefits. Therefore, this book deals with how you can better understand the other's needs.

As helpful as tricks and panaceas may be in other areas, so ineffective are they when people are concerned. What is good for one may not be good for the other.

In each situation, you will be able to observe, if your communication behaviour is helpful or not. When you understand the other

person's reactions also as a kind of feedback, you can draw conclusions, and in consequence adapt your behaviour.

In this way, clarity about one's goals in combination with orientation towards the dialogue partner will lead to communication success.

Christian-Rainer Weisbach Petra Sonne-Neubacher

www.professionelle-gespraechsfuehrung.com

Content

Prologue V

1. From Efficiency to Effectiveness 1
2. Recognising Your Own Conversational Manner 19
3. Four Ways of Listening 39
4. Body Language 63
5. Guidance and Regard 79
6. Resistance with the Dialogue Partner 101
7. Transactional Analysis and Successful Communication . 119
8. Conversation Killers 135
9. Conversation Savers 161
10. Four Ways to React 187
11. From Cause Analysis to Purpose Finding 215
12. Behaviour is Goal-Oriented 233
13. To Take Someone at His Word 251
14. From Persuasion to Conviction 267
15. Delivering Unpleasant Messages 293
16. Chances in a Complaint 321
17. Positive Talking 333
18. Talking from the Other's Angle 353
19. The Art of Causing Change 379
20. Deductive Communication 397

Epilogue 413

1. From Efficiency to Effectiveness

"Another book on communication!" one or the other reader may think when he looks at the title. In my seminars I am often confronted with doubts and disapproval when employees have been selected to undergo a training course to improve their communication skill. Understandably, I am often asked, "Why now, all of a sudden?" Our jobs permanently involve communication, and we know all too well, which role communication plays in assessments, delegation, setting objectives, planning, co-ordination, and motivation.

Indeed, it is worth considering that something so central (and I am not only referring to the importance but also to the amount of time consumed)

- is so rarely developed systematically by parents and the school system,
- is not covered in a school subject such as "communication education",
- is more or less left to chance in determining the quality of our professional communication,
- as our most important asset, is probably in an area that has never been "trained" systematically.

These may sound like buzzwords. One might object, claiming that communication is not everything and has been over-emphasised in recent years.

I still remember the objections of an established executive:

"What is the use of communicative competence? It's the numbers I must get right! In my eyes someone who places social questions before operational realities is a mollycoddle, though you mustn't say this aloud. When a supervisor doesn't demonstrate communicative competence, he is badmouthed as authoritarian. And why? Because he is mainly interested in success and not in people – but that is exactly what makes a "competent" manager. First the results, then communication. Strategic goals are not met by mawkishness. The focus has to be on growth and productivity, when a company wants to gain in size."

This objection is not only common; it is also to be taken seriously. To clarify this, let us look over the shoulder of a representative of this way of thinking, when he shows how to lead successfully.

Phone call of the managing director: "Mr. Quick, in your department you have a Mr. Black who speaks Spanish so well. For our new subsidiary in Santiago de Chile we need someone with these qualities. Please find out whether Mr. Black will be available for this job for about two years. And let me know before Wednesday, it's urgent."

Quick: "Alright. You can count on me."

Drops down the receiver.

Talking to himself: "My goodness, Black isn't half lucky. I wish I'd been offered something like this at that age. Black, the lucky devil. Well, then I'll give him the good news."

Takes the receiver and dials.

"Quick here, good morning, Mr. Black, I hope you're making good progress and are on schedule with the Newton project? – – –

But that's not why I'm calling you. It's about our new subsidiary in Santiago de Chile, for which we have chosen you. You have probably read in the Intranet, that we will be represented out there starting in January. Now, your name has been suggested for this exceptional opportunity, and I have the honour to inform you of this. Congratulations. – – –

Mr. Black? Are you still there? – – – You didn't react; I thought we had problems with the line again. – – –

What do you mean, you have questions? Aren't you happy about it? – – –

Well, ok. But then you need to come now, I have another meeting at 10."

Puts down the receiver.

"Funny. He's not sure. This is rather unexpected. – – –

Strange chap. And I thought he was a man of action, a man of vision. Well, I'll have to give him a piece of my mind then."

Knock at the door.

"Come in! Please take a seat. Ok, let's start from the beginning: Mr. Black, as you know, with growing international contacts we must increasingly take on the role of a global player in our markets, which has the consequence that contacts are followed by obligations – and this leads me directly to our subject. Our future business will still maintain its focus in Germany, but we have to keep other countries in mind, especially in Latin America. This is where demand is growing most gratifyingly. Just think how well our business in Mexico is developing.

Now, this is the reason why the executive board has decided to start up another subsidiary in Chile – And this subsidiary is in need of a top-class expert, and one who speaks Spanish and who is willing to roll up his sleeves for two or three years and do the pioneer work of effectively representing our company in this new market. And, Mr. Black, you will not be surprised that we have thought of you.

Black: "This comes as a bit of a surprise. We have just started the Newton project – this will take at least four months to complete – and now, all of a sudden, you want me to ditch it and to go to South America. It's impossible, who will take care of my job here?"

Quick: "Now, that's not your problem. Mrs. Abel will be happy to take over the project – That isn't really a legitimate reason."

Black: "But Mrs. Abel, of all people, then you'll really put the cat among the pigeons. Pardon me, Mr. Quick, for being so candid, but you won't be at all happy with Mrs. Abel."

Quick (*irritated*): "That's not the point. We are offering you the enviable opportunity of a responsible job overseas, and I am getting the impression you are going to chicken out."

Black (*angry*): "That's most certainly not true. This is all rather sudden, and it annoys me that, for such an apparently important project, the required people are selected just four weeks in advance." (*Shakes his head*).

Quick (*ironically*): "And how much time in advance would Sir like to have? Ask your colleague, Mr. Lawson, he flew over to London for a presentation – and do you know when he returned? Three years later. He didn't make such a fuss. His wife took care of the move to London all on her own. You could learn a lesson from him!"

Black (*furious*): "Fair enough! If there are such wonderful people, why don't you ask one of them?! I am sure there is more than one Lawson in the company, who doesn't mind moving to South America with his wife and children. You cannot count on me for this trip." (*Stands up*)

Quick (*with suppressed anger*): "As you wish. I hope you won't regret this very emotional decision. But all right, you want it this way. Have a nice day then." (*Turns back to reading files while Mr. Black leaves the room*)

"What a bull-headed jerk! I only mean well with my subordinates, and they have nothing else to do but walk all over me. Well then..."

Black (*leaving*): "That was definite! I think I'll buy the *Adviser* on my way home."

Evidently this conversation was disastrous. What is more, considering that the employee will probably quit his job, it was anything but effective.

Before you receive concrete hints and suggestions regarding professional conversation leadership, I would like to ask you to answer the following question first:

- **What do you expect of this reading material? Or more precisely:**
- **What must this book contain so that you will say afterwards: "That was really worthwhile. I'm glad that I decided to read it"?**

Perhaps you do not just want to reflect for two minutes, but take a pencil and note down your thoughts. The following space will save you the search for paper.

When I ask similar questions in my seminars, the answers read as follows:

Lead more efficient conversations.
Convince more quickly.
Not to let arguments in discussions get out of hand.
Convince others so that they do not feel persuaded.
Influence others, without it being obvious.
Lead no unproductive conversations.
Learn to listen better.
Become more successful.
Improve my communication behaviour.

The goals listed here can only be reached with extreme difficulty. In order to better understand the point being made, a small digression is necessary.

In the following free space, please draw a picture with some strokes whose central statement reads:

- **On this page you do not see a tree.**

If you asked a child to give the picture a name, what would he or she probably call it? Would it say: book page without tree? Or would the answer be: on this page you can see a crossed-out tree.

The difficulty of this task is due to the fact that our brain consists of two hemispheres, which during development became differently specialised. While the left hemisphere contains the **language centre**, including logic and reason, the right hemisphere is responsible for **visual and spatial information** and also for intuition and feelings. Both hemispheres are connected with a bundle of nerve fibres called the *Corpus callosum*, and each hemisphere finds its characteristic way to solve problems, according to the respective specialisation. Now, denial is a logical function that can only be processed in the language centre, i. e. in the left hemisphere, whereas the right hemisphere does not know what to do with negation and all words derived from it, such as "never", "no", "not", "nowhere", "nothing". In the drawing exercise, your right hemisphere immediately imagined a tree, which in fact should not be visible, but in your imagination it could not be deleted any more.

In the comedy "The Love Potion" by *Frank Wedekind* the private tutor Schwigerling makes use of this phenomenon in order to regain his liberty. Prince Rogoschin thinks he is a gypsy, and thus expects him to understand the art of brewing effective love potions. The prince decides to exploit to the latter expertise, after all his advances towards his ward, Countess Trotzky, have failed. When Schwigerling confesses that he is not capable of such miracles, the prince orders him to be arrested and threatens him with a death sentence if he is not willing to brew the desired love potion. After many mysterious preparations, Schwigerling offers the desired drink to the prince. However, for the efficacy of the potion, it is imperative that while drinking it, the prince must not under any circumstances "think of a bear". However, due to his excitement, the man in need of the love potion is not able to turn his thoughts away from the ominous bear, he literally stammers: "*My head swarmed with bears*" so that he himself annihilated the effect.

You will probably meet a similar problem in the following exercise where the solution depends on what a picture you visualise.

▶ **Crossing the Rhine**
Near Coblenz two men wanted to cross the river Rhine. The boat that lay at the river bank was so small that it was only able to carry one person at a time. Both crossed the Rhine in this boat and subsequently continued their trip.
How did they manage this?

Everyone who has thought about it a while without finding a solution tends to believe the problem cannot be solved. If you are still searching for a solution, it might help perhaps to consider, which image you created in your mind, so that you could ask yourself whether another picture would also make sense.

In one of my recent seminars I asked the participants about how they imagined the scene, and it was impressive how many details could be envisaged. For example, when I asked about the weather, I received answers such as, "it is summer", "like now", "autumn fog", "winter with snow and ice" – the Rhine bank was described to me as "rocky", "green meadow with little bushes", "a narrow, long wooden footbridge with a railing" – The men appeared as "clothed like two hikers with backpacks and walking sticks" "tall, lean shapes in black coats and hats pulled down over their faces", "looked like two shepherds" etc.

I admit that the first sentence of this little story leads to an image, in which the two men stand next to each other at the Rhine bank in front of the little boat. Clearly, the exercise cannot be solved with this picture in mind. However, whoever thought of a setting, in which both men stand at the opposite banks of the Rhine, lets one cross the river from north to south and the other in the opposite direction afterwards and asks rather surprised: where is the problem?

A short time after the first edition of this book, a reader expressed her anger: "This solution is quite unreasonable, even illogical. One could read in the story that both men want to cross the Rhine together and together definitely means jointly." Surprised, I asked where the word "together" appears, so she took the book at hand and read to me: "Near Coblenz two men wanted to cross the river Rhine together." Uncertain if maybe the word "together" had found its way into the book unnoticed during the printing process, I asked her: "Where is the word together?" She opened the book up again and read to me angrily word for word: "Near-Coblenz-two-men-wanted-to-cross-the-river-Rhine-together. There you are!" But this time I had glanced into the book and I repeated my question. She used her index finger and sought through the text: "Well, there! Strange, now it is gone." Flabbergasted she looked at me and did not understand the world any longer

This event reveals, how strongly our imagination, so to say our visions, can influence our logical thinking. The philosopher *Hegel* 150 years ago summarised this perception in a bonmot:

> "If the imagination is strong enough, reality cannot resist."

▸ **The following exercise may have a similar outcome: connect the 9 points with 4 straight lines, without dropping the pencil.**

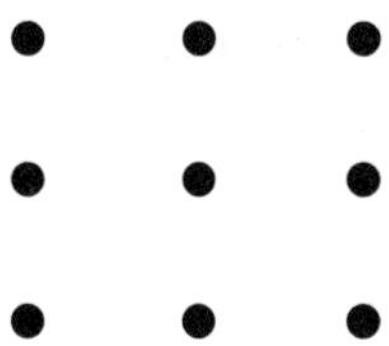

Independent of our consciousness, the brain constantly creates images, no matter whether these are suitable or not. (In chapter 12

"From Persuasion to Conviction" I go into the details of this aspect).

It seems that the right hemisphere with its images takes the lead in stress situations. In spite of all reason and logic, overlap is created between the images in our head and the emerging reality.

The following anecdote will illustrate this:

Before a speech to a large audience, a colleague leaned over to me and whispered: "I hope I don't fall over the many cables." Shortly afterwards it was his turn to give his presentation. He had only reached the third step when he slipped and – to the amusement of the audience – found himself lying lengthwise on the floor.

What had happened? His right hemisphere parallel to the whispered sentence had created an image. My colleague had already seen himself stumble. In the following excitement, the right hemisphere, which is also responsible for the control of our body movements, took care that picture and the reality matched.

It may sound paradoxical, but when we define success as a match between imagination and reality, the stumbling colleague had been successful. Viewed in this way the prophesied and therefore imagined defeat proves to be a success once it occurs. I admit that with this idea I am touching a delicate point, since the importance of one's own responsibility for the imagined future cannot be underestimated. Whoever believes he is able to achieve something is just as right as someone who believes that something is impossible. We use the word pessimist for people, who always look on the dark sides of life and paint everything black. Yet the so-called pessimists are able to prove time and again that their opinion was correct, for it finally turned out exactly so. Be it pessimist or optimist, both are successful in as much as they form their individual reality in such a way that at the end they are always right. In chapter 10, I want to review this phenomenon more closely.

Perhaps you know of similar incidents in sports. If you throw a ball but are not certain whether you will hit the target, you will usually miss. The moment you aim, you are in the matter with only partial attention. A part of your brain is already concentrated on missing and the possible consequences. For an athlete there is hardly anything worse than trying

- **not** to lose the baton,
- **not** to hit the high jump slat,
- **not** to jump with the wrong foot etc.

Even in an egg and spoon race, the representation of a falling egg usually leads inevitably to the premature end of thc coursc. Similarly consciously trying to avoid letting coffee swash over the rim of the cup represents a visualisation of the undesirable.

In another context you may have experience in doing what should be avoided. In route directions it is often added, to give complete information, into which street one should not turn. In the fervour of finding the right way, you may notice only after turning that this was indeed the wrong street.

At the beginning of this chapter, you had been asked to define your goals. In the following, you can test to what extent you have developed images that are beneficial and/or troublesome regarding goal achievement.

Of the listed remarks the following are **inappropriate** due to being **negations**:

Not to let arguments in discussions get out of hand.
Convince others so that they do not feel persuaded.
Influence others, without it being noticeable.
Lead no unproductive conversations.

So clear the goal seems to be, so very much does the related image mislead to persistence. Who does not want to let arguments get out of hand, first of all imagines very clearly **out of hand discussions.**

Who does not want to persuade is oriented to imagining **persuasion**. Furthermore, the wish to influence without it being noticeable includes the picture of a **noticeable influence**. In the last sentence our right hemisphere sketches **unproductive conversations**.

In no way should the impression emerge that you must avoid each form of negation in future. However, this guide can help you to identify unintentionally developed images, which might stand in contradiction to your intentions.

You can observe how much we are used to formulating our goals in a negative way when you ask somebody, what he would change in his life, if he, for example, had three wishes or won a million in the lottery.

You might like to consider this question now and note down your answer before you go on reading.

At birthday parties, the question as to what one would do with a million is frequently posed as a parlour game. The following answers are particularly memorable:

"First of all I would stop working."
"That would be a dream. I would no longer have to live in my small apartment."
"I know at once what I would wish for: to stop smoking, to stop getting angry with my children and not to let my boss get away with treating me badly."

The objectives listed at the beginning of this chapter also contained the following sentences:

Learn to listen better.
Lead more efficient conversations.
Convince more quickly.
Become more successful.
Improve my communication behaviour.

Who would deny the good intentions of these statements? "Better", "faster", "more successful" are typical words for well-sounding goal specifications. However, for our right hemisphere they are unsuitable: How do you imagine someone, who has achieved his goal of learning to listen better?

The comparative adjective is used as a form of contrast. The sentence "learn to listen better" contains the unspoken addition: "I would like to be able to listen better than I can now, or for example, better than my boss can, etc.". Viewed this way these sentences contain also a hidden negation. Who for example "wishes to convince more quickly" is already orientated at a speed that is not quick enough, resulting in the wish to become quicker. In the slogan "Know more, want more, do more", the left hemisphere is made to imagine an extension of knowledge, willpower and ability, but simultaneously the right hemisphere imagines the as-is state, which is scarcely intended to become the **to-be** model. In addition, the negative words: "fewer", "slighter", "more weakly" fix us unintentionally to the state that should be avoided.

"I want to smoke less."
"It would be good for my health to drink less."
"Less job stress would be wonderful."

Defining your goals **effectively** means stating the facts that will indicate you have met your goal.

The wish to practise listening skills, can for example, be formulated this way:

"I would like to learn to listen in a way that I am able to repeat the essential content of a remark spontaneously in my own words."

The wish for "more efficient conversation" can be put:

"I want to learn to express my ideas to my dialogue partner during the first two to three sentences of a conversation, in order to establish whether additional concerns on his part exist and how long the conversation should last. When I am able to do that, I would like to learn to restrict the conversation both to the specified topics and to an agreed time limit."

Such a statement of objectives does not sound particularly pleasing and in many passages may even sound quite baroque. Nevertheless, this **detailed circumscription helps our right hemisphere**. The more clearly and conceivably we state our goals, the easier it is for our right hemisphere to refrain from imagining something on its own. On the other hand, a clear, well-formed image acts like a magnet, focussing all of our energy onto the goal.

Perhaps you have already observed that in difficult conversations the time actually needed is also influenced by one's vision. If the specification reads: "I will spend 30 minutes on this conversation" or:

"I want to make an effort to lead this negotiation to an acceptable agreement in at most 30 minutes"; you will most probably achieve your goal (assuming you regard the time limit as realistic).

The following formulations are, however, in stark contrast to the above: "I will bring this conversation to a conclusion as quickly as possible" or: "I will endeavour to lead this negotiation to an acceptable result very rapidly." – "very rapidly" or "as quickly as possible" leaves our imagination, i.e. our right hemisphere, with sufficient room for interpretation that it will be expanded at the first hurdle. If then dealing with the subject matter actually took 40 or even 50 minutes, this would still be "very rapid" and/or "as fast as possible", though not saving any time. In investigations on time and self-management it can be observed again and again that a **job of work expands to fill the time available**.

In the following, I would like to give you the opportunity to re-formulate typical "goals" into appropriate ones. You can compare your suggestions with my proposals on the next page.

Typical goals	**Your suggestion for an appropriate description of the goals**
(1) "I want to work less."	
(2) "I want to be more relaxed and less tense whilst doing my work."	
(3) "I would like to have more influence in team discussions and to be better at convincing my colleagues."	
(4) "I must not be so unconcentrated. I must learn how to focus on the important things."	
(5) "I want to overcome dreading discussions on delicate personnel matters and especially to be more resolute when criticising others."	
(6) "I do not want to lose my concentration when disturbed during work and I want to be more satisfied with my job."	

On the next two pages you will find my proposals for re-formulations:

(1) "I want to work less."
Concentrating on the undesired situation of working too much has to be replaced by a vision that is not only conceivable, but at the same time creates acceptance, e.g.

"I want to leave my office at 5 p.m. every working day and for the rest of the day I want to relax, either by doing sport, or going for a walk with my wife, or by going on an extended pub crawl."

(2) "I want to be more relaxed and less tense when doing my work."

"Independent of the amount of work I would like to be as relaxed at my desk as I am in bed in the morning, shortly after waking up."

(3) "I would like to have more influence in team discussions and to be better at convincing my colleagues."

The formulations "more influence" and "better at convincing" create an image of little influence and little power of persuasion. An entirely different image is generated by the following sentence:

"When I have ideas and introduce them to my team, I want to have my colleagues' attention right up to the end of my presentation and for them to indicate with their questions that they are thinking my ideas over. In addition, I would like to put my ideas in such a form that my colleagues understand the respective benefits at once."

(4) "I must not be so unconcentrated. I must learn how to focus on the important things."

The image of an erratic, unconcentrated, or even absent-minded person can be replaced by a more positive vision. This is more likely to be the case in the following:

"Starting tomorrow morning I will bring my daily work into order. Then I will begin with the work that has the highest priority for me. I will remain with this work until it is done, no matter how often I am interrupted by others. Before I start another job, I will review whether my ranking, which reflects the urgency of the unfinished tasks, remains unchanged and then continue with the second task. Even if in this manner I only complete half of the jobs in my working day, I will always leave my desk with the feeling that the most important and urgent tasks have been dealt with."

(5) "I want to overcome dreading discussions on delicate personnel matters and especially to be more resolute when criticising others."

The perception of "delicate criticism in a conversation" suggests an image depicting a lack of assertiveness. In consequence the right hemisphere requires a positive instruction, such as the following:

"Starting tomorrow morning I will use direct conversation as the best means of influencing my subordinates. In addition, I will show my satisfaction with good performance and also initiate a conversation with the respective colleagues, as soon as deficiencies occur. In these critical conversations, I will let the employee know from the very outset how I would like his work to be in the future, so that he can recognise immediately that he need not justify the mistake, but rather learn from it."

(6) "I do not want to lose my concentration when disturbed during work and I want to be more satisfied with my job."

Whether something is defined as a "disturbance" or "interruption", depends on our personal interpretation. Yet in each case, our right hemisphere creates a corresponding image. You can well imagine how somebody who is discontented and continuously losing his train of thought appears. However, what would the positive image look like? The following formulation is just as laborious as the previous, but it offers positive stimulation to the right hemisphere:

"Being available for questions should be a part of my working day. I want to deal with complicated matters in a defined period of time. In future, I will go into seclusion every day between 10 and 11 o'clock. In addition, I will redirect telephone calls and shut my office door. I will have reached my goal when I work on easy and undemanding tasks mainly during the times that I have to be available for others, while the large and difficult tasks are dealt with when I am alone at my workplace. During these times my telephone will be redirected to my colleague Kurt, and in return I will be prepared to receive his calls for two hours a day. In order to achieve this goal this year, I will bring a written proposal to the next departmental discussion and I will recommend that such "hours" become introduced in general."

> If you phrase objectives, the outcome should always include:
> WHO does WHAT with WHOM until WHEN to achieve which RESULT?

You are probably surprised that so far there have been very few hints regarding "**leadership** in professional conversation" in this first chapter. Yet before details are discussed in the next chapters, I would like to come back to the title of this chapter: **From efficiency to effectiveness**.

Both concepts have become rather fashionable, and unfortunately they are increasingly often used as synonyms although they definitely do not mean the same. Whereas **efficiency** is the **power to get results**, **effectiveness** stands for the **results actually obtained**. In other words: **efficiency** is an **action-based** concept, while **effectiveness** is oriented to the **objectives**. An example from mechanics can illustrate this: The degree of efficiency of a machine is a measure of its effect, for example the torque of the motor. However, this includes no statement about what the machine is used for and what is expected to be achieved with it.

Transferred to human work, efficiency means to **do the things right**. However, it is evident, that solely doing things right is not enough and occasionally one also needs to **do the right things**. The latter is a question of effectiveness.

In a quotation often accredited to *Mark Twain*, the common definition of efficiency reads:

> "After we had finally lost sight of our goal, we doubled our effort."

So it is not enough to lead conversations efficiently, since this only means that the effort used in the conversation was big. Usually conversations are led to achieve goals (even small talk is more than an entertaining pastime).

This chapter should also clarify that the best conversation leadership remains a patchwork if it does not include a clearly defined goal. Although at first sight it may seem trivial, the following statement by *Martin Luther* is particularly pertinent:

> "You can only achieve your goal, if you have one."

How you enhance your effectiveness

Efficiency is an expression that is oriented towards an activity. **Effectiveness** is oriented towards a goal and describes a **result**. Goals formulated effectively are:

(1) positive: Define exactly what you want (e. g. I am in good health, I will manage the project etc.)
(2) absolute: Goals must not contain a comparison (such as being better than him, working less etc.)
(3) specific: You must have a clear understanding of how you know you have achieved your goal (e. g. How can you measure, feel, see, . . . ?)
(4) independent: You either have the required knowledge and capabilities or the possibility to adopt them
(5) tolerable: What consequences will achieving your goal have for you and your environment – are you prepared to live with these?

Goals are nearly never given an exact wording. People believe it is evident that they know what they want. For conversation and negotiations it can be very useful to test whether you have a clear understanding of your goal (effectiveness) or more an idea of the way towards it and of the actions required (efficiency).

Questions that help to distinguish goals from means and methods:

- What will this lead to?
- What will be different?
- What will be the result?
- What is your expected benefit?
- Are there other advantages?
- Which other objectives will be met?

If you will have formulated your goal effectively you will know:

- WHO does WHAT
- with WHOM
- until WHEN
- to achieve which RESULT?

When answering the following six questions you will focus on your goal and clarify your expectations:

Fixing your goals:

- What is my desired outcome?
- Which result would also be satisfactory?
- What is my interest in the result?
- Which long-term benefit do I expect from the result?
- What are the additional objectives?
- How do I want to feel after the conversation and how will the others feel?

2. Recognising Your Own Conversational Manner

The term conversational manner in a dialogue refers to a behavioural trait that results from attitudes and personal convictions. It is an **expression of individual personality** and is hardly influenced by the specific situation. The reaction of many people in conversation is spontaneous. On careful listening, you will notice that an individual's reactions in conversation are generally constant, irrespective of the dialogue partner or subject.

This may have aroused your curiosity, and you are now interested in learning more about your own spontaneous reactions in a discussion. To this end, I have put together a little test based on suggestions by Roger Mucchielli*, in which you can ascertain how flexibly you react to different conversation beginnings.

In the following, you will find ten conversation clips as they might occur in everyday life. For each opening sentence of the dialogue partner, you will find six different reactions, each leading the conversation into a certain direction. If you read the six remarks, please indicate the answer that most closely resembles your own characteristic reaction. Should none of the remarks satisfy you, which is quite possible given the plethora of different possibilities, simply mark the response that comes closest to your reaction. If you mark the answers spontaneously, you will require about 15 minutes. At the end, you will find some instructions on how you can evaluate this test on your own.

---

* Roger Mucchielli: Das nicht-direktive Beratungsgespräch. (i. e. Non-Directive Counselling) Otto Müller Verlag, Salzburg 1972.

Conversation Clip 1

One of your subordinates, a reserved man of 44, who has been doing his job quietly for the last eleven years, addresses you one day after his morning break and says:

"Er, I've got an idea, and I'd just like to mention it. Er, regarding the parking mess in front of the gate every day, I just thought, we could draw lines on the ground, so that the customers do not park directly in front of it."

Your answer

(1) Could you please tell me more about it, where exactly, which colour, how expensive, and who could do it?

(2) That is really great. Finally an employee who thinks about this problem. Very good, that you mentioned it to me.

(3) Yes, I will write down immediately what you propose. Or even better, let us go to the courtyard and take a look. I think we should solve this problem at once.

(4) Well, now I am curious. You have probably seen this somewhere else, and now you think that we could adopt this solution without any problems.

(5) If I understand you right you have got an idea how we could prevent our customers from parking in front of the gate.

(6) Well, I don't think this is such a big problem that we have to daub the whole courtyard. Yet, I appreciate that you have thought about it. Let us consider it without being too dramatic.

Conversation Clip 2

In a meeting one of your salesmen tells you in a very frustrated way about his fruitless attempts to get a customer to sign a contract.

"... and he simply didn't listen, he did not even take a look at the brochures. Pushed them back to me over the table and said, I was a nice guy, but he would stick to his old brand."

Your answer

(1) Well, that's no wonder, you can't just push some brochures to a customer, but you offer him a three months' trial period!

(2) If he is neither listening nor takes a look at the brochures, I assume that you didn't really talk about the product and thus ran out of arguments.

(3) At the moment you are angry and disappointed, because you could not get anywhere with this customer, although you tried really hard.

(4) First things first: How did your meeting come about, what were your first remarks, and what was his initial response? Try to be precise, word-for-word.

(5) Don't upset yourself. Difficult customers are our everyday business. You will be able to meet your goals I am sure. Each of us has bad luck sometimes.

(6) Now listen, with such a customer it always helps to stick his company logo on to our product so that it really catches his eye.

Conversation Clip 3

One of your employees, who has been with the company for 33 years, addresses you just before five o'clock as you are walking by:

"I say, Sir, what is your opinion about early retirement, I mean, do I have to take it or would I be allowed to stay?"

Your answer

(1) Don't tell me you worry about that. In your situation you can be confident about your future.

(2) I suspect that you are worried about being pushed out because of your age, and now you would like to know where you stand.

(3) How did you get that idea? Who told you that we will make use of early retirement? You'll have to explain that to me in detail.

(4) Then you should make up your mind quickly. We need to know where we stand. If you would like to retire earlier, my proposal would be that we both sit down with the Human Resources Manager.

(5) I welcome your coming to talk to me about it, because I think it is important that we discuss this on time. Very good, that you have already thought about it.

(6) Well, the bark is always worse than the bite. So don't make haste, you really don't have to worry, since we cannot do without you right now.

Conversation Clip 4

One of your employees, in his early thirties, comes to you early in the morning and asks nervously:

"Boss, may I have a week's holiday. Preferably right now, tomorrow would do as well. I'll be back next week, ready for action."

Your answer

(1) Well, if you are in such a hurry, I assume something is wrong. Don't worry. As far as I know you have some vacation days left, so I won't mind you having a week off, but only starting tomorrow, is that alright?!

(2) Well, let's take a look how many days you are entitled to. (Looks it up.) You have got 16 days left, if you want, you can have one week, but not starting today or tomorrow, who will do all the work? You can leave on Wednesday, but tell me on time when you will be back.

(3) What is the matter with you? Something wrong with your wife? Trouble with the children? Good heavens, we can talk about it, we do have a heart.

(4) At the moment you seem to be having trouble, and you hope that a week off will help. I have the feeling that you would prefer to leave at once.

(5) Well, if you are so nervous, something must be wrong. Before I let you go I would like to hear what your colleagues say.

(6) Say, what do you think you're doing? Just imagine if everybody burst into my office and asked for an immediate vacation. I don't mind you having a vacation, but there are rules in a company and we have to stick to them.

Conversation Clip 5

One of your subordinates, in his mid twenties, with your company for seven years addresses you rather shyly in the courtyard:

“Sir, since you seem to have time at the moment, I’ve got a question: What do you think about me doing my master craftsman’s diploma?”

Your answer

(1) When do you want to start? What plans do you have? I need to know more details so that we can clarify what this means in financial terms.

(2) So you are toying with the idea of starting up on your own one day.

(3) You would like to talk with me when we are not being distracted and find out what I think about your plans.

(4) Listen, since you are not the only one, I propose we meet up with the other two colleagues. Three going for the master craftsman’s diploma is rather a lot. It would be best if the three of you came to my office after lunch, so that we can talk it over.

(5) Cheer up old boy, nothing to be nervous about. Nobody needs to be shy about his plans to become foreman.

(6) It’s very good that you have made this decision. Gaining qualifications always secures your future.

Conversation Clip 6

One of the supervisors reporting to you, in her mid forties, always performs to your satisfaction. However, you cannot remember if she has been on a training course during the last few years. You propose that she should take part in a 3 x 3 day course for managers, and she answers curtly:

"No, no, that is nothing for me. Let the younger ones go, they can learn something in it, and let me stay in the office. Who else could run the show in my absence?"

Your answer

(1) I don't think it would do me any harm to work in your area again. You go on the 3 × 3 day course and I'll stand in for you. Is that alright?

(2) That sounds more like an excuse to me. I think it would do you good if you went on a training course. It's not a good idea to put the company before your personal development.

(3) That sounds as though the idea of going on a course is unpleasant merely because you're in your mid forties.

(4) Come on now, you're not that old. You shouldn't worry about being regarded as belonging on the scrap heap.

(5) When did you last go on a course? What was the subject? I'd be interested to know if you had such bad experiences that you're no longer interested in going.

(6) You seem to think that after 3 days of absence we'll have changed everything behind your back and even replaced you.

Conversation Clip 7

One of your trainees comes for her certificate and asks hesitantly:

"I just wondered, er, if you have a vacancy for professional training, er, how does one find out about it or how does it work?"

Your answer

(1) You seem to have enjoyed your training here. If you want to recommend us to others, please feel free to do so.

(2) Finish school first and then come back three months before the end of term with your last report and then we will see.

(3) I wouldn't worry about that yet. We will see when the time comes. Just keep your chin up, you'll certainly find a vacancy. During your training here we were all very satisfied with you.

(4) You would like to start your professional training with us, and you're afraid that you haven't applied on time.

(5) It is not good if you specialise so early. You have trained with us, now get some experience with other companies, before you decide where to go.

(6) Which job do you want to do later? I am also interested in knowing what your references are like?

Conversation Clip 8

Two of your employees have had a bad row, and you have been asked to arbitrate.

Employee Norman (annoyed): "I won't let anybody humiliate me like that, especially not him!"
Employee Bates (coolly): "What's wrong with being objective and saying that you haven't got a clue and that you still have a lot to learn?"

Your answer

(1) Ok, one thing at a time, Mr. Norman, what exactly was said. Please tell me the whole story from your point of view.

(2) Mr. Norman, if I have understood correctly, you feel as though you've been made a fool of, because this happened in front of a customer.

(3) Gentlemen, there is nothing wrong with criticism, but this really must not happen in front of our customers, if you see what I mean.

(4) It seems to me that this is a case of rivalry, which has deeper causes. Mr. Bates, I have already realized that you sometimes have problems with Mr. Norman since he started working in your department.

(5) Now, if the two of you are not able to cooperate, we should consider whether a separation might not be the best solution. I think, Mr. Norman, we could find other duties for you.

(6) Now then gentlemen, calm down. We all want to get along with each other. Come on, let's have a brandy. You can shake hands and we'll talk about it in a civilised manner.

Conversation Clip 9

During your lunch break a colleague sits down beside you and complains bitterly about her new supervisor:

“She is such an idiot! If I wanted to, I could easily outshine her, but nobody listens to me. They will soon see, what she’s like.”

Your answer

(1) Be patient, some people need time to get used to each other. Maybe you’ll get along better after a while.

(2) You wanted the job yourself, and now you are angry because you have been overlooked.

(3) Your new supervisor seems very unqualified to you, and you would like to show her, how to do the job properly. However, at the moment you don’t harbour any hopes that you will change anything.

(4) You are not playing fair. It does not help at all if you waste your energy trying to undermine the authority of your supervisor.

(5) Where does she come from? What did she do before, and do you happen to know why she left?

(6) In such a situation it is always best to take notes on each incident and then go to your department head and present it to him. If you do not want to take that risk, there is also the possibility of giving a hint to the editors of our internal newsletter. Then they will take care of it. And maybe the promotion of your supervisor is just what the works’ committee is waiting for.

Conversation Clip 10

You have one of your subordinate's notice to leave in hand, and you have asked her to come and give her reasons.

"I feel very uncomfortable about giving my reasons, especially to you of all people."

Your answer

(1) Somehow you feel awkward about giving your reasons especially to me.

(2) I would suggest that you be quite frank with me about your reasons and that you make your decision afterwards.

(3) Honesty always pays. You can be open and honest with me.

(4) If I understand you right, you are saying that you want to quit for personal reasons only.

(5) Please don't worry. Nothing from our conversation will leave this room. You can rely on my discretion.

(6) But this is exactly what I am interested in: What made you want to leave?

Data Evaluation

Begin by shading the number corresponding to your most favoured reply for each conversation clip in the table below. The clip number is indicated at the top of the columns. Do not take any notice of the letters in the first column at this stage.

	Clip 1	Clip 2	Clip 3	Clip 4	Clip 5	Clip 6	Clip 7	Clip 8	Clip 9	Clip 10	Total
A	2	1	5	6	6	2	5	3	4	3	
B	4	2	1	5	2	6	1	4	2	4	
C	6	5	6	1	5	4	3	6	1	5	
D	1	4	3	3	1	5	6	1	5	6	
E	3	6	4	2	4	1	2	5	6	2	
F	5	3	2	4	3	3	4	2	3	1	

Now you have noted the test results. In the “Total” column please add up how many fields you have hatched per row. The single values of the numbers are not important. Now you can see whether your answers are distributed evenly or whether there is a tendency, for instance with more than five answers in one line

Whoever, for example, has hatched six fields in line A and four in line E knows that 60 % of his spontaneous answers are based on A behaviour and 40 % fit E behaviour.

You are probably interested to know what the letters A to F refer to in the solution of your test. If you look five pages ahead, you will find the corresponding explanations. On the following pages you can evaluate what feelings the various answers can evoke in the dialogue partner.

For example in Conversation Clip 9 a colleague sits down beside you during a lunch break and complains bitterly about her new supervisor:

“She is such an idiot! If I wanted to, I could easily outshine her, but nobody listens to me. They will soon see, what she’s like.”

Let's take a closer look at the first reaction:

"Be patient, some people need time to get used to each other. Maybe you'll get along better after a while."

At first sight this answer appears to be consoling. That's quite right!

However, do you really know that the colleague needs comfort and encouragement? Someone who is so angry will perceive this well-meant encouragement more as patronising. One could even assume that at that moment the colleague is not so keen about being on better terms with her new supervisor. We can hardly expect that the colleague will respond as follows to this remark:

"Yes, you are right. It is probably best to wait for a while and try to get along with her."

Encouraging or **comforting** remarks can easily sound like "Cheer up!" or "Keep your chin up." However, who does not feel down or discouraged, can readily interpret such reactions as exaggerated and in consequence indignantly turn away.

> Take anger and annoyance seriously. Encouragement often sounds like playing things down.

What about the second reaction?

"You wanted the job yourself, and now you are angry because you have been overlooked."

How does this remark appear from the colleague's point of view? Even if we suppose that this is the truth, you run the risk of receiving the following response:

"That is not what I am up to. I just think it's wrong how somebody who is as thick as two short planks can be given such a position. One has to consider the consequences, and anyway ..."

Reaction 2 is based on the **interpretation** that the colleague is so angry, only because she has not been promoted and is jealous of her new boss, since she now occupies the vacancy the colleague had desired for herself. The colleague would have to be very self-critical and go against her better judgement to admit that frankly. We do not object because an accusation is wrong, but rather because people usually do not like being seen through – particularly by a business colleague. This would be even worse, if the colleague had had no ambitions of becoming a supervisor and our suggestion was a complete misinterpretation. One can assume rather correctly that the conversation will come to an abrupt end.

If you want to avoid interpretation, ask for clarification.

Let's analyse the third reaction:

"Your new supervisor seems very unqualified to you, and you would like to show her, how to do the job properly. However, at the moment you don't harbour any hopes that you will change anything."

Although this response contributes little in terms of content, it does indicate to the colleague that you have been listening very attentively. This **listening** (in the following chapter I will distinguish between descriptive and active listening) is used to clarify whether the dialogue partner has any hope of influencing this awkward situation.

By paraphrasing and active listening you indicate that you wish to understand your dialogue partner. You show how much you are trying to understand the problem from his point of view.

What about the fourth reaction?

"You are not playing fair. It does not help at all if you waste your energy trying to undermine the authority of your supervisor."

Here the colleague suddenly finds herself in a situation where her behaviour is **judged**. As soon as one of the partners voices his or her evaluation of a situation, the other is automatically forced to take a position. This can be approval. However, it is often observed that many people have a strong tendency towards individualism and respond to an uninvited opinion in a relativizing if not rejecting manner. Thus, I can well imagine that in our example, the colleague who is named "unfair" justifies herself or shows in another way that she is, of course, fair, for example:

"No, I am not trying to put anybody down, however unqualified she is. It's just sad to see how the whole department is going to the dogs ..."

With a **judgmental** remark, be it praise or blame, you introduce a moral component into the conversation that can easily distract from the essential and also forces the dialogue partner to deal with your opinion without having had the opportunity to explain his or her point of view in detail.

A different response would have been possible:

"Where does she come from? What did she do before, and do you happen to know why she left?"

Now interest is shown. Now one comes to the point. Clear questions focus a conversation. But what is essential in this case? Does the bitterness of the colleague vanish if she establishes, where her boss comes from? Does it help, if the question is asked as to what the superior did prior to her current job? Moreover, the one who asks takes the initiative in the conversation and you can get the impression that the answers to the questions will automatically lead to a solution to the problem. If only this were the case!

If your dialogue partner does not understand the questions, he might only too easily interpret this situation as an **interrogation**, leading to the corresponding discontentment. Furthermore, one runs the risk that the questions are answered only hesitantly or superficially, since your dialogue partner does not yet understand the consequences of his possible answer.

And what about the last reply?

"In such a situation it is always best to take notes on each incident and then go to your department head and present it to him. If you do not want to take that risk, there is also the possibility of giving a hint to the editors of our internal newsletter. Then they will take care of it. And maybe the promotion of your supervisor is just what the works' committee is waiting for."

Superficially regarded, one might think that the colleague will get exactly what she wanted. However, it does not take much imagination to foresee that the well-meant advice is "unfortunately" impossible to realize, as illustrated in the following:

"Well, you don't know our department head. If I did that, I could forget all chances immediately. And as far as our internal news letter is concerned, they made such a big mistake at the beginning of the year, that wouldn't be any use at all ..."

An idiom says: "Advice is never nice". This is especially true for **unwanted advice**.

The quick, usually hasty offering of a **solution** or advice can restrict your dialogue partner. He senses that he is being pushed into behaving in a certain way. He therefore often falls silent and in addition tends to reject the solution, even if it were useful when viewed objectively.

This little test for finding your spontaneous reaction tendency deals only with the beginning of a conversation. You might get the impression, that I favour exclusively "understanding" as a conversation reaction. This is merely true for the beginning of a conversation. **Each of these reactions has its value at an appropriate time**. In other words, in professional conversation leadership you can easily give advice, but only if your dialogue partner lets you know he is open for it or even directly asks for it. Questions can also be the means of choice, especially in an analysis of the circumstances. As long as your questions are intelligible for your dialogue partner, conversation control may even seem helpful to him. If a dialogue partner is doubtful or sad, encouraging and constructive reactions are not only appropriate, but also required. Sometimes dialogue partners express themselves so confusingly that the meaning of what they say can only be grasped using interpretation skills. In some conversations, the partner also expects an evaluation in the form of approval or rejection. Here appropriate timing is also important. Did your dialogue partner ask for an evaluation or is he forced to listen to your personal opinion?

After this detailed review of the conversation reactions, it is time to hand you the test solution. On the next page, you will find a grouping of the reaction tendencies that are represented by the letters A to F. Since these six replies are frequently used in conversations as the first answer, one also speaks of "answer biases", as the first answer can trigger a general disposition that influences the further progress of the conversation.

Reaction tendencies in conversations

(A) Your answers are **judgemental**, i. e. they imply a moral point of view and include either agreement or disagreement with the dialogue partner.

(B) Your answers are **interpretations**. Since your mind is searching for an explanation, you only hear what you want to hear and emphasize what seems important to you. It may happen that you change the other's statement or alter its meaning.

(C) Your answers are **consoling or comforting** and are intended to encourage the other person, calming him or her down or trying to find an agreement. You feel pity and you believe that one should rather not dramatize the situation.

(D) Your answers are **investigative**. You try to find out more and lead the conversation into the direction that seems relevant to you. You may be suspecting the other person of hiding the most important facts or of wasting time. You are in a hurry and your questions are too direct.

(E) You tend to give an immediate **solution**. You react with action and pressure the other person into doing something. You find your preferred solution immediately. You do not wait until you know more. This is the surest way to get rid of the other person and his problem.

(F) Your answers indicate that you try to **understand** the other and make an effort to see the situation with his or her eyes. You want to make sure that you have understood correctly. This attitude encourages the other and makes him or her tell you more.

Whoever does not like to depend on his or her intuition, will self-critically examine to what extent the dialogue partner is really interested in what you are so intent on saying.

Such an "examination" could, for example, sound like this:

- "I am wondering whether you are interested in my opinion (view, estimation, judgement) of the situation."
- "I am not sure whether I have understood correctly (suppose correctly)."
- "I am wondering whether you expect advice from me."
- "I have some questions in mind, but I am uncertain whether they might help."
- "I would like to encourage you, but I fear this might be misunderstood as playing things down."

You can be certain that your dialogue partner will answer directly and will look at you attentively, if he is really interested. However, there is no hiding the fact that in such a self-critical assessment, you will often come to the painful realization that you will get no opportunity to add your contribution. Your dialogue partner might for example say: "Yes, that's very interesting, did you know that I…" and then he goes on and on and on.

One means of becoming aware of various different reaction tendencies is to sharpen one's perception. Conversation Clip 9 has already been discussed in detail. I propose that you classify the other nine conversation clips again and distinguish the six respective replies in such a way that you make a note on the classification next to each answer, before you compare them with the solution. You might well notice that, having read this chapter, you would now mark very different answers. Firstly, you could practise once again using these examples. In a next step with real-life conversation reactions (your own as well as those of others), you should be able to learn to recognize the various types of answer. After only a little practice, you will notice how your sharpened perception for conversation reactions will also influence your own conversational manners.

3. Four Ways of Listening

Some readers might be surprised, since they would not expect a chapter on listening in a book about professional conversation leadership. Yet, in contrast to other ways of influencing a discussion, such as questions, advice, comments etc., listening proves to be the best way to **lead** a conversation. It is significant that **professional listening skills** are emphasized in all research studies on the success of outstanding leader type personalities.

In the following, I will distinguish between four different forms of listening and their effect on the dialogue partner:

(1) "I understand" listening

This is in fact not really a type of listening, but rather a **prelude to a statement**. However, as it is believed to be impolite to interrupt somebody directly, it has become a habit to silence him or her with "neutral phrases" like "I understand,..." or "Yes, you are right, but...", or the popular "Yes, I am of exactly the same opinion, you know, I..." and similar expressions.

Maybe you can think of other examples, such as the following scene that took place in a shop for electrical equipment:

Customer: "Some time ago, I think it's six weeks now, I bought a low voltage light fitting from you, quite a large one with 200 Watts, this means 6 meters right across the room, right...

Vendor: "I understand, and now you want to install additional spotlights. Follow me, please, I can show you a special offer that we have just had delivered."

Customer: "Yes, but I only wanted to know about the energy consumption if I only install a few spotlights." And so on.

Does the following scene, captured from a neighbouring table in a canteen, remind you of similar instances?

Colleague A: "Oh boy, what a mess, now they have changed our schedule for the third time in a row. I don't know! Sometimes I don't know if I'm coming or going. First we were told we have six weeks for completion, then five weeks, and yesterday they told us everything needs to be done by the end of the month. And the worst of it is, Kramer has had surgery on a slipped disk and won't be coming back for at least four weeks."

Colleague B: "Oh, I can understand that. Oh boy, am I glad that I managed to get my act together and leave you to take the job in the lab. We do not have such problems, you know, we do..."

In the case of "I understand" listening, you can observe the listener nodding briefly, making a sitting up movement and straightening himself, or taking a deep breath – all indications of the listener's wish to speak.

I am not objecting to showing one's understanding, but when the phrase "I understand" or "I can understand that" is followed by nothing else, it serves as a kind of lingual full stop. A pause or an encouraging look motivates the dialogue partner to go on talking.

What is surprising about this **pseudo-listening** is, how mindlessly the dialogue partners talk at cross-purposes and fob each other off with empty phases or accept that the other is only pretending to listen. Presumably, this particularly bothers nobody, since these standard phrases are so commonly used. Thus, nobody thinks twice about "With my sympathy", except when the speaker finally realizes how little sympathy he really feels. Then he will promptly think of "With my sincerest sympathy".

(2) Receptive listening

*Duden** defines receptive listening as: "To focus attention to words and sounds". This attention has to be made visible and audible, so that the dialogue partner realizes that he is being listened to receptively. This includes silence as the first step. We have to distinguish between "being quiet" and "keeping silent", since even without saying something we are quite well able to:

- comment on what we hear, e.g. by exhaling audibly or moving or even shaking our head
- express impatience by drawing breath and bending forward

* German language compendium

- express lack of interest by keeping ourselves occupied with something else or looking elsewhere.

This type of silence is not indicative of receptive listening, whereas "true silence", in which we pay full attention to the dialogue partner, is. How intense our attention really is, is apparent from our face-to-face interactions. Maintenance of eye contact with the speaker, without staring at him, coupled with slight nodding express unmistakably, that we are listening receptively. Nodding one's head does not mean agreement, but indicates solely that we follow the other person's thoughts.

If eye contact is missing, as for example on the telephone, an audible replacement by short listening signals like "Hm", "Aha", "So", "Oh dear", "Yes" or "No" etc, is required. Everybody knows the situation in telephone conversations where you leave out the "Hm" for a while. After a short time, you can guarantee hearing "Are you still there?" from the other end of the line.

You can also observe how often people use such listening signals, though they scarcely keep eye contact. This pseudo-listening occurs frequently when superiors listen to, or at least ought to be listening to, a subordinate. The superior flips through his mail or signs various documents, uttering "Hm", "No, how interesting!", "So", while the subordinate is made to continue talking.

We should not deceive ourselves; **the level of our attention,** i. e. whether we are following a conversation intellectually, **is visibly expressed by our body language**. Not only our gestures, but also our facial expressions indicate how attentive we are. Be it the forehead that we wrinkle because we have objections to a remark, be it our lips that we compress, because we have heard enough, the lifted eyebrows if we are surprised or the wrinkled nose, if something displeases us. Whether we are bored, or already

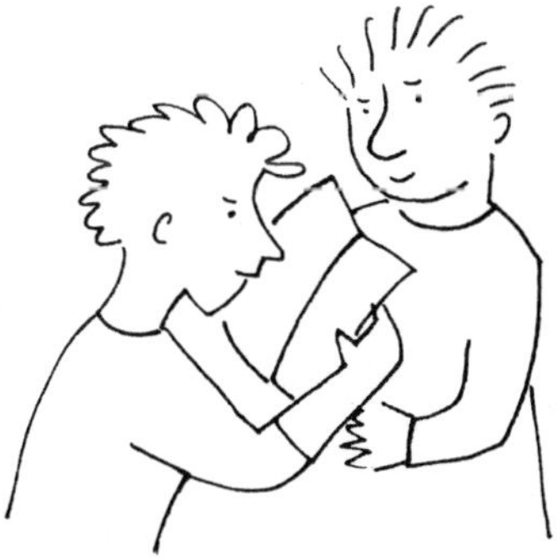

thinking about how to reply, we always show – usually unconsciously – whether we are listening receptively.

I overheard the following conversation at a neighbouring table in my favourite pub. I paid particular attention to the receptive listening. For clarification, I have also included possible reactions as they are frequently used.

A: "Well, the vacation was alright."
B: "Mhm."

B could very easily have mentioned his own vacation and the heavy rain, the sunshine or whatever, for example, "We had a lot of trouble with the hotel!"

A: "I mean, not only regarding the weather, but also otherwise. On the whole, we got along with each other rather well."
B: looks at *A* attentively and nods.

B could have shown interest with a question such as, "Where have you been?" or, "How long have you been away?" and a dialogue on vacations in general would have started.

The beers arrive and they say cheers

A: "I mean, quarrels do occur from time to time. Happens in the best families, right?"

B misses this direct invitation to say something. How easy would it have been to change to one's own problems like: "You can say that again, you wouldn't believe what was going on at our place last week… "

Instead *B* keeps his eye on *A*, nods and murmurs "Mhm".
A: "In fact I do not know whether it started during the vacations or later at home." *A* turns his glass from side to side and seems to reflect.
B: remains silent but keeps looking at *A*.

You could imagine a question like: "What's the matter?" or "Don't beat about the bush, what happened?"

A: "Yes, I think it was at home. Everything was fine between us

there." *A* begins to play with the beer mat and looks down at the table.
B: remains silent.

If he had been impatient, *B* might have come out with: "What are you on about", or something similar.

A: "You know, we have been through quite a lot, and this has very much kept us together."

To my great astonishment *B* did not satisfy his curiosity with e. g.: "Tell me, what have you been through?" but nodded and looked attentively at *A*.

A: "And now I really don't know what caused it. Somehow, I still just can't believe it."

I must admit that even I became slightly curious and found myself asking "What is going on?" in my mind, but the reaction was totally different:

B: "Hm" and kept calm eye contact with *A*.
A: "You know, we have broken up. The day before yesterday. All of a sudden. This really struck me out of the blue."
B: "Oh dear!"

If *B* had wanted to show off his knowledge of human nature, he might have said: "But, you can tell when something like that is coming, there are always plenty signals."

A: "You probably cannot imagine how I feel. I have not eaten anything for two days now, I feel sick, and I cannot even think of sleeping. I only toss and turn all night."

From my position at the next table I was surprised that *B* did not even think about objecting to the idea of him lacking imagination, maybe in the form of: "Of course I can imagine, don't you know that last autumn I…"

In fact, *B* just looked at his friend, nodded slowly, and said: "Yes."
A: "I don't really want to live any longer."

Normally the dialogue partner would be quickly dissuaded from this thought, with either "Come on, you won't commit suicide just out of love sickness, just think of…" or "Oh, I know how you feel, it was just the same some time ago when…"

B did not say anything, but simply looked gravely at *A*.
A: "Damn it, I feel horrible."
Instead of the well meant "Now look, all will turn out well, such things happen to all of us sometime!"
B actually said: "Oh, yes."
A: "Do you know, in a way it's funny, we do not know each other all that well, but in fact you are the first person I am telling this."
B nods turning down the obvious question: "And why did you tell me, of all people?"
A: "Do you know what worries me most? The visit of my parents next week. How do I explain, that there will be no wedding in October? I've no idea what to do."
B: "Mhm"

Even in this case the expected advice such as, "Just cancel the invitation with some excuse", was not given.

After the release of the first edition seminar participants who found B's behaviour rather absurd often surprised me. They made comments such as: "No normal human being would behave in that manner!" Or they implied: "He is really not interested at all." – "Probably he has had an encounter with the girl friend himself." – "Anyway he is listening to the story the xth time." – "He is most likely thinking of his own problems and is not paying any attention."

You might now consider whether you had similar thoughts whilst reading this dialogue. But before you read on, please answer briefly to the following question:

▸ **What exactly is worrying A? What is his problem?**

The following were the most frequent answers to this question:

A is lovesick.
A is suffering, due to the unexpected break-up.
A cannot cope with the new situation.
A is desperate because his girlfriend ran away.

A's thoughts of suicide are seen as a consequence of the break-up. Yet, it is surprising that *A* explains what is concerning him **most**. Moreover, the fact that the wedding would not take place, was the topic of the further conversation. *A* was thinking almost exclusively about his mother, to whom he now had to explain somehow that he would not marry the woman whom she favoured as a daughter-in-law, because she had walked out on him. Up to this point, the conversation had lasted less than five minutes. In the progress of the conversation, *B* actually proved not simply to be a monosyllabic "Mhm"-sayer, but enquired sympathetically about the "parents problem." Due only to his patience, could A's worries be discussed in any depth, incidentally without him necessarily being conscious of it. This form of receptive listening allowed a discussion about vacations, experiences, relationship problems, love sickness, health troubles and suicide intentions to be avoided.

(3) Descriptive listening

In contrast to a word for word repetition, in a circumscription the statement that has just been heard is repeated **in one's own words**. This sounds much easier than it really is. You may have already established that we are able to repeat whole sentences word for word without much practice. We do not even need to have understood the context. What is important is that we are allowed to do the literal repetition directly afterwards. However, if we are to repeat in our own words what we have actually understood, we will not usually get far without practice.

Descriptive listening is the simplest and most certain way **to avoid misunderstandings** from the outset. Some may object that such responses bring nothing new into the conversation and are therefore more or less redundant. However, those who have experienced how pleasant descriptive listening can be, would not accept this reason-

ing. If you repeat the content with your own words, you support the conversation. Through your circumscription you indicate that not only did you listen, but that you also grasped the essentials of the statement and are ready to talk further about the subject.

The following start phrases are suitable for descriptive listening:

"For you it is important that..."
"Do I understand you right that..."
"You mean, if..."
"I have understood that you..."
"What you have said I understand such that..."
"If I have understood you correctly, you are referring to..."

These circumscribing statements are remarks that refer entirely to what your dialogue partner has said.

The most difficult aspect of descriptive listening lies probably in holding back your own opinions, views, evaluations, questions and advice for a moment.

These difficulties may be explained by the fact that we are capable of intellectually processing about 400 words per minute. This matches the reading speed of an untrained adult. By contrast, people usually speak substantially slower than this. Thus, from a purely mathematical point of view, the average language speed of 200 words per minute (which means talking fairly quickly) challenges our receptive capacity to an extent of only 50 %. The remaining 50 % does not lie idle however, but manifests itself in the form of our personal attitude, in the pre-formulation of our response, or in contemplating something unconnected with the conversation. If we listened consistently with the one half of our receptive capability and followed our own thoughts with the other half, this would probably not affect our comprehension. However, in general, after a few seconds our own thoughts become much more interesting than what we hear, thus consuming more than the remaining 50 % of our capacity and correspondingly we listen with diminished attention. In the extreme case, we only just realize that our conversation partner has (finally) finished and that we can go ahead with our reply.

From the Greek philosopher *Socrates* we learn that he was a master of exact listening. In an argument (about immortality: "*Phaidon*") his student *Plato* lets him say for example the following:

"That is what I assume you are trying to say, Cebes. I am repeating you on purpose, so that nothing may escape our attention, and that you may, should you wish, add or subtract anything."*

Here it is evident that not so very much the "weak point" of an argument is being sought, but rather an exact **understanding of the dialogue partner's viewpoint** is being striven for. This form of communication, a fight in the sense of an exchange of views, reached its height in the 13th century, in the so-called scholastic disputations. At the time, there was a rule for these debates that forced the participants to listen. Nobody was allowed to reply immediately to an interjection of the dialogue partner. Before doing so, one was obliged to repeat the opposite position in one's own words in order to unequivocally ascertain what the dialogue partner had meant.

This "medieval practice" can also be used today for training purposes:

▶ **With your dialogue partner, select a topic on which you have opposing opinions and begin a discussion according to the following rule: One is only allowed to reply if one has repeated with one's own words, what the partner has said in his last statement, and if he signals by a clear "yes" that he feels as though he has been understood. Those who are not accustomed to this rule will be glad if a third person takes on the role of an "arbitrator". A neutral person is more likely to pay attention to compliance with the rule in the heat of a real discussion than the participants. Furthermore, he can assist in clarifying whether the repetition was correct or not.**

* from translation of Plato's *Phaedo* by Benjamin Jowett, 1871

In the following dialogue from one of my seminars I played the role of the arbitrator:

A: "I would welcome it if we established a speed limit of 100 km/h on all German motorways, with a maximum speed of 120 km/h. Here we could take a leaf out of the book of the former GDR, since their accident rates were very low. Apart from the lower number of accidents, such a speed limit would lead to reduced pollution. Cars would not have to be so powerful and we could save a lot of money that is currently splashed out on road construction."

B: "Now, if I understand you correctly, you want to implement GDR rules and spoil the party for drivers."

C: "If I may just interrupt, first you are to repeat, before you give your comment."

B: "Why, that was actually repeated. – Well, fine, so you state that with a speed limit – bother, now I've forgotten what I wanted to say. Could you please repeat your statement."

A repeats his statement almost word for word.

B: "Now once again; you want to establish a speed limit of 100 km/h on motorways, because this is how it was in the GDR and because of this, you believe, they had less accidents. Let me tell you right away, that this is not correct, since they had much less traffic."

C: "This was not descriptive listening."

A: "Yes, there were a few things missing."

B: "What, even more? Ok, so try again."

A repeats his position another time.

B: "You prefer a maximum speed of 100 or 120 km/h, because this would lower the accident rate and reduce pollution. Furthermore, you believe that vehicles could be constructed more economically and – I have forgotten the rest."

A: "We could save money, which is wasted on road construction."

B: "Oh yes, but I have a very different view. First of all, our economy is dependent on the car industry and by introducing a speed limit, we would not only lose thousands of jobs, but we would also be no longer competitive internationally. Moreover, the accident statistics are not at all correct, since most accidents happen in city traffic where you drive at only 50 km/h and where people are inattentive and consequently cause accidents more frequently."

A: "You are against a speed limit because you fear that our economy would suffer from it, both from the point of view of job losses and competition. In addition, you doubt that going slower leads to less accidents, because at the same time the concentration of drivers decreases causing an increase in the number of accidents."

The conversation went on in this manner for another 15 minutes.

> "Descriptive listening" indicates that you have understood the content.

(4) Active listening

Active listening is the fine art of listening. Here, one pays attention not only to **what** the other says, but also to **how** the other talks and behaves. Feelings, hopes, and wishes are not usually expressed directly, but are hidden in almost every remark.

In active listening, you ask yourself:

"What are my dialogue partner's emotions?"
"Which aspects of what he has just said are important to him?"
"What is preoccupying him?"
"Which interests is he pursuing?"
"How does he feel?"

In order to answer these questions, you will have to try to understand the thoughts, and even the feelings of your conversation partner.

In contrast to descriptive listening, active listening does not involve repeating the entire statement, but rather an attempt is made to **summarize the emotional content**. Through your active listening, you signal that you have realized your dialogue partner's emotions.

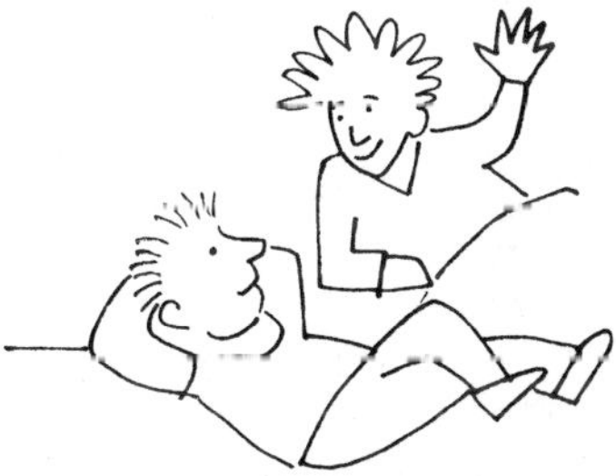

With such an expression you show that you are endeavouring to focus entirely on the other person. You indicate that you are trying to understand the other's point of view and situation.

> "Active listening" is the key to the dialogue partner. It creates a climate of trust and solidarity.

One goal of professional conversation **leadership** is the creation of an atmosphere in which the other **feels as though he has been un-**

derstood. You can experience how difficult it is to grasp this emotional condition intellectually, if you try to list the reasons that are crucial to you to feel understood. People can be especially stubborn if they do not feel emotionally understood. You can observe this most easily with little children.

Imagine the following situation: a two or three year old runs along the street, stumbles and all of a sudden lies on the ground. The child begins to scream. The mother or father rushes to help the child to stand up again and try to calm and comfort it. Typical sentences in such scenes are: "It does not hurt, it does not even bleed…", "Just stop screaming, it will stop to hurt right now…", "Big boys don't cry" or "If you stop crying, you will get some sweets…" Experience tells us that in such situations children scream even louder and cannot be calmed down at all. What is the reason behind this? If we consider what the child might feel after falling so suddenly, it is evident that it most probably isn't pain. First of all a stumbling child (incidentally, an adult, too) feels shocked. It has been running, and now it is lying there on the ground. The shock that went through the body is not acknowledged with a single word by the parent. Instead, a pain is denied that the child has not yet registered.

Whoever responds to the feeling of shock in this situation, shows that he has grasped the circumstances. The following story serves to clarify that acknowledging feelings in no way dramatises the situation, on the contrary:

In this case, his mother could not comfort a three-year-old boy after a fall. He sat on her lap and cried bitterly. On commenting: "Well, Raphael, you were really shocked when you suddenly slipped from the stairs" he said with a totally different voice: "Yes, stupid step!", and immediately the boy stopped crying. Promptly his grandmother added: "Look, Raphael, it does not hurt any more", and the crying started again – this time even louder.

Not only children react in this way. We adults attach just as much importance to being taken seriously, and in many situations we can be rather unpleasant if our feelings are not addressed in an appropriate manner.

I often hear the expression: "Don't add fuel to the fire." This implies a concern that negative feelings might be made worse by a sympathetic response. Indeed, one can observe again and again that people tend to exaggerate their emotions until they feel understood.

Whoever is not prepared to try **active listening** with adults may discover how quickly it can lead to change in perspective with children.

A four-year-old girl falls off a swing and does not duck her head quickly enough. The shock of falling is followed by a painful knock on the head as indicated by the loud crying. The alarmed father puts his daughter on his knee and tries to understand the child's situation: "I can well imagine how shocked you were, when you fell off, and then the swing hitting your head, that must have hurt terribly." To the astonishment of the observer the child turns to the father with her face wet with tears and asks: "Will I get a lump?" – "You'll definitely get a lump, after such a heavy blow on your head." After a brief pause, the little girl, who suddenly changes her perspective, replies: "I don't want to have a lump. You have to put some ointment on it immediately. Come on."

But note, the sequence of events is relevant:

> First, you demonstrate your understanding by active listening, then your dialogue partner will change his or her perspective.

The following example will illustrate this:

It is Dave and Doris White's wedding anniversary. During breakfast they have agreed to go to the theatre in the evening. Doris is happy, pays an extra-visit to her hairdresser, and dresses up nicely for the evening. However, it is after eight o'clock, when her husband finally comes home. She is livid. When he enters the living room, as always whistling cheerfully, she bursts out:

"You are so damned selfish. You only think of yourself and your bloody career."

Neutral and pragmatic remarks will only heat up an already difficult situation. So Dave will add fuel to the fire if he answers:

"I am really sorry, we had a very important meeting, and you know if Dr. Bird is determined to get something done, we have to bear the brunt." Or:

"Now calm down, we can go to the cinema instead." Or:

"I have a proposal for you: I'll take you out to dinner in a fancy restaurant, and you can be sure it will be a great night."

We can assume, that after these remarks the accusations are even more emphatic. Whoever realizes that Doris White's emotional response reveals how important the planned evening out had been for her can only empathise:

"You are very angry about me mak ing you wait for hours. I realize how much it must hurt you when my job is so important to me. I guess you feel like an 'also-ran'."

"Yes, I feel as though you've not taken me seriously and that is no state of affairs. But I don't want to argue with you now. Let's have a glass of wine while we go on talking."

Active listening can also be used in far less dramatic situations.

What experience do you have of situations, in which you have legitimately complained in a shop? What comes to mind when you think about the reaction of the salesman, the service personnel etc.?

It is highly probable that your subsequent behaviour as a customer was dependent not only on whether you got what you wanted, but also on whether you had the impression that your complaint was taken seriously. I will come back to this point in detail in chapter 16.

Imagine the following situation: a customer has bought a floor lamp. Since the lamp is in its original packaging, he takes it home and assembles it there. Unfortunately, when he tries it out he finds that the lamp hums audibly. His emotions will immediately rise, without the man in our example necessarily being aware of them, and he will probably be disappointed. Perhaps a feeling of helplessness emerges of the type "Oh no, what have I done wrong now?" or he feels annoyance, because taking back the lamp will cause him a lot of trouble. In this case, the customer picks up the telephone in order to report the damage at once.

"Hello, this morning I bought an Italian floor lamp from you, and after assembling it I found that it hums."

"Well, I'm afraid that is impossible."

Even if the salesman is right, that such a humming is **actually** impossible, he is not in the least responsive to the customer. Understandably, he stresses his point again:

"Come on now, I think I am able to judge whether this thing hums or not, alright?!"
"Yes, if you are sure, then you will have to bring it back, and then we will see."

Of course the salesman is quite right: he will most probably not be able to stop the humming over the telephone and it is therefore more sensible if the customer returns the lamp to the shop. Nevertheless, his reply was not sufficient to show the customer that he has been understood. What will follow now is an angry customer who in his annoyance will take the lamp back to the shop and directly after arriving will shout:

"Here is this humming thing! And now I want a decent lamp for my money, is that clear?!"
"Hey, please calm down, what's the matter?"

For the salesman it is most important to establish what the problem is quickly. However, the customer is now even more under the impression that he has not been understood and explodes.

"I am willing to explain, but only if you go and get me someone competent."

How easily the situation would have been handled by active listening. If the salesman had practised dealing with trouble, complaints, and claims through active listening, he would have come up with the following sentence without much effort:

"Oh how annoying! You have made all that effort, and now you are disappointed that the lamp does not function properly." The customer would almost certainly have been more matter-of-fact. He might have replied:
"Well, it is not that bad, but I wanted to tell you immediately, because I will not be able to come before next week."

Active listening captures the dialogue partner's emotions.

Imagine a colleague announcing during lunch:

"I don't know why I'm not making more progress with my work. Perhaps I should give it up."

Whoever wishes to react sympathetically should not reply with statements such as:

"Keep your head up, everything will work out well."
"Why, where is the problem?"
"I would do the following..."
"I can imagine, it is because..."

In **receptive listening** you should simply look at your colleague attentively, to indicate that you are listening and that you are curious to learn more.

In **descriptive listening** your reply might be:

"You would prefer to cancel the job, since you cannot see any progress."

In **active listening** you mention the emotions:

"You seem to be discouraged." Or
"You appear to be at a complete loss."

As another example please imagine your colleague saying with a broad smile:

"I still cannot believe it, my application for leave has been granted."

Here, too, you can choose from a variety of reactions none of which has a listening character. For example:

"Now, don't jump for joy too early, you never know..."
"Well, we are not planning to go anywhere this summer, but..."

"Where are you planning to go?"
"I would not talk about it too much, that'll just cause trouble."

Who wishes to listen actively, not only hears the joy, but also the fact that the dialogue partner had worried that the application might not have been granted. The following comment might thus be appropriate:

"I can imagine how relieved you feel."

Since, as you well know, practice makes perfect, in the following table six remarks are listed with which colleagues might begin a conversation with you. In the next 15 minutes you can practise active listening by formulating an appropriate reply to each comment. Afterwards, you can compare your ideas with my proposals.

Example	Your answer
(1) "The organisation of our new project is taking so much time, and progress so far has been slow; I do hope that I can manage everything."	
(2) "Fortunately the colleagues in the team to which I have been transferred have a similar idea of cooperation as I do."	
(3) "The boss had to argue with me about this recent time limit problem in front of the new trainee, of all people."	
(4) "If Mr. Adams gives me a dressing-down like that again, he will get what he deserves!"	
(5) "I have no idea how we can keep the deadline."	
(6) "To get everything done on time, I had to work overtime without even grumbling about it, and what did he say? Nothing! Just nothing!"	

(1) “The organisation of our new project is taking so much time, and progress so far has been slow; I do hope that I can manage everything”

The word “hope” suggests worry, doubt, uncertainty or anxiety. A possible reply would be:

“You are wondering if you can make it on time.” Or:
“In spite of your effort, you are anxious about being able to manage everything.”

(2) “Fortunately the colleagues in the team to which I have been transferred have a similar idea of cooperation as I do.”

Here the insignificant “fortunately” indicates relief or fears that collaboration might be a problem. Therefore, active listening could sound like:

“You sound relieved.” Or:
“You were afraid it wouldn’t work out.”

(3) “The boss had to argue with me about this recent time limit problem in front of the new trainee, of all people.”

This remark suggests shame of being shown up in front of somebody else. This unpleasant feeling can be addressed directly, for example with:

“It is quite compromising to be shown up in this manner.” Or:
“You felt quite humiliated.”

(4) “If Mr. Adams gives me a dressing-down like that again, he will get what he deserves! “

In addition to the wish for revenge you can find indignation and bitterness about the unjustified treatment. Possible reactions might be:

“I can imagine how it grieves you to be treated like a child.” Or:
“You are hopping mad about Adams.”

Behind the indignation and annoyance we can, however, assume another feeling. In the situation in question, the colleague had been given a dressing-down without being able to say something appropriate or to defend himself, otherwise he would not have to seek revenge. Another possible response would therefore be:

"You really felt at his mercy in that situation."

This last remark makes clear that further discussion will not so much pursue the thought of revenge, but will rather deal with the options that the "speechless" colleague will have in future situations in order to defend himself appropriately.

(5) "I have no idea how we can keep the deadline."

In this remark the little word "how" indicates that the colleague has not yet resigned and has still some hope, but his doubts are gaining weight.

Here are several suggestions as to how you might address the pressure of time:

"You feel under pressure." Or:
"You have doubts as to how it can be done." Or:
"You don't have much hope."

Somebody who overlooks the "how", may formulate a reply suggesting resignation, such as:

"You see no way, how this can be managed." Or:
"You have already given up."

(4) "To get everything done on time, I had to work overtime without even grumbling about it, and what did he say? Nothing! Just nothing!!"

On the one hand this sentence contains disappointment because of the lack of gratitude, on the other some bitterness that "working overtime work without even grumbling" was taken for granted. Thus, there are two possible ways to answer, for example:

"You are disappointed that you did not get any reaction." Or:
"I can imagine that it hurts you when your extra work has been taken for granted." Or:
"You are bitter about so much ignorance."

This task becomes considerably more difficult, if instead of having 15 minutes to prepare written replies, you have to react instantly and verbally as would be the case in a real life conversation.

To avoid any misunderstanding, I wish to stress that **active listening** is neither a trick nor a technique to manipulate others, or to steer their behaviour or thinking.

Active listening focuses on the dialogue partner.
One's own intentions, wishes or opinions have to remain in the background.

A prerequisite for active listening is a message that includes some emotional depth. Otherwise things will become grotesque:

A stranger asks a local: "Excuse me, how do I find the railway station?" To which the other, being up-to-date in psychology, answers: "You are uncertain where to find the station." Slightly impatient the stranger asks: "Yes, can you tell me how to get there or not?" But the "psychologist" does not give up that easily: "You sound a little irritated and you're asking yourself, whether I will be able to help you." Unnerved the stranger turns away and murmurs: "Something as stupid as this has never happened to me before." But even this is answered by pseudo-active listening: "Now you sound extremely angry."

The basic mental attitude of active listening is to focus completely on the other person. Active listening is therefore not an examination technique, but is rather an attitude that expresses respect for and attention to the other. Most people find it very pleasing to perceive that they are being listened to attentively and with patience. Even if they are reserved to start with, in most cases the initial "ice" melts quickly in the warmth of concentrated attention.

Nevertheless, I have to acknowledge that with active listening one can of course spy out a dialogue partner. However, I warn you that the price for this "betrayal" is very high. Whoever experiences that the views and feelings openly expressed in a trusting atmosphere are used against one later, will avoid making a similar mistake with this partner again; in future he or she will be extremely wary.

How to get to the point:

Descriptive Listening

If you want to **avoid misunderstandings** the easiest way is to repeat what you have heard in your own words (paraphrase).

If you do this you make it known that you not only listened but also captured the essence of the content and that you are willing to continue talking about the topic.

Your dialogue partner will feel respected and will enjoy being listened to carefully. In most cases this impression will encourage the other to go on talking, so that you learn more about his or her thoughts and feelings.

If you are uncertain as to whether you have really understood your dialogue partner you will most easily achieve common understanding by first repeating what you have comprehended without adding your own opinion on the topic.

Your dialogue partner will be much quicker in getting to the real point if, while explaining his own thoughts, he doesn't have to deal with your assessment.

With descriptive listening you can show that you have understood the content of a statement.

You concentrate on "What does the other want to say?"

On the so-called Line of Agreement, your dialogue partner spontaneously reacts to your statement with a "Yes".

The following **phrases** are useful for **descriptive listening**:

- "In other words..."
- "If I understand right, you mean..."
- "It is relevant for you that..."
- "You value..."
- "For you it very much depends on..."
- "I have understood that you..."
- "If I got it right, your point is..."
- "Do I understand correctly that..."
- "You mean, if..."

• "What you say I would understand in such a way that..."
• "It is very important for you that..."

These phrases focus solely on what the dialogue partner has just said. The essence of this way of leading a communication is to concentrate on the dialogue partner and to abstain from giving well-meant advice and from stating your own assessments, opinions, or objections.

Whoever concentrates on the dialogue partner's point of view usually discovers, paradoxically, that he or she also starts to show interest for the other side of the conversation.

Active Listening

In active listening you not only focus on what the other is saying, but also how he says it and how he behaves. Emotions, desires, and wishes are very rarely stated directly, but resonate in nearly every statement.

As an active listener you ask yourself:

• "What does my dialogue partner feel?"
• "What is so important for him in what he has just said?"
• "What are his concerns?"
• "What are his interests?"
• "What are his intentions?"
• "What mood is he in?"

To answer these questions you have to try to understand your dialogue partner and to empathise with him.

> In active listening you prove that you have comprehended the emotions, which have been linked to a statement.
> You concentrate on "How is the partner speaking and acting?"

In contrast to descriptive listening you do not repeat the statement but try to **summarize the emotions** you have recognized.

By doing this you signal that you have understood your dialogue partner's feelings. You thus indicate that you are making an effort to try to respond to him or her.

Phrases, which express active listening typically, begin with:

- "You are afraid that..."
- "You are in doubt, whether..."
- "You are angry about..."
- "You are not certain, to what extent..."
- "You are startled by..."
- "You are shocked, because..."
- "You are scared by..."
- "It annoys you that..."
- "You could explode, because..."
- "You are sick of..."
- "You are worried about..."

Most people find it very pleasant to notice that they are being listened to with attentiveness and patience. Even if they are reserved to start with, you will usually find that this "ice" melts in the warmth of concentrated interest.

4. Body Language

According to a classic experiment from the year 1972, the overall impression you get of a person is influenced to 55 per cent by body language, to 38 per cent by the tone of voice, and to merely 7 per cent by content. Whoever wishes to lead conversations professionally, would be better off paying attention to his own and his dialogue partners' body language.

We are constantly receiving body language signals, mostly without even noticing. For example, we do notice when somebody looks depressed – even if we are unaware of the fact that this perception is caused by the drooping shoulders, the bent back, and the dropping corners of the mouth.

We do not only receive, but also send signals. This is mostly done subconsciously, and for this reason it is much more difficult to lie with gestures than with words. How easy is it to say: "I really like you". Yet, how difficult it is to look into the other person's eyes in such a way that he or she will believe you, if you are not being sincere. Thus, a message conveyed by body language is generally more credible than words.

Body language can reveal contradictions. Maybe our words say "No", but our eyes and our positive posture will disclose that our emotions have already said, "Yes". Whoever has noticed this will easily elicit the "Yes" from us. Conversely, the voiced "Yes" of a dialogue partner does not mean anything, if the body says "No", when he retreats and closes up. In meetings and conversations – be it private or business-related, with customers, employees, or colleagues – it is essential to interpret body language and to use this knowledge in order to facilitate communication.

Body language is a means by which our body can communicate with its environment. The body follows an inner purpose or a feeling, or it responds to an external impulse. It either transmits an emotion or reacts in a positive or negative way to environmental stimuli. One can guess from the body signals of a person whether he or she is sad or happy, tired or interested.

When body language and verbal expression match here, they complement each other. For example, when I say: "I'm angry!" and at the same time bang my fist on the table. Or, when I welcome somebody with the words: "It's so good to see you" and rush to embrace him. In these cases, the two languages form a unit and reinforce the message. Who acts in this way will appear sincere, trustworthy, and convincing.

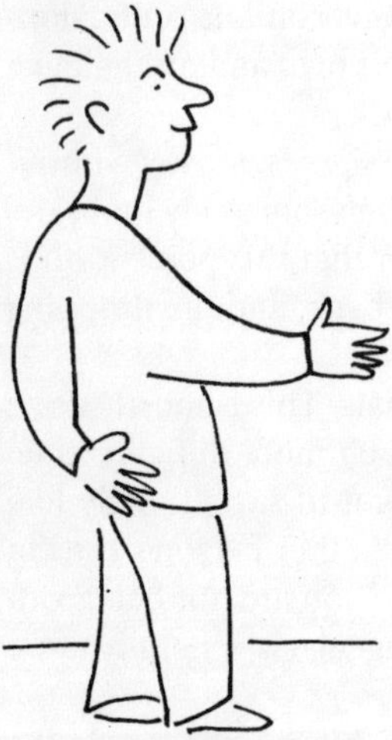

In a different situation, body language can replace words. For instance, when we nod instead of saying "Yes" or when we shake our head to express a "No". this clearly shows that we can also talk with gestures.

In the third case, the two languages contradict each other – a hint at a conflict. One says one thing and thinks another. Yet, this difference will be noticed. Contradictory messages cause distrust and uncertainty. Who is saying one thing, but his body language is transmitting something different, risks being viewed as insincere and will not be convincing.

Therefore, it is better to be careful when trying to conceal your real opinion with well-selected words. Our body will not always tell what we really think, but it will reveal if we are being dishonest. This will suffice to arouse suspicion. Our dialogue partner is unlikely to tell us about his negative impression. However, they say first impression always counts. And in the next discussion the other person will be far more difficult to convince.

So far we have talked about two aspects of body language; sending and receiving.

However, body language not only affects the listeners, but also the one who is talking. Body language has an auto-suggestive effect on one's own emotions. The signals we send out will not only be received by others but also by ourselves, and we also react to them. If I adopt a positive and open posture, this will also influence my own emotions and attitudes in a positive way. Conversely, a crestfallen composure will depress me. Many people subconsciously take on a bent posture when they knock on their supervisor's door with a weighty problem.

When clients come to me for the first time, they have to pass a broad window on entering the room. Automatically, they look at the horizon. Many pause for a moment, take a deep breath, and enjoy the view. Yet, when they sit down and concentrate on their concerns, they lean over and I recognise all the signs of a heavy burden.

The lack of success of some sales representatives can be ascribed to the fact that their whole attitude signals that they are not really convinced of the quality of their product. You can observe the same in meetings and discussions: Somebody gives a presentation. However, before he has really started, you have stopped listening. What has happened?

The speaker wants to say something, but he has mentally devalued his statement as unimportant in advance. I do not want to imply that this has been done consciously. He merely lacked the conviction as to how important his contribution is and what effect he wants to have on his colleagues. Since he does not consider his own contribution worth the effort of – admittedly time-consuming – preparations, I use the term mentally devalued.

Thus, the colleague starts to speak even though the attention of the audience is not yet focussed on him, and he does not even have their eye contact. He explains his ideas without inner conviction. His voice is low and somewhat monotonous, and his posture seems stiff and almost defensive. This leads to the impression that rejecting his ideas would not unsettle him much. Indeed: he hardly shows any signs of disappointment when he is interrupted and somebody else – almost offensively – contradicts him.

The colleague may complain about the lack of attention and may accept with resignation that nobody had listened to him. However, he has to ask the question what he has done to make his message effective.

I admit that he may feel alienated and reprimanded, if he has to account for his unsuccessful body language. Maybe he will understand that his gestures almost encourage others not to listen to him or to ignore him. Instead of harbouring the faint hope of meeting amicable people who can read his mind and promote his badly stated ideas, it would be more effective to optimise his own behaviour.

In this context we should call to mind the importance of the research mentioned in the first paragraph, which states that only 7 per cent of the overall impression are influenced by the content. Nevertheless, we are also responsible for bringing across the remaining 93 per cent.

When we communicate, we want our statements to have an effect. If my message comes across, I will have an effect on my dialogue partner. This change will be visible in gestures, facial expressions, in other signs of an inner process, or by verbal expression and can therefore be observed.

Whoever wishes to affect somebody has to cause a change in the dialogue partner and elicit some sort of feedback response. If this does not occur, I can interpret it as an evidence that my statements have been too weak or lacking in clarity.

While you are talking, your dialogue partner will look at you and listen. His eye movements are signals you can take into account.

In a conversation, different types of pauses arise, which require different reactions. In the following, five typical kinds of pauses will be described more thoroughly.

(1) "It is your turn"

This type of pause arises when your dialogue partner has finished speaking and wants you to go on. In addition to phrases like "What do you think?" or "I'd be interested in your point of view" or seeking approval like "Don't you think so, too?" and similar sentences, eye contact is primarily important. **The "It is your turn"-pause is ac-**

companied by eye contact, to which a slight nodding is added (normally just a hint of a nod).

The following type of conversation pause is very different:

(2) "I am thinking."

This pause arises when your dialogue partner has stopped talking but only to consider whether he has mentioned everything, wondering which way to put the next thought, or perhaps he is already anticipating your answer.

In this type of pause, the line of vision makes the difference. Your dialogue partner will not look at you. On the contrary: his view seems to be fixed to the ceiling. He is not really looking at the ceiling or up to the sky, but is rather **turning his eyes diagonally upwards in a relaxed manner**, without really seeing anything. You can perform a little experiment to show this: Ask an acquaintance to calculate the following arithmetic problem in his head and to look into your eyes while doing so.

▶ **3 plus 2 times 2 plus 3 times 17.**

While you are being looked at unerringly up to the result of 13, the eyes will normally turn upward on reaching the calculation "13 times 17" if your partner has not already started to laugh, because he notices that he is unable to calculate and to keep eye contact at the same time. If you have found a mathematical mastermind, you can augment the result of 221 by the request to multiply this by 17.

Allow your dialogue partner his time for cogitation. He will end the pause himself and will continue talking. Alternatively, the "I am thinking"-pause turns into an "It is your turn"-pause, which will always occur, if your dialogue partner finds out that he has already said everything he wanted to say.

The following pause is a similar case in point:

(3) "I am reflecting"

In contrast to thinking, during which the eyes usually turn diagonally upward, there is a process that can best be described as "reflection", in which the **eyes** normally **turn diagonally downward**. Reflection is a kind of "inward listening", caused by questions like: What do I perceive? What is so important to me? How will I feel? While by turning our view upward we call visions into our memory, in the truest sense of the word visually remembering them, constructing them by imagination, or envisaging how something might be. With the view turned downward we reflect a mood, even without being aware of it.

Perhaps you can persuade your "experimental subject" once again to answer the following questions in his mind:

"What annoys you early in the morning?"
"What did you have for lunch the day before yesterday?"
"What does honesty mean to you?"
"What is the colour of your neighbour's eyes?"
"What do you feel when you are rebuffed?"
"Where would you like to travel?"

You might be surprised to find, how his eyes move alternately up and down.

> You can react to the signals of your dialogue partner. If he looks diagonally upward or downward, a pause in the conversation is required.

It has to be admitted that such a conversation pause can sometimes last "a dreadfully long time". Depending on emotional tension, pauses of more than five seconds may give you the urge to say something. However, only the "It is your turn"-pause is a real request to continue the conversation. In this situation you are under pressure to speak, since it is embarrassing when your partner has finished talking and you are incapable of reacting. Yet, anyone who is aware of the thinking pause and the reflection pause will feel no stress at all. On the contrary, he can remain relaxed until he is signalled to go on.

When you can recognize the different conversational pauses, it becomes clear what was so strange about the conversation in the pub in the previous chapter. Dialogue partner *B* waited until being invited by *A* to contribute to the conversation. Only because *B* was, as is unusual, able to restrain himself, *A* got the chance to lead the conversation to his problem "How do I tell my parents", which he may not even have been conscious of at the beginning. At that very point, *A* looked at *B* and started a dialogue, in which *B* actively participated.

> You are only asked to continue talking when your dialogue partner maintains eye contact and remains silent. In two thirds of all pauses in a conversation it is not your turn. You should relax and remain silent.

However, there is another type of pause, which significantly differs from the others:

(4) "I am ashamed"

This pause always arises when your dialogue partner suddenly stops talking because he realizes that he has embarrassed himself, or he has let slip something he was not allowed to tell you under any circumstances, or because he feels ashamed. However, in contrast to the relaxed view directed diagonally downward, the view here goes vertically downward, usually in combination with a lowered head; alternately, it wanders purposefully to a point in the room which catches the attention of the eyes. In this situation of distress, your dialogue partner will hardly look at you although he waits eagerly for you to say something. Depending on the situation, one person may enjoy allowing the dialogue partner to stew in his own juice while others might end the embarrassing silence.

For the sake of completeness, another pause has to be mentioned, although it is rather rare.

(5) "Let us be quiet"

In this case your dialogue partner has ended his contribution; a pause arises and it is assumed that further conversation will not disturb the emerging silence. In the cliché, it is the situation as on a bench with a view of a landscape or a sunset at the seaside. Exactly this look into the distance is also observed when you are requested non-verbally to sit together in quiet. Shortly after a seminar a participant sent me a letter with a transcript that he allowed me to quote here:

The following conversation between my wife and myself took place last Sunday morning at breakfast after a late night party:

She: "Listen, I have got to talk to you. I can't bear to be laid into the way you laid into me last evening at the Kelleys."

In the emerging pause I would have liked to reciprocate: "That's nonsense, me and laying into you." However, although my wife had glanced at me at first, she now looked at the table in front of her. A little while later she continued:

"See, I had the impression that you and your colleagues were making fun of me."

I nearly let slip the following remark: "Now this is too much. You bring me into an impossible situation in front of my colleagues, I try to save face by hinting at your alcohol level, and now you blame me."

But since my wife's look dropped to the table cloth at the end of the sentence, I abandoned my defence and gave only a "Mhm".

"I admit I had drunk a bit too much, but that is no reason to show me up."

This would have been a perfect opportunity to remark acrimoniously: "A bit too much is an understatement." Yet her look directly down at her plate indicated that something was embarrassing her. A short while later she continued:

"Moreover, you know exactly why I drank so much. If you had not started to flirt with Lisa before my very eyes, everything would have been different." With this sentence my wife looked again down at the tabletop. She fingered her rings and said shortly afterwards:

"Maybe I am making too much of this, but each time I get this stupid feeling of jealousy. Since this incident this dogs me somehow."

While my wife occasionally glanced at me while she was speaking, her look went noticeably to the floor at the end of the sentence. A long pause arose, in which it was hard for me to remain silent and to wait. Yet, I remembered the training part in the seminar and therefore only looked at her with concentration and nodded. Finally she went on unsolicited:

"I know it is nearly two years now, but in such situations I notice that I have not got over it."

You can imagine that now – just two minutes after the beginning of the conversation – we talked or better had to talk about something entirely different...

Maybe this transcript will motivate you to use one of your next conversations for practice. Concentrate only on talking when your dialogue partner has stopped speaking and is looking at you during the emerging pause. If you can manage to take up the conversation thread immediately, few dialogue partners will notice your unusual behaviour.

Who in a conversation monitors the **eye movements** of the other and reacts to the emerging pauses appropriately will be surprised: The atmosphere will become relaxed and in addition the conversation will gain profundity, some dialogue partners will even start to open up in a manner never seen before. I admit that this is not desirable with all people or in all situations, but we are all masters in stalling a conversation, so no further remarks on that point are required.

Anyone who has had sufficient practice in monitoring the eye movements of the dialogue partner, will soon transfer this particular perception to other areas. While you are talking, your dialogue partner is looking back at you, and his eye movements are signals you can react to.

Maybe you would be interested in doing a little experiment in one of your next conversations. Each time your dialogue partner signals thinking or reflection, you stop talking. The three typical reactions are:

- Regaining eye contact, in the sense of an invitation to go on talking;
- Using the pause to make a contribution to the dialogue (you can assume that in most cases this will be a question regarding what you have just said). Your dialogue partner has reflected on something you said and got caught up in his thoughts;
- Not noticing the pause at all. In other words, your dialogue partner is so absorbed by his thoughts that it might take some seconds before he regains eye contact.

You cannot tell what someone who is looking diagonally upward while listening is thinking about. Maybe he is following your train of thoughts or assesses the consequences. Yet, it cannot be excluded that he is thinking about something completely different, for example how he can close this conversation as soon as possible or what he wants to have for dinner. However, if you pause you can end the uncertainty. If your partner has been following your thoughts he will ask a question or a voice comment. If he was elsewhere, he will gratefully perceive the pause as the end of your contribution and continue where he had left off in his thoughts. This might be extremely disappointing for you since you hardly had the chance to say what seemed to be relevant to you some moments ago. Yet, what is the use of a partner who only pretends to listen and in reality is following his own thoughts.

After a training course on how to lead conversations a participant sent me the following dialogue minutes:

When I came home around eight o'clock my wife asked as usual: "How was your course?"

Remembering what we had learned about body language the day before, I did not intend to answer with the usual: "Pretty good", but to use my new knowledge, and so I explained to her:

"There was a lot about body language in conversation and which reactions are possible. A research study was mentioned where they measured the length of pauses in conversations. If I remember correctly, more than 80 % of all pauses were shorter than six seconds."

I wanted to go on explaining that according to the study, such pauses are usually ended with a yes/no-question, and just managed to stop myself, as my wife's eyes really did move upward to the ceiling. I waited expectantly. Then, after a few seconds she looked at me again and said:

"That's not very much. I've often wondered when people reflect on what they're saying. Like yesterday evening in the talk show with – you know who I mean – they talked non-stop. I only got half of it."

"Yes, and that is what we were learning about this afternoon, that in conversation we tend to prepare our response while the other is talking and begin replying immediately after he has finished. It is very common that we do not take in everything because we are thinking about something different. Many discussions are more like two separate monologues than a dialogue."

Here I paused again, since I noticed that my wife had already been looking up towards the ceiling for some seconds. She looked at me enquiringly and said:

"That business with the pauses makes sense to me, but how does it work? It occurred to me that when I tell you a long story with all the details and I have finished I expect an instant reaction from you. If you just looked at me without saying anything I would hit the roof. I would assume that you hadn't been listening properly."

"That is exactly what we were taught. You are completely right: When you have finished, you expect an instant reaction, though this reaction does not have to be a statement. In most cases it would be sufficient if I answered: 'Give me a moment to think about it.' or 'Before I give you an answer I would like to think it over' or something similar.

But while you are talking, you pause briefly, for example to think something over, or because you are searching for the right words, or you are not sure whether you really want to give all the details. And during these pauses...

Here I had to stop again, I even had to interrupt myself in mid sentence to see how she reacted.

"That's right! I can't stand it when you interrupt me before I've finished speaking."

"And now I know why this is. Not all pauses are the same. When you look at me, this means you're inviting me to talk. But when you pause without looking at me I'll keep my mouth shut in future or wait until you continue or look at me."

A chapter on "Pauses in Conversation" would only be complete if I briefly addressed the fundamental problems with daring to pause in a dialogue.

In a diagram below, normal behaviour in a dialogue can be represented like this:

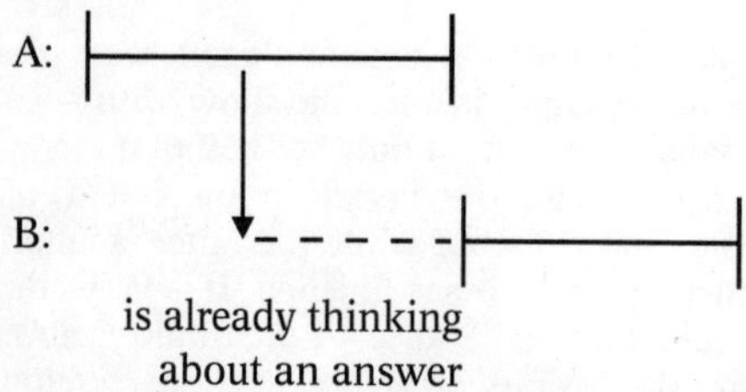

The German author Heinrich von Kleist appropriately named this type of online thinking "the Gradual Completion of Thoughts by Talking".

If you want to listen to the end you necessarily have to pause before you go on talking, like this:

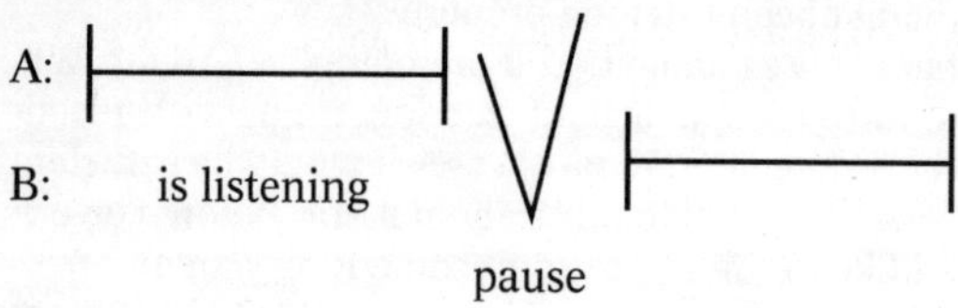

In this case, you risk making your dialogue partner either think that you do not have anything to say or believe that you are incompetent or uninterested. You can prevent this by briefly mentioning before you start thinking that you are going to say something in a few moments, for example using the following phrases:

"Let me think about this a short while."
"I would like to structure this first."
"I need a moment to think about it."
"I have an idea, just wait a second."
"Stop! I have something in mind."

As a diagram, the situation looks as follows:

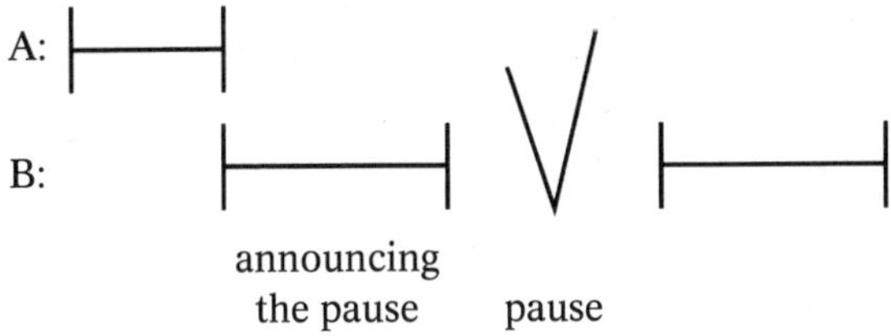

I have noticed repeatedly in conferences and heated debates, that the climate of the discussion changes suddenly, if one of the participants uses such phrases. Naturally, supervisors can be role models and, using such a sentence, contribute much more to a constructive conversational atmosphere. However, all employees can contribute and demonstrate that taking time to reflect is no disgrace but adds to clarity and mutual understanding.

Whoever uses the **announcement of a pause in combination with descriptive listening** will often find that a brief summary is usually sufficient to make the dialogue partner give a more precise statement. In this way the debate on speed limits from the previous chapter could be continued like this:

B: "Now, these were the four arguments for a speed limit: accidents, pollutant emission, construction technology and road construction. I need to think them over, before I continue."

A: "With respect to the ubiquitous lack of money, road construction seems to be the most important argument to me. With a uniform speed, our existing motorway network could bear much more traffic."

B: "You are considering possible savings in the extension of the infrastructure. This is an aspect I would like to briefly think about." (pause ...)

Using this conversation technique you can quickly bring conversations with controversial content to the point. It appears that descriptive listening in combination with announced pauses contributes to saving time. If you focus the conversation on the aspects that are really important to your dialogue partner, you will be able to avoid useless discussions.

How to get to the point

Pauses in conversation

In two thirds of all pauses in conversation it is not your turn to speak. You can remain relaxed and silent.

"It is your turn"

You are only asked to say something when your dialogue partner looks at you and remains silent. Then, and only then!

"I am thinking"

As long as your dialogue partner remains silent and keeps looking diagonally upward, this means he is thinking things over. Wait until he has finished, he will be grateful.

"I am reflecting"

if your dialogue partner looks diagonally downward, this means that he is listening to his inner feelings, such as what is important for him in that moment, whether something sounds right, or how he can assess what he has just heard. Allow him time to reflect.

> React to your dialogue partner's signals. Eyes turned diagonally upward or downward are a request for a time for cogitation.

While you talk your dialogue partner will look at you when listening. His eye movements are signals you can react to.

Stop talking when you find his eyes signal that he is thinking or reflecting.

Three typical reactions of your dialogue partner will be:

- To regain eye contact in the sense of an invitation to continue speaking;
- To use the pause to say something (in most cases this will be a question about what you have just said). Your dialogue partner has started to think about your statement and got caught up with a certain thought;

- Not to notice the pause at all. In other words, your dialogue partner is so absorbed in his own thoughts that it may take some seconds until he is ready to regain eye contact.

Hint: Anyone who is uncertain as to whether the dialogue partner is really thinking, would be well-advised to address this directly, e. g.:

"You are just thinking things over."
"You have something on your mind."
"You want to consider this for a little while."
"Something is bothering you."

5. Guidance and Regard

In chapter 3 which dealt with listening, it emerged that you cannot pay anybody a higher compliment than to listen intently and attentively. It was shown that listening is a complex process. In addition, mere reception of what has been said is enhanced by an interpretation of the content. You may ask yourself, what is meant by a remark, assess it and react correspondingly. In other words, we do not react to what we hear but to our interpretation and assessment of what has been said.

Whatever answers you may give; it can be plotted on a scale with the following extremes:

Regard ⟵——————————————————⟶ Disregard

Whether you are aware of it or not, each of your statements also reflects your **relationship** to the dialogue partner. The degree of regard, recognition and respect is not only expressed in words but also by your intonation, your gestures and your facial expressions.

How often have you experienced in conversations that your dialogue partner started to form an opinion in his mind while you were still talking. The other agrees spontaneously, nods for example, smiles, or shows his agreement in another way – or he disagrees with your arguments and shows this by shaking his head, frowning, or showing other signs of disapproval. Indeed, sometimes you may have had the impression that the rejection of your arguments and the rejection of you as a person were not clearly separated. Imperceptibly, a lack of regard for your arguments becomes a lack of respect for yourself.

The entrance dialogue between the supervisor, Mr. Quick, and his subordinate, Mr. Black, made this very clear. Mr. Quick cannot understand the reaction of his colleague at all; he who means always well, suddenly meets with resistance, which he promptly takes very personally, and so finally threatens "Well then . . .". The same is true for Mr. Black, who meets with a total lack of understanding from his supervisor and gains the impression that not only his hesitating, but also he as an employee is not being accepted.

Why, when dealing with regard and disregard, is so little distinction made between an idea and the person stating it? This is related to our need for generalization. By **generalizing**, we reduce the complexity of our environment to manageable units. Yet, this simplification also has a downside: We are usually unaware of the fact that behind our opinion lies a **subjective estimation**.

Statement	**Estimation**
"I think it is good."	"It is good."
"I would never have come up with such an idea."	"This is absurd."
"I agree."	"This is completely right."
"I don't like that."	"This is nonsense."

If something is "nonsense" in our eyes, it implies that we regard our own position as correct and correspondingly we strive to make the other person understand this. In other words, with opposing points of view, the esteem for our own opinion goes hand in hand with a disregard for the opposing position. This is usually caused by the fact that we are convinced of the correctness of our own opinion, otherwise we would not voice it at all. At the same time, you can observe that the more vehemently someone attacks the opinion of others, the shakier his own arguments are. Sometimes you get the impression that having an opposing view to them is equal to attacking their position, or even their integrity, and therefore needs to be fought against determinedly. Or put positively: the more certain you are, the more calmly you can react to remarks that contradict your own convictions.

These facts are in no way intended to make you avoid opposing somebody else's opinion in the future or leave them uncommented. If something is important to you, if, for example you want to change something, you will gain influence as long as you **take yourself seriously**. Depending on how important something is to you, you will be able to plot your remark on a scale with the following extremes:

Giving freedom ⟵——————————⟶ Control

The more you want your dialogue partner to agree with your argument, the more you will try to control, or conversely grant the other the freedom to see things differently if coming to an agreement is unimportant to you.

If now both behaviour scales are combined, the following coordinate system results, in which the four quadrants represent four different conversation or leadership styles.

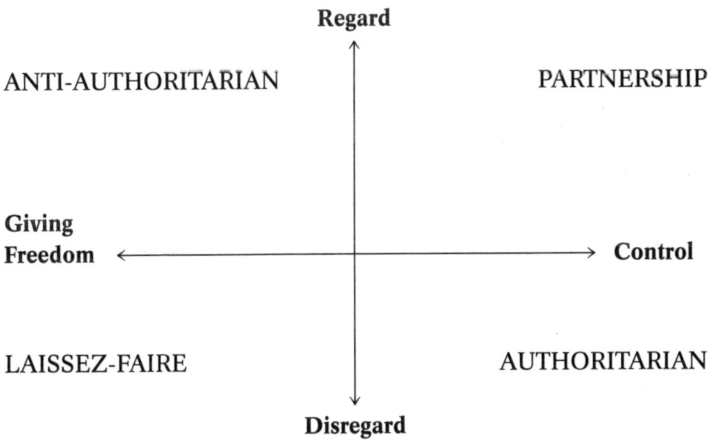

When the controlling influence is combined with disregard, the resulting style, which is most certainly known to you will be **authoritarian**. If, with the same disregard, the freedom of the other remains

unaffected, this leads to a behaviour that is called indifference or **laissez-faire style**.

The opposite of the authoritarian behaviour is the renunciation of control, meaning to give freedom and regard, this leading in its purest form to the **anti-authoritarian** style, which in the past twenty years has led to considerable misunderstandings: the renunciation of control favoured by the anti-authoritarian movement turned out all too often to be only a lack of responsibility combined with fear of possible rejection. To illustrate this, I want to give an example from one of my recent seminars:

A student (in her 10th semester of education & social studies) had prepared and presented a three-hour seminar unit. Her failure to give clear instructions led the seminar group into complete chaos. In the concluding discussion, I confronted her with the comment: "I had the impression that for some reason you shied away from telling your colleagues how you had planned the unit." – "That's right, I don't like imposing my ideas on others." – "You evidently dislike that sort of thing." – "Well, yes, it would be authoritarian." – "In other words, you prefer to avoid appearing authoritarian under all circumstances. What surprises me is that you automatically assume you are imposing your will on others, if you are only trying to communicate your ideas clearly." – "I would not put it quite so blatantly." – "Okay, now let's consider what would have happened, if you had directed your fellow students deliberately in the direction, which you had deemed suitable."- "I don't know, but perhaps some would have rejected that or tried to assert themselves against me."

One might have the impression that taking control is rejected for fear of being rebuffed when one's own ideas are formulated. In other words: the **renunciation of control** also resembles a **conflict avoidance strategy** in order to reduce the possibility of being insulted.

And finally there remains the combination of control and regard, which is named the **partnership** style. In a partnership relation the other is generally allowed to have a different opinion, without any loss of regard. However, one's own point of view is argued for decisively; since with all respect for the partner one should not go so far as to abandon one's own position. Reduced to a common denominator:

> Self-esteem is a prerequisite of regard for others.

This prerequisite may be substantiated by a brief philosophical excursion: according to *Hegel*, humans differ from animals in the desire for other people's appreciation, i. e. in wanting to be "accepted". Above all, man wants to be acknowledged as a human being, a being that has a certain worth and dignity. In addition every person has the desire that not only his own intrinsic value is acknowledged, but also the worth of the people, things or principles he values. This ability to recognize the worth of the inner self and to demand appreciation for it is commonly referred to as self-esteem. In his Politeia *Plato* describes the ability to feel self-esteem as emerging from the part of the soul named Thymus (feeling – emotion). It is a kind of innate **sense of justice**. The need for self-esteem and appreciation is accompanied by the emotions of fury, shame and pride. *Plato* believes anger to arise if one is treated less respectfully than one's own self-estimation, shame when one acts against one's self-respect, and pride if one is judged in accordance with one's inner worth. Viewed this way, regard for others at the cost of self-esteem produces the feeling of shame while lack of regard from others leads to the emotions of annoyance and anger. Thus, the self-esteem of an individual depends on how much appreciation he receives.

Probably, the partnership style will only rarely have occurred to you. In a partnership style dialogue, the result of a conversation is not fixed from the start. The task is to find out if a given goal can be achieved another way, as implied by the proverb: "All roads lead to Rome". A result is not a purpose in itself. Nevertheless, one often has the impression that deviations from the way – not from the goal! – are rated as a dangerous loss of authority. If you already know or have decided, how to deal with something, you no longer meet the

conversation partner as an equal, but you rather want his unconditional acceptance of your position.

The following example is meant to clarify the conversation reactions:

In a business with 60 employees an accountant was hired four months ago, and he has proven to be especially efficient and experienced. The owner has already noticed repeatedly that the accountant does not care too much for coming on time in the morning. By coincidence he meets him in the parking lot one day, nearly twenty minutes after the beginning of normal working hours. The colleague seems to notice the critical glance of his boss, walks over to him and says:

"I hope you don't mind if I sometimes come in a bit late."
Typical authoritarian reproaches might be:
"The working day starts at 8 am, for you as well!"
"If you're late one more time, I'm afraid I'll have to reprimand you."
"Are you always going to take the liberty of coming late?!"

Ironic or sarcastic remarks also belong to the authoritarian style:

"Maybe it has slipped your attention that work starts at 8 am here."
"If you don't mind working elsewhere in future, I don't mind you being late."
"If it is too hard for you to come on time, I must have over-estimated your capabilities."

With the same disregard and lack of control, laissez-faire comments might be:

"Everyone does as he pleases."
"If you think it's necessary."
"Why do you bother asking me? You come late anyway."

In an anti-authoritarian reply the supervisor gives up control but shows regard for the accountant:

"For me the most important thing is that all my employees are happy at work. If it is important to you to be allowed to come late from time to time, I can accept that, especially since I am sure you know how to organise your time."

With a partnership style answer understanding for the employee's position is shown, but at the same time one's own point of view is stated unmistakably:

"I do believe that it may be convenient for you to choose your own working hours. However, since you ask me directly, I will tell you frankly, that it is important for me that you start at 8 am, too."

With this remark, the positions are made clear, and no more. For this is exactly where the last remark differs from all previous ones: here the accountant has the chance to further explain his point of view. I admit that this automatically leads to a longer conversation. Indeed, this is exactly the point where many managers prefer the authoritarian style, since the case is decided and the colleague has to come on time (or he must leave). The following reply would be conceivable from the employee's side:

"I don't follow you there. You want me to complete all my work correctly and on time. It doesn't matter if I come at eight or at half past, especially since I often stay later than six in the evening."

Suddenly the employee's behaviour appears in a new light. This does not necessarily lead to a concession, the supervisor could answer:

"I do not have any doubts regarding your performance, on the contrary. I only have problems with making an exception. I am afraid that your colleagues may take you as an example and claim that I tolerate you being twenty minutes late."

This way it is made clear to the employee that punctuality is not requested as an end in itself, but is related to concrete business requirements and with related fears. Now he could answer:

"Okay, I can understand that. But if my colleagues argue that way, I would appreciate it if they would also cite my late working hours in the evening. What would you if I were to talk to them about this point? I cannot imagine that any of them would like to stay as long as I do, and this is the reason why they all arrive early in the morning and call it a day punctually."

One can presume that this accountant will continue arriving late at work in the morning, without any effect on the quality of his work or other problems arising from it.

And if in this example the partnership style can lead to a compromise, which favours the accountant, another consequence is also conceivable if you change the argumentation slightly. The supervisor could enhance one of the above-mentioned sentences like this:

"I don't have any doubts regarding your performance, on the contrary. I only have problems with making an exception, and this is connected with your role as our accountant and with the fact that you are the supervisor of two experts. I can well imagine that you are able to find a solution for dealing with the working hours internally. On the other hand you are also a role model for other departments, and I would prefer my managers to set a good example. In addition, you know that we have many visitors early in the morning, and I fear that conclusions may be drawn about your late appearance regarding the correct settlement of our transactions. In the worst case, someone might think: 'If the accountant is allowed to come, when he wants, then what about the rest of the team.' You ought to know how dependent our business is on a good image'."

In the beginning the partnership style may seem unusually time-consuming. It is, however, highly probable that from now on the accountant will appear punctually, without any grumbling. On the contrary, the employee can understand his boss's arguments and therefore changes his behaviour voluntarily, which would not have been the case with the authoritarian style. The latter approach would risk that the accountant arrives on the minute from that day on, but expresses his displeasure in other ways, for example in observing closing time, even if important transactions have not yet been completed.

I would like to summarize the advantages of the partnership style especially in the cooperation with subordinates with the following:

- with the partnership style you arouse interest and commitment,
- show that the goals you set are worth achieving,
- raise the hope of being successful,
- wake hidden capabilities and
- make others identify with a common goal.
- With the partnership style you reduce the number of problems in everyday cooperation

In the following example, first try to find four different reactions before comparing your answers with my proposals.

▶ **You are the leader of a team of 5 experts. There is a business directive which regulates that vacation is only allowed, if at least three colleagues of the group remain to deal with the ongoing business. Ms. Short, a young specialist, who joined your group eight weeks ago from another department, requests an appointment, in which she asks for vacation as follows:**

"I would like to go on a fortnight's vacation in three weeks time. Now I found out that the other colleagues have already planned their vacation and that there is no possibility for me to take mine before November. Can you make an exception? It is very important to me because I have been given a once in a lifetime opportunity to fly to Kenya at short notice."

What would be your authoritarian answer?

Which reproach can you think of in laissez-faire style?

And how do you answer when you lose control but want to show regard?

How could you use the partnership style?

My replies are only intended for orientation and are by no means the only valid ones.

The wish to control can be expressed according to the extent of disregard, from subtle to dominant:

"My dear Ms. Short, I would gladly grant you vacation, but you know very well, the directives do not allow it. Don't worry, you'll probably have more luck next time." or:

"What are you thinking of? The other colleagues have planned their vacation on time. I cannot change everything, just because of you. I'm afraid it's impossible!" or:

"I am not sure I have heard correctly. Do you want me to get a dressing-down from management? If everybody wanted an exception, we would close the store down."

Finding an authoritarian answer may not have been hard for you. When combining disregard with giving freedom, people hardly ever hesitate:

"You want to go to Kenya for two weeks. If you believe that you will endear yourself to our team, go as you please." Or:

"I have no other choice. In the worst case, you will go on a sick leave and have a vacation anyway." Or:

"You do not realise what situation you've put me in. Well, who cares, so long as you have fun."

If you combine regard with lack of control, an anti-authoritarian answer could sound like:

"Two weeks in Kenya, that is a unique opportunity, and I can understand very well that you do not want to miss it. In such a situation I think I will have to make an exception to the rules."

In the classic situation of a team leader, the last answer will be rather unrealistic because his supervisor will ask him questions, if performance problems arise in this group. Therefore the team leader will hardly forgo his right to control.

However, if it is combined with regard, he could for example reply in the following way:

"I can well understand that at the moment you want to realize your vacation plans. It is important to me that the ongoing work is completed without delay. If you go on vacation at the end of the month, as far as I know only two colleagues will be present. This automatically means that some work will not get done. On the other hand I realize that you should not suffer from any disadvantages related to joining our group. How about asking one of your colleagues if he would postpone his vacation? I would be prepared to go and ask him."

With this partnership style answer, everything is still open. It is possible that the colleagues agree to a postponement or find an agreement which guarantees that during the period in question no tasks remain pending. However, if it turns out that the three colleagues have already made bookings for their vacation, the partnership style answer secures a basis for future collaboration. It is hardly to be supposed that the employee will reproach her team leader, if the Kenya vacation is impossible, since he showed understanding for her position and tried to find a solution acceptable for all people involved. In addition the colleague was even requested to assist with finding a solution. In the best case, a solution that is satisfactory to everyone will be found. In the worst case, she will have to cancel her vacation. Nevertheless, she will recognize how difficult it was to realise her request, since not even she could find a solution.

This partnership conversation style can be used not only in working life. The combination of influence and regard can also solve conflicts in partnerships and the family in a way that is acceptable for all participants.

With the following case dealing with family life you can again note down possible answers, before comparing them with my proposals.

▸ **You are mother or father of three children aged 15, 12, and 10 years. For the summer holidays you have planned a three-week vacation with the whole family. One Sunday evening your eldest daughter discloses to you:**

"In the summer holidays I would like to go on a four-week camping tour with Dorothy. Her parents have already allowed it. May I go?"

If you select an authoritarian answer you might say:

Your laissez-faire behaviour may sound like this:

For an anti-authoritarian answer you may have found the following reproach:

A partnership style reply could be expressed with the following reaction:

As an authoritarian father I would spontaneously think of the following answer:

"You know how much I like to have you with us during the holidays. As I see you so rarely, I do hope that you will come to the seaside with us just to please me." Or:

"I can hardly imagine that Dorothy's parents have agreed to that. Even if they have, I do not think a camping tour of four weeks is an appropriate way for a fifteen-year-old girl to spend her vacation." Or:

"Are you mad?! Four weeks of camping, I won't hear of it. You know exactly that we are going to the seaside for three weeks, so forget about that nonsense."

As an authoritarian father, I will however have had many discussions with my teenage daughter. So I can well imagine switching from authoritarian behaviour to the laissez-fair style, like this:

"Your family does not mean anything to you any more." Or:
"I don't care, you are a hopeless case anyway." Or:
"As long as you do not expect us to finance your holiday, you can do, what you want."

An anti-authoritarian answer would be hard for me because my daughter's wish annoys me and giving her her freedom would mean abandoning my own point of view:

"I can understand you wanting to go on a camping tour with Dorothy. We are probably a bit unexciting, and you find your younger sisters a bit restricting."

This is probably the answer the daughter wanted to hear. Nevertheless, a stale taste remains if boundaries don't need to be explored and when each wish is granted immediately. Only the partnership style answer gives the daughter the chance to fight for her interests and to deal with the conflicting point of views.

"I am sure that you are really excited about going on a camping tour. For me it is important that I spend at least part of my vacation with you, and moreover I am a bit surprised to hear that you and Dorothy want to go on your own."

After this opening, the positions are clear and the daughter can help to find different solutions. A camping adventure of the daughter and her friend in the vicinity of the family's holiday resort or a joint family vacation (with or without Dorothy) and a following week of camping in a setting that reduces the parents' worries would be possible solutions. Even the renunciation of the camping vacation does not have to be excluded since the daughter can modify or abandon her wish the sooner when she is certain that her wish has been understood and accepted.

A kind of paradox can be found in partnership style communication:

As long as you do not accept the dialogue partner's point of view he will tend to persist and defend his view instead of dealing with your explanation.

> When showing regard, you create a base for a rational view of the conflict, with which your dialogue partner can voluntarily forgo or change his point of view.

It is always fascinating for me to observe how quickly people adopt an appreciative communication style, when they realize that taking a controversial point of view seriously or even accepting it does not require abandoning one's own position.

To most readers it may appear somewhat mechanical at first if I reduce appreciative control to: **"You want X and I want Y."** You may have noted that here the respective points of view are consistently connected by the word "**and**". The conjunction "and" gives the same weight to both positions and at the same time makes clear that the decision is really an open one. In chapter 13, I will address the much more frequently used "but", with which we already indicate beforehand what the decision will turn out.

What is your reaction if a four-year-old girl addresses you as follows:

"You want to relax and read the newspaper, and I want you to read me a story."

The effectiveness of this type of conversation leadership can be found in the fact that the respective remark deals with the concerns of the dialogue partner from the outset.

I confess that my daughter would have had hardly any chance, if she had attached more importance to her wish to hear a story than to my need for a rest; my defiance would have been assured. In the following chapter I shall deal with avoiding resistance.

In order to avoid the impression that the pattern of appreciative control is only useful in the private sphere, I want to cite a colleague as an example of someone who tried for a long time to convince his supervisor to acquire a certain computer program. When the colleague made use of appreciative control without regard to the case history, the reaction of the supervisor changed:

"During the last four weeks you have repeatedly said that our current program is quite sufficient, since we can quickly process all routine work. What's more, I would like to work with a program that in addition to the normal features provides other functions that are needed only occasionally. Are you interested in comparing programs? I believe you are interested in a smooth handling of our day-to-day business."

"I do realize you do not give up that easily. Please provide me with a list of operations our present system does not perform, and add your estimation, as to how much time manual processing would require. I can decide best if you add up that for one year, since then acquisition costs and loss of time can be compared."

In chapter 14, "From Persuasion to Conviction" I will describe the pattern used here in greater detail.

> The strategy of appreciative control represents a way of problem solving, with which you can integrate adaptation and insight and obtain lasting change.

From your own statements and from those you find in this chapter you may have noticed that regard can be graduated.

Unconditional regard is the most difficult to realise. Independent of the respective point of view of the dialogue partner it is shown that he has the same right to voice this position and that he fights just as legitimately for its realization as we do. Our attentiveness and acceptance is therefore not tied to anything in return. In the intimate sphere we call this state of unconditional regard 'love'. Probably the best-known definition is found in I. Corinthians 13, verse 4–7 of the apostle Paul:

"If I love people, I will be patient. I will be kind to them and I will not want to have their things for myself. I will not tell them how good I am. I will not think that I am better than they are. If I love people, I will be polite to them. I will have kind thoughts about them. I will not think only about what I want for myself. I will not get angry with them often. And I will not keep a list of all the wrong things that they do to me. I will not be happy when those people do bad things. If I really love them, I will be happy when they do what is right and true. And if I really love people, I will never stop loving them. I will always believe that they can do right. I will continue to hope for good things in their lives and I will always be patient with them."

Conditional regard can be realised much more easily. Here the other gets our full acceptance and attentiveness as long as he is in agreement with our ideas and goals. Many educational processes follow this scheme: "If you behave well, you will get..." In everyday leadership life the analogous formulation becomes: "Since you performed so well, I would like to give you..."

If brought up in a constant climate of conditional regard a child's: "If I am good (dutiful/busy/good at school), my parents will love me" becomes the adult's striving for achievement in the sense of: "If I behave in accordance with the expectations of my superior, I'll get recognition". The point is not to abolish the regard associated with achievement, we just need to understand that leading a conversation in such a way can easily cause unreflected adaptation or defiance.

Even more frequently we meet the **conditional disregard**. Here we let our dialogue partner feel that we reject him momentarily because of his "misconduct". Reproaches and criticism are only too often coupled with disregard, in formulations like: "Since you have bad marks in the test, you are not allowed to..." or in the working life: "It is because of your error, that I unfortunately have to..." In such a climate people learn to avoid painful disregard through avoidance of mistakes. Unfortunately the elimination of errors alone does not necessarily lead to desirable results. Another danger is the camouflage of mistakes, for only discovered mistakes lead to disregard with all the unpleasant accompanying circumstances.

Finally the **unconditional disregard** has to be mentioned. Independent of the other's actual behaviour it is made clear to him that he has no right to have his own point of view. The other can do what he wants; he is always a "loser" and does not count. The impression may arise that this concerns a rather extraordinary form of behaviour. Far from that! What did the father say to his daughter?

"Are you mad?! Four weeks of camping, I won't hear of it. You know exactly that we are going to the seaside for three weeks, so forget about that nonsense."

Or the authoritarian team leader to Ms. Short:

"I am not sure I have heard correctly. Do you want me to get a dressing-down from management? If everybody wanted an exception, we would close the store down."

At the end of this chapter, I propose that you self-critically analyse your training results for the conversation with Ms. Short or with the daughter and decide which form of esteem or disregard they express.

Criticizing with Regard

Always begin a criticism conversation by making clear, what your goal is. To this end the focus will not be the critical points but rather the chances of improving something.

Criticizing somebody without naming the preferred state always leaves behind a stale taste. The other feels rejected, embarrassed, criticized, and insufficient: a *win – lose situation* emerges. The one who is criticized loses – even if it is only his "face".

Whoever conceals his real intentions, loses the chance to cooperate in order to be successful.

To avoid an aggressive or distrustful conversation climate, try to achieve a relaxed conversation atmosphere.

Five Rules for Criticism

(1) **Describe** the situation, do not rate it.
(2) **Show understanding** for the other instead of acting indifferently.
(3) Regard the other as an **equal**, instead of demonstrating your superiority.
(4) Be **problem-oriented**.
(5) React **spontaneously** to the other's statements instead of preparing a strategy.

> You can keep criticism on an objective level, if you resist the temptation to try and change the other person.

Whoever wants to achieve a goal, will voice criticism in three steps:

(1) Explain the goals:

In the first step, you clarify whether both sides are pursuing the same goal. If that is the case, compare, how each of you imagines the result and how you want to achieve it.

If the goals are different, you can stop this conversation immediately. Instead you can think about how a common goal could come into being and how it should be conceived.

(2) Check the means:

Even if the other does something you do not like, you can show him that you respect him *nevertheless* by letting him explain how his means would lead to achieving a goal. You abstain from reproaches (which would only cause defence) and make clear that you have a serious interest in the other's intentions and ideas.

(3) Find a common approach:

If you have confidence in the other you will let him participate in the search for a solution and ask him for his proposals. He *is* to take over responsibility! In this case, mutual understanding is also possible, and it creates a *win – win – situation*.

If you do not trust the other to find a solution, you can forgo the criticism anyway. It saves time and energy if you immediately look out for someone, whom you regard as more appropriate.

6. Resistance with the Dialogue Partner

There is hardly anything people react so sensitively to than to a restriction of their freedom.

Anyone who perceives that his **window of opportunity is constrained against his will, is bound to express resistance**; this resistance, also named reactance, can even be expressed in the mere expectancy of an assumed restriction of one's freedom, as a kind of anticipated answer to a possible restriction in the sense of: "Nip things in the bud!"

This resistance which serves to restore the lost (or feared to be lost) freedom, can be expressed in four ways:

Defiance

Doing exactly what is not supposed to be done, according to the motto "Now more than ever", restores the threatened or restricted freedom. Although the word defiance is most frequently used when talking about children (There is an entire development phase that is named phase of defiance), this defiance will also be found with adults, only that they will like to call it "critical awareness", while elderly people are often said to be "stubborn". Yet, whatever the label may be, it is always a matter of intended violation of given boundaries, an insistence on one's own point of view – as an expression of resistance – against the restriction of individual freedom. In the defiant reactance the message always reads: "Not with me!"

If you just consider how you react to speed limits:

- Do you drive at 30 mph if signs have been put up accordingly?
- Do you mind the speed limit in an urban area, even on an empty road?
- And do you stick to the speed limit on a freeway, just because it is prescribed?

These are examples of typical defiant reactance to the restriction of our freedom as a driver. The German motoring organisation ADAC has the slogan "Free way for free citizens!". The wide acceptance of this slogan is due to the fact that it claims free choice of the appropriate speed (on a freeway) for everybody.

Orientation towards the excluded alternative

Is the freedom of choice reduced because one alternative is excluded, e. g. through a ban, excuses, or pressure, just the alternative which would be eliminated gains attractiveness. You find a typical example in sales: a special offer usually includes a hint of limited supply that is to wake a disposition to buy. In addition many customers tend to be interested especially in the product, which the salesman draws back out of the narrower choice. For example, many a salesman uses the lack of decisiveness of a customer, in that he slowly retracts the most expensive one in a set of articles in order to direct the attention on two or three positions more favourable in price. Promptly the customer will turn to the retracted item. However, with some salesmen, this sounds only clumsy:

"This is our top model, but I don't think you will be interested in it." Or:

"This equipment is usually asked for by our more sportive customers. So may I show you our standard model first?"

You will already have repeatedly experienced that alternatives, without regard to their actual advantages, become extremely unattractive, if you are put under pressure to choose them. Perhaps herein lies also an explanation for why people usually react to unwanted pieces of advice and solutions with a "Yes, but...", this "but" takes care of the threatened alternative, that possibility, that would be excluded by following the advice.

Regarding this reactance behaviour a seminar participant told me that her past summer vacation went totally wrong, because her husband niggled about everything for three weeks. Meanwhile this made sense to her, since she had provoked the resistance of her husband downright. While he was absent she had made the pending decision on “Do we go to the mountains or to the seaside this year?” together with their children and thus confronted him with accomplished facts. While in the preceding year he had proven to be a seaside enthusiast, he now complained about the eternal sun, the heat, that much too warm North Sea, the meals, the lodging, the support offers, and the gym, always with the hint, that it would be better in the mountains, much more variety, more healthy climate, just much, much better.

Indirect restoration of freedom

Here the restriction of the behaviour latitude is apparently obeyed to, in some kind of adapted manner. However, simultaneously one’s own freedom is demonstrated, but secretly. For example, when children read with a pocket lamp under their blanket, although their parents have switched off the light for bedtime. The parents know nothing about it, but the message of this typical child behaviour actually is: “You could have left the light on as well, I will read anyway.”

A similar indirect restoration of freedom you can also find in many a constricting sales conversation where the customer suddenly thanks the salesperson for the detailed “consulting” and ends the conversation by declaring that he needs some time to think things over or asking the representative shortly before contract conclusion to leave the filled out documents behind, he would send them later (which will hardly ever happen).

A seminar participant told me that he always had problems with leaving a shop without buying something after he had received time-consuming support. He avoids the assumed restriction of his freedom, which would be to have to buy something, by for example reserving two pairs of shoes in a shoe shop and leaving the shop under a false pretence such as lack of cash or the need to talk to his wife, but indeed, he never returns to that specific shop. He confessed that this strategy has a definite downside, since for fear of being recognized he will never enter these shops again.

Open aggression

Finally the resistance can be expressed by open aggression. Who threatens the freedom of another person or even actually restricts it, must reckon with an attack. Aggression does not need to show itself in an assault. Certain statements are especially apt for that, too. Someone who denies the other's competence clearly demonstrates that he does not allow himself to be restricted in his freedom of action. Whether the sentence reads: "You know nothing about that" or "What you say is ridiculous", it is always shown to the other that he has no chance to prevail with his course of action, which in some way is perceived as a restriction of freedom.

Some time ago in a seminar, I became the target of such an attack myself. Out of the blue a participant interrupted me and asked me in an extremely toxic tone: "Tell me, Professor, what is it good for, what you maunder about all the time?" Later it became clear to me that this behaviour was not at all out of the blue, but had a previous history. The same participant had appeared twenty minutes late in the morning, and I had given him no opportunity to explain anything; instead I glanced at my watch, shook my head disapprovingly and went on.

In spring 1988, in what at that time was still the Federal Republic of Germany a census was carried out. A large part of the population did not experience such an inquiry as a restriction of individual freedom and returned the properly filled out questionnaire on time. However, the other part of the population experienced this as a restriction of freedom imposed on them against their will and reacted with resistance in accordance with one of the four reaction possibilities discussed above. Many started to hesitate first, when on the part of the state something was suddenly advertised at enormous costs and with all means, which should have been understood. You may just ask yourselves how you will react, if next week you find an advertisement from the ministry of finance with the slogan:

"Pay your taxes, too!" or "Taxes are important. Take part!"

With the census all four forms of restoration of the individual freedom could be observed. There was the classic **defiance** behaviour; freedom was demonstrated through not filling out the questionnaire. The toughest still proudly present their unanswered questionnaires although they had been threatened with a 10,000 Euro fine.

Orientation towards the excluded alternative became the choice of all who did meticulously, what should have been prevented. So it was stated specifically, that the questionnaire should not be folded, which they promptly did. Ink was used instead of a pencil, cover sheet and questionnaire were handed back separately, the code number was detached, the format changed and more.

How high the percentage of those was, who reacted with **indirect restoration of freedom**, cannot be determined, but for quite a while one could be told on occasions that questions became answered of course, only just not truthfully. The type of heating was for example answered with "indirect solar heating", which probably is a paraphrase for window, or pets were included in the number of cohabitants or the number of square meters was altered or more.

Open aggression, the last reaction possibility on restricted freedom, in many cities was actually shown. So census officials were beaten publicly, or documents were stolen and it is reported that in Stuttgart an entire census office went up in flames.

Whoever supposes that his freedom of choice is in discussion and at the same time is able to and wants to decide independently, will react to the assumed or actual restriction of freedom with resistance, i. e. reactance. This is expressed in the form of defiance, orientation towards the excluded alternative, through indirect restoration of freedom or through open aggression.

If in leading conversations you want to ban the danger of causing reactance to the greatest extent possible, you will put your attention on the interaction, i. e. you will strive to choose your formulations in a way that your dialogue partner hardly feels restricted in his freedom.

Which **kind of statements** is it, with which you unintentionally restrict your dialogue partner's freedom?

There is a long list of possible terms and phrases with which we **provoke reactance** right away.

We can for example observe that many people are not able to put pieces of **advice** into action. Recommendations, even if they are logical or based on scientific background, first of all narrow the behaviour latitude. The freedom to remain oneself is restricted by each recommendation, every suggestion. This problem occurs for example with medical advice, where it can be observed quite frequently that patients disobey given recommendations, "forget" to take their medicine or modify the prescribed schedule individually, thus showing subtle avoidance reactions. So it could be proven in investigations that dependent on the type of disease up to 92 % of all patients do not mind the treatment proposals of their physicians.

Reactance has nothing to do with acting in bad faith or unreasonableness although this false conclusion is frequently drawn. It is based on the simplified assumption: Someone who is reasonable and wants to do right does always what is best for himself.

So the point is not to perceive the retention of a problematic behaviour as bad, displaced, or daft, but rather to realize that people usually pick what seems to be the best choice out of the possibilities they are aware of. What an outsider thinks to be right, does not have to be accepted by the one who is concerned. Whoever wants to change problematic behaviour, has to deal not only with the obvious negative consequences but also with the primary and secondary gain from illness, which I will discuss in detail in chapter 13.

But not only **pieces of advice**, **directions**, **requests**, and **recommendations** cause resistance, also with **pointing out causes** and **inter-**

preting possible backgrounds dialogue partners may feel constricted. Their reaction will turn out to be correspondent. Even the popular **questions** can provoke reactance easily. Since both the direction of thoughts and the horizon of possible answers are purported to the one who is questioned, he is forced to answer within the limits of the question. This becomes especially clear in the 'why' questions since they frequently lead the other into justifications, trying to give plausible reasons for their actions. That **blame** and **criticism** can be interpreted as a massive restriction of freedom, needs no further explanations. Yet, also **praise** can provoke reactance if the subject suspects that it is not meant as a recognition of his achievements, but to control his future behaviour, which includes a future restriction of his freedom.

In addition there is a list of verbs which direct, without leaving alternatives. Serious examples are the three insignificant words

must (to have to)
shall/should (ought to)
must not

Such words cause resistance when the speaker means to protect himself against an attack on his integrity. In addition to the linguistic possibilities of defence, there are the manifold forms of body language that express the reactance reaction: the dialogue partner folds his arms, gives you the cold shoulder, shakes his head, or the conversation is interrupted under a pretext.

The directions given by **must**, **shall** and **must not** fail to cause reactance only if the freedom of choice is not in discussion and there is no desire to decide on one's own in the specific situation. If for example a doctor places an absolute ban on smoking after a patient has just survived a heart attack, this massive restriction of freedom will cause reactance only with a small number of patients, for whoever wants to stay alive, has hardly any need to decide differently from what was prescribed in this case.

Once I made an experience with an electrician, which taught me to be extremely carefully with the word "must". Before he started working on the installation, I had shown the workman where I wanted to have which outlets, switches, and light connections. What I said was: "And

here you must put a switch, there you must put an outlet" etc. Up to that hour, I was of the opinion that the workman's freedom of choice was not effected. Far from it! Some days later it turned out that the outlet for the extractor hood was exactly in the place, where the wall needed to be cut through. On my annoyed: "You knew upfront that the outlet would be in the way!" I got the instructive answer: "You said, I must place an outlet there, and now you come and complain."

Not only the words **must**, **shall** and **must not**, but also verbs like **to force**, **to strive**, **to try**, **to overcome something** etc. leave little chance to evade. All these verbs exert a certain pressure; the typical associations with achievement, judgement, and assessment are interpreted as a restriction of the personal freedom of action.

If your dialogue partner experiences that his freedom of choice is not restricted, that for example, for a direction a number of ways to carry it out exists, that he can decide freely, he will use this freedom and will experience the given situation as inoffensive.

Allow your dialogue partner his decision latitude.

Even if this sounds like splitting hairs, the three words provoking reactance, **must**, **shall,** and **must not**, can be exchanged with three other words that are able to relax the conversation atmosphere and let a climate of mutual regard emerge:

can (could)
would
would like

You can decide to what extent the difference in the following example sentences is more than "language cosmetics".

"Here you must put another outlet for the extractor hood." Or:

"Could you install the outlet for the extractor hood in a way that it is covered later?"
The well known call from the kitchen: "Dinner is served." Or:
"Could you come down for dinner, please?"
A salesman answers to the customer's complaint about lack of service: "You must not look at it this way, you should rather consider, that this product is..." Or:
"You want a better service agreement and would like to rethink your decision..."

In leading everyday conversations, there are further idioms that seem to be insignificant and rather harmless and let one hardly suspect that they are able to start momentous processes.

For sure you will have run across the following phrases repeatedly:

"I think you agree." Or:
"I presume this meets with your approval."

In leadership it can be observed frequently how such formulations evoke resistance in form of **indirect restoration of freedom**. In other words, subordinates react to such remarks with an approving nod and say "Yes, indeed" and then do what they believe is correct.

But things turn out very differently with the following alternative:

"It depends on whether you agree."

Here the possibility to disagree is specifically allowed to the dialogue partner, thus excluding any opposition based on restricted freedom and giving the dialogue partner the chance to agree voluntarily.

Where excessive paternalism may lead, can be observed in totalitarian systems, in the ways people try to indirectly restore their freedom.

This principle of the freedom of choice is also named the **illusion of an alternative**. Herewith two or more comparable options that however look into the same desired way are offered simultaneously. Usually a dialogue partner will react within the set frame and accept the indirect suggestions. In simple form this may sound like:

"I think you can decide best what would be the optimal solution for you, acting according to A or choosing B."

What first sounds like disinterest and has the appearance of laissez-faire turns out to be goal-oriented leadership. For the dialogue partner's freedom is limited to the choice between A and B, and in the same time this remark implies that the dialogue partner will definitely make a decision and will become active.

Very similarly appointment agreements can be handled. To leadership in professional conversation belongs the offer to be allowed to choose between two possible dates. Maybe you have already reacted indignantly when for an appointment at the dentist the assistant just told you:

"Next Wednesday, 6 pm!"

How much less patronising sounds:

"What would you prefer, Wednesday 6 pm or Thursday 4 pm?"

With the following words a colleague managed to have his especially critical audience do a silent exercise:

"You can either think my lecture over, or you can make notes on it."

Thereupon the overzealous and often sharp questions died down, and instead concentrated silence fell upon a round of twelve managers for almost three minutes.

In another situation a seminar leader succeeded in moving a shy group towards cooperation by saying:

"Do you want to note down your hopes and fears immediately on the cards, or would you want another moment to think about it in order to formulate them more precisely? If you want, you can use the pens, and there are also sufficient cards in the supply, so that none of you needs to bother with writing in small letters."

Within the set frame, the participants reacted in each case with writing their hopes and fears down, some at once, others later, and everyone grasped a pen and noted only few clearly readable catchwords per card.

The use of indirect suggestions allows the dialogue partner to make use of his freedom latitude within a set frame.

Since the need for freedom can never be understood as to be absolute, but rather expresses itself within given boundaries, the important principle of voluntariness can even be followed where the boundaries are extremely narrow. Even an appointment request for the same day can be formulated causing little or no reactance:

"If you like you can come at once. Or would you prefer to come in an hour?"

It has already been mentioned that **questions** often act as **conversation killers**. Perhaps you have already observed that in conversations you have answered rather vaguely to questions, whose meaning was not entirely clear to you, or that many a question appeared rather inquisitive to you and you felt rather hassled. When leading a conversation professionally pressing and embarrassing the dialogue partner through direct questions is forgone. Instead questions appear in form of a reflexive sentence, which looks like a statement to the dialogue partner.

"I am just thinking about, ..."
"I am asking myself, to what extent ..."
"I am uncertain, if, ..."
"I don't know whether ..."

As a rule you can reckon with a reaction of your dialogue partner. Only he does not answer to a direct question, but **can** rather react to your reflexive remark without having the feeling to be constricted in his behaviour latitude.

In seminars about **leadership** in conversation, I often experience the atmosphere in the beginning as rather tensed. Normally the participants do not know each other and look at me in a rather strained way. After some remarks, which are free of causing reactance, the tension diminishes visibly:

"Good morning, I want to welcome you and wish you a really nice day. Today we have come together to hear about leadership in professional conversation. I don't know with which expectations you have come here this morning, ..."

Here it is implied that everyone has expectations.

"... moreover, I am wondering which hopes you may have regarding this training course."

Includes that everyone has specific hopes related to the seminar.

"... and at the same time I am asking myself whether I will be able to satisfy all your wishes."

Everybody has wishes, and if not all at least most of them will be satisfied.

"Some of you have already had experiences with similar training courses and will find it easy to begin. Others may draw comparisons and will have problems because of that."

Here a double implication is made: it is permitted to draw comparisons with other courses, but it may be a drawback, which eases the decision to forgo comparisons voluntarily.

"Others will hear about the subject of leadership in conversation for the first time, and have come here with curiosity and great expectations mixed with shy restraint and the concern that they might not be able to understand everything at the first attempt."

Here it is implied that everyone will understand the subject sooner or later, in addition the indirect suggestion takes effect that all mentioned feelings are alright and that I specifically express that negative feelings such as doubt, shame, fear, or anxiety are acceptable.

"I am curious to learn from you how you will make active use of professional conversation",

Everybody will make active use of it.

"... and some of you have already decided to participate actively from the start, while others want to wait until after the coffee break."

Everybody will participate actively.

And so forth.

Here, I admit that it needs continuous practice to formulate one's thoughts without causing reactance. Many seminar participants declared that they achieved their goal most quickly, when they subjected themselves to the effort to plan and note down a presentation sentence by sentence. In this type of preparation, many an inconsiderate and also unnecessary provocation of resistance can be eliminated beforehand.

An essential aspect of this technique of leading a conversation is to be seen in that independent of the chosen alternative control is retained. In this course of action, the dialogue partners can show no form of resistance, since everything they might do or feel has specifically been allowed to them already.

Or how in *Zen* it is said: "To give your sheep or your cow a spacious meadow, is the best way to control it."

Maybe you have noted during reading how the phrases **"at the moment"** or **"yet"** or **"in the beginning"** prevent a static situation.

Three additional examples may support this:

"At the moment your view is totally different."

The existing disagreement is noticed and addressed so that the dialogue partner feels understood and says, "Yes". This affirmation includes a confirmation of the time limitation, for anyone who views something very differently **"at the moment"**, can easily come to new conclusions in the next.

"You have not yet made up your mind regarding this question."

The hesitation is addressed sympathetically so that here a "yes" will most probably be the answer, too. However, at the same time this "yes" includes acceptance of the "yet". Anyone who is still undecided can make a decision in the next moment.

"If I understand you correctly, you don't want to give a comment now."

Here, too, the dialogue partner who keeps silent will feel understood and will nod or say "Yes". It is possible to prevent a static state of silence by using the unimpressive "now". Who would like to say nothing **now**, can speak his mind shortly afterwards.

From insurance representatives I was able to learn that customers, who are more or less pressed to the conclusion of a contract, make use of their one-week right of withdrawal in a rate much higher than the normal average. A professional contract conclusion with a hesitant customer will sound more like:

"I am just considering whether you feel taken by surprise, and whether I may not have explained the specific points to you in enough detail. Maybe this is just too quick for you and you would not want to sign

the contract now." (While saying this he can slowly take the contract form away and pack up the documents quietly, but definitely.)

The probability that the customer now takes up the pen is extremely high. Who did not intend to sign anyway will in any case be delighted at the easy termination of the conversation, which is a good base for future conversations.

To the Roman emperor *Marc Aurel* the stoic dictum "AD UTRUMQUE PARATUS" (prepared for either case) is credited.

Since in conversation often only one side is favoured, the **orientation towards the excluded alternative** is rather common. It is alarming how rarely the actual topic is the problem and how often the real issue is an unconscious attempt to restore individual freedom. To be prepared for either case, has nothing to do with lack of preference; it can avoid unnecessary disputes and broadens the horizon of the conversation.

Three examples from three entirely different areas may illustrate this:

At a fair a visitor attacked an energy consultant with the following words:

"You are all monopolists. We do not need nuclear power stations. We could as well generate electricity by wind wheels, like the Danes have been doing it for years. They produce 90 % of the required electrical power by wind energy."

The energy consultant in the first moment tended to take the opposite position and to explain to the customer that not 90 % but only 0.9 % of the Danish energy demand is covered by wind power, yet he quickly realized that he would merely conjure up a dispute conversation on "correct" numbers, so he opened up for the customer's view instead and answered:

"We could indeed produce electricity with wind power plants, and in our region we have an especially favourable wind situation. If for example you take the 23 wind power stations in the North Sea Wind Park, at wind force 6 you can produce with those one Megawatt-hour. So to replace one 500 Megawatt reactor we would need around 10,000 wind engines."

To the astonishment of the energy consultant, the formerly quite rude customer became entirely reflective and began an earnest dialogue.

In the second example a teacher was told at the beginning of a factory visitors tour that just that morning all road markings had been repainted and that he would be requested to take care that none of his 30 students (12 and 13 years old!) would step on the fresh paint. A prohibition would not only have provoked the students' resistance so that all lines would have been covered in footprints, but would probably also have made necessary unpleasant and futile interrogations to find the "culprits". Instead the teacher managed to make the following announcement:

"Site management has just explained to me that the road markings have been freshly repainted and begged that nobody would step on the lines if possible. Well, I cannot prevent that one of you does it anyway or thinks it funny to jostle one of the others. Anyway, I'll go ahead."

He spoke without turning his head afterwards. None of the pupils stepped on the line during the two-hour site tour.

The third example may appear very dramatic to you because it concerns the question of life or death in the truest sense of the word. It concerns the announcement of a suicide in form of saying goodbye. Perhaps you are surprised to learn that in Germany alone such conversations take place about 20,000 times per year, sometimes only on the telephone. Typical for such a conversation is the lack of willingness of the addressee to take sides with the suicide and to understand his hopelessness and forlornness. Instead the hearer tries to cajole him, to talk about better times or to exert moral pressure, with reference to the children, the partner, the parents, etc. The reaction will look very different if the freedom of action is not additionally restricted, for example in this way:

"If you have decided to end your life, I am convinced that it has been no easy decision, but that you have agonised about it and do not see another way at the moment. I do not know, what made you consider this step now, but I'll take you seriously up to the last minute. I am wondering what can I do for you at the moment, except that I stay here now."

Such a preamble is no guarantee that the suicide throws his intention overboard, but it is a possibility to begin a dialogue. The outcome of the conversation cannot and must not be defined beforehand, otherwise it would not be open for both sides. Being open in this case does not mean to approve of committing suicide, but only to recognize that one acts within narrow boundaries, and that the slight influence is entirely lost, if the suicide turns to the excluded alternative that wins attractiveness increasingly.

How you can deal with resistance

Resistance with the dialogue partner

There is hardly anything people react to so sensitively as to a restriction of their freedom.

Whoever perceives that his window of opportunity is constrained against his will, is bound to express resistance. This resistance that serves to **restore the lost** (or feared to be lost) **freedom** can be expressed in four ways

- **Defiance:** Doing exactly what is not supposed to be done, according to the motto "Now more than ever!" restores the threatened or restricted freedom.
- **Orientation towards the excluded alternative:** Just the alternative, which would be eliminated, gains attractiveness.
- **Indirect restoration of freedom:** Here the restriction of the behaviour latitude is apparently obeyed, however, simultaneously one's own freedom is demonstrated, but secretly.
- **Open aggression:** Finally the resistance can be expressed by open aggression.

> Allow your dialogue partner his decision latitude, for the freedom to remain oneself is restricted by each recommendation, every suggestion.

If you aim at avoiding reactance with your dialogue partner, give him the opportunity to make a choice. Use

can		must
would like	instead of	should
want		must not

If there is no real choice of method, you can nevertheless allow the freedom of choice in that you offer an alternative in the same direction.

"You **can** settle this now, or perhaps you would rather **want** to do it in the afternoon."

Instead of: "This has to be done today."

Since it can always be observed that people change the easiest if they are allowed to remain as they are, you best **do without advice, directions, recommendations, requests, blame, and criticism.** Just as you avoid verbs like: force yourself, overcome yourself, strive, and exert yourself. These words can exert pressure and become interpreted as a restriction of the personal freedom of action.

With the following phrases you can avoid resistance:

- "You could **try** xy."
- "When you **look at** xy..."
- "Maybe you would like to **test** how..."
- "If you want to **get an impression** on..."
- "When you **compare** x to y..."
- "You **decide**, when..."
- "You **define**, to what extent..."
- "If you **check it**, you..."

7. Transactional Analysis and Successful Communication

Smoother communication and more effective cooperation can be achieved when we understand, what takes place between dialogue partners. It is not the mere content of the conversation, i. e. what is actually said. This is added by facial expression, body language, and the mutual feelings, which are not always manifest, but do play a role in conversation at all times.

It seems that dialogues follow specific rules and that answers and reactions to opening statements are in a way pre-assigned.

A psychodynamic model, the so-called transactional analysis, can help to better understand communication processes. According to transactional analysis our behaviour can be subdivided into three clearly separable sets of behaviours. These sets are also called ego states. One differentiates between Parent, Adult, and Child ego state. These three ego states each resemble a combination of thoughts, emotions, and behaviours.

The ego state that develops when we are born is named Child ego state. In the beginning, each newborn acts solely spontaneously. It wakes up, cries, drinks, wees, and drops to sleep again spontaneously. However, this universal spontaneity does not last long, because parents strive to teach their children certain rhythms and to adapt them. This adaptation process is usually whitewashed as “education”. Thus in the first year of life the Adapted Child ego state emerges beside the Natural Child. It is almost evident that required adaptation leads to rebellion. This ego state is sometimes called the Defiant Child.

These behavioural patterns,

adopted in early childhood, will not be abandoned when growing older. Any time we feel boisterous, are curious, seek adventures, or are impassioned, we act out of our Natural Child. A typical example can be found in the jubilation “Goal!” on the soccer pitch, where our Natural Child can truly act out its feelings.

And the way we learned as a child to confess bad marks in a test with hanging head, low shoulders and closed legs, the same Adapted Child state can be found decades later in similar situations, when for example we are criticised for a mistake. With some people one can directly notice when they talk to their supervisor on the phone, so heavily expresses their body language their repression. Recently, a school headmaster confessed to me that he had found himself several times to be standing up when receiving a phone call from the ministry of education.

However, adults can also act very defiantly, although in this case one likes to talk of critical awareness. The same behaviour can be found in the “stubbornness” of old age. With defiance the voice sounds strained and much higher than usual. Between the moaning voice of a three year old pouting:

“It’s my mother’s fault when my fingers are cold. Why doesn’t she make me wear gloves?!”

and the equally complaining voice of the employee, who feels treated unfairly, when he grumbles:

“You wait, there is only so much you can take, always special requests, but nit-picking when I am concerned. I’ll teach him…”

there is hardly a difference in quality.

Our Child ego state incorporates three aspects:

- The Natural Child approaches everything in a natural and unprejudiced way, without thinking about possible consequences.
- The Adapted Child is dutiful and submissive.
- The Defiant Child does not want to comply, is rebellious, and fights given norms. This ego state expresses the negative form of adaptation.

During the course of further development another ego state emerges in each human being, which is called Parent ego state.

Everywhere in the world children imitate their most important contact persons, which usually are their parents. Parents are on one hand perceived as giving orders or dominating, which part is named Critical Parent, on the other they are observed as loving, caring, and tender, which part is called the Nurturing Parent.

And so all children in the world lull their dolls and teddy bears to sleep (= Nurturing Parent) only to beat them moments later (= Critical Parent) or to be strict with them in another way.

By and by through numerous repetitions of parent behaviour all those phrases that have been addressed to the child countless times will be followed without thinking, such as:

"Wash your hands before dinner!"
"Don't speak with your mouth full!"
"Children hold their tongues while adults talk."
"Do your homework first, then it is time to play."
"Brush your teeth, before you go to bed." etc.

One day finally our mother's and father's words are replaced by an inner voice, which sounds amazingly similar to those of our parents and which makes us act "appropriately".

Maybe this is what Faust means when Goethe makes him say:

"Two souls, alas! are lodg'd within my breast."

The soul of "I will" (= Child) and the soul of "I must" (= Parent).

This Parent ego states acquired during childhood will accompany us through our whole life. Any time we act out of a position of strength, of dominance and power, we are in our Parent ego state. It is evident, that after all those painful experiences during childhood, when one's parents and elder brothers and sisters always were allowed or able to do so much more than oneself, this ego state is perceived as very strong. It may sound overstated, but in our Parent ego state we experience ourselves as omnipotent,

exactly as almighty as we as an infant perceived our parents to be everyday.

- In our Parent ego state we incorporate values, norms, commandments, bans, and our socialization, in which case we talk about the Critical parent.
- But our Parent ego state also embodies benevolence, comfort, warmth, and support, which is named the Nurturing parent.

No matter whether we talk out of the Nurturing or the Critical Parent ego state, we generally feel in a position of strength, power, and superiority. This may explain, why this ego state is so extraordinarily favoured by many people.

But at the side of the voices of to want to and to have to steps another inner voice which develops during childhood and is named Adult ego state, although a child of that age will be far from being rated as an adult. The Adult ego state considers possible consequences of an action and makes purpose-oriented decisions.

The following example is to clarify this:

A driver is circling around the town centre for quite a while in search of a parking space. Since it is raining he wants to stop as closely as possible to the dry-cleaner where he is going to pick up his coat. Finally a gap! Just before he stops the engine, he notices a huge "No parking" sign. Promptly his Critical Parent pipes up: "You must not stop here." To which his Defiant Child replies: "Come off it, it's only for a second." The Critical Parent insists: "If everybody would do this. That's not what you want." And the Defiant Child answers cheekily: "I'm not everybody!" Here the Adult joins in: "Stop! Could we please check the facts. How likely is it that we will be caught and have to pay a fine? Do the other cars have parking tickets behind the windscreen wipers? This is not the case. How expensive is parking in a no parking zone? How likely is it then we will be caught? One to one. In how far is it worth it?" Etc.

What has been demonstrated here in an explicit way, happens all the time inside of us. There are two voices inside of us: One that says I and stems from our child ego state, in form of "I want… "or "I will…" Another voice says YOU, it originates in our Parent ego state and serves as a means of current control. These inner dialogues – also referred to as thinking – sometimes sound like this:

Adapted Child: "I don't get it. Damnit, why didn't I let them explain it to me properly. Somehow it is so complicated. I believe, I will never manage it."

Nurturing Parent: "Come on, you will make it. Until now you always completed everything on time."

Defiant Child: "O come on, I'll drop it, this is so stupid!"

Critical Parent: "Stop stop stop. Now pull yourself together and make an effort. It would be ridiculous if you could not do it. Stiffen your upper lip and go on!"

Finally the Adult ego state makes itself heard by checking the situation and by considering, which behaviour might lead to which consequences.

- The Adult ego state stresses a rational view: it calculates, weighs, and decides according to requirements of reality and not based on uncontrolled, but on verified and integrated emotions.
- Main task of this ego state is a check in the sense of:
  What happens if...?
  In how far is this statement true...?
  Which advantages and disadvantages result from...?

It represents the rational autonomy of a person.

The ego states with their different aspects can be recognized by words, gestures, voice, posture, and actions. Content becomes less important than expression. In short:

> Whoever feels and acts like he did when he was a child, is in the Child ego state.
>
> Who thinks, acts, and feels like he has observed with his parents, is in his Parent ego state.
>
> Who deals with present reality, collects facts and assesses them objectively, is in his Adult ego state.

This model consists of three attitudes, everyone can adopt in varying situations. The following scene is to illustrate how quickly ego states can be switched:

Through the open door I overheard a struggle in the office between two colleagues. Mrs. Heaney in an angry tone: "I mean, you should already be able to handle such incidents without me. I have explained it to you so many times, and you act every time as if you see it for the first time." (Critical Parent)

In this moment another colleague comes back from the bakery and Mrs. H. calls with totally different voice: "Oh, may I have a bite?!" (Natural Child)

I enter the office and Mrs. Heaney says, the mouth full of cake: "Mr. Weisbach, good that I meet you, the comment for the university calendar needs to be handed in by Friday. Could you give me your complete data before then." (Adult)

First the impression may come up that there are desirable and undesirable ego states, but none of these is good or bad in itself. Whether an ego state is problematic can only be told from the context of the ego states of dialogue partners in a real argument.

Predominance of the Critical Parent can typically be found with teachers, pastors, policemen, judges, or federal prosecutors, while the Nurturing Parent can be acted out in a social or health care career. The Adult ego state usually dominates with managers or scientists. Preference for acting out the Natural Child can be related with artists, whereas the Adapted Child is significantly asked for by the military forces.

Communication will always be without problems when the other is addressed out of the same ego state the interaction started with.

In a training course class my Child ego state uttered:

"With this great weather outside I don't want to stay inside at all. I would propose having an extended lunch break and continuing the course in the afternoon in the park." Almost the entire course reacted spontaneously with: "Great", "Good", "Fine", "Super".

Talks at a regulars' table in a pub are usually held from the Parent ego state:

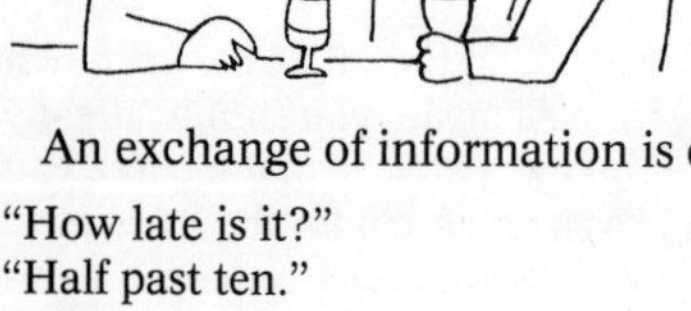

"If you ask me, real unemployment does not exist. Those are all slackers and illicit workers."

"Exactly, none of them really wants to work. As I always say, seek, and ye shall find. But anyone who gets that much dole, has no need to strain oneself."

An exchange of information is easiest done in the Adult ego state:

"How late is it?"
"Half past ten."

Problems arise when out of the Parent the dialogue partner's Child ego state is addressed, especially when it is the Adapted or the Defiant Child. Why is that so?

What we learned quickly in childhood – to react to our parents' requests in an adapted or defiant way – is now that we have grown up an important part of our manners. The awkward feelings, which are caused by inferiority and powerlessness, still accompany any adult who is addressed as the Adapted Child against his will.

Typical comments out of the Critical Parent sound like this:

"Are you not able to or don't you want to?"
"What do you have your head for?"
"Come on, hurry up. How long do I have to wait!"
"This is not your business, alright?!"
"You will see what you get."

More friendly but similar in effect are statements from the Nurturing Parent:

"Hand that to me, you can't do it anyway!"
"My respect. I really value what you have achieved!"
"Come here, I'll fill the form in for you."
"Don't worry, women usually have problems with that."
"Cheer up, you'll bounce back soon."

Many judgemental statements, be they positive or negative, can be characteristic for the Parent ego states, as long as they contain an opinion about a person, and especially an opinion that has not been formed by weighing different aspects in the Adult ego state, but more or less automatically, like a reflex. Most of the common "conversation killers" I will deal with in the next chapter stem from the Parent ego state and repeat, what we have captured from our parents and teachers during our childhood.

All these behaviour patterns lead to reactions in the other that come from his Adapted or Defiant Child and are related to feeling not good, not lovable, not okay.

If such Parent egos state attacks are responded to with defiance directly, or the protest is saved for a more favourable point of time, depends on the individual pre-experiences and the particular interlocutor. Some people could win the world championship in the collection of “payback points”, i. e. they carefully remember every single case of humiliation, paternalism, or mortification. And like a shopkeeper cannot foresee when the customers will come to encash their payback points, also the “private payback points” will be cashed at the least favourable moment, just when it really poses a problem to the other. A typical example is the termination of a work contract.

A former head of a department told me that his career dropped at the very point a highly qualified member of his team quit his job just when a very complicated project had to be completed in extremely short time. The future of the department head depended on the project results. When he reported to his supervisor that the specialist would be leaving and asked for extra time he got the answer: “If you have staff problems in such a moment, you do not seem to be the right man in the right place.” The leaving employee was able to take revenge for all he had had to swallow during several years.

The unpredictability of the tit-for-tat response is what makes the use of the Parent ego state so dangerous. Some people tend to react at once, while others have developed a kind of ability to suffer in silence, which only at first sight looks like forebearance and patience. One day they will also present their payback points, and what they have collected may have a devastating effect.

An interaction will be without any problems, if we act out of the Child ego state voluntarily. A request for help we are not entitled to ask for will preferably come from the Adapted Child.

Having lost a button from my leather jacket could make me talk to my assistant out of the Parent ego state:

“Mrs. Help, could you be so friendly as to sew the button back on, I have to give a lecture in a minute.” With this question I am in danger to get the answer: “I don’t think that’s part of my job description, Sir.”

Out of the Adult ego state the “button problem” sounds like: “Oh, I have lost a button. I cannot hold the lecture like this. Do you have a sewing kit?” The most probable answer will be something like: “Here you are.”

Most promising is a helpless voice, nearly crying, out of the Adapted Child, something like: “Oh no, that’s impossible. Now the button has gone off. What do I do now? I cannot go to the lecture with a flagging

sleeve. Bad luck." And now Mrs. Help takes her sewing kit from her handbag and says:
"Come here, I'll sew it right back on." In such a situation I will of course not collect "payback points" even when Mrs. Help hands the jacket back some minutes later with the words: "Tell me, Professor, what would you do without me?"

> To behave weak and helpless is usually the easiest way to make other people help us. In no other ego state but in the Nurturing Parent one can act out one's superiority with such a clear conscience.

That this has not necessarily to be so will be demonstrated by the following scene in a highway rest area:

A young woman in a light-coloured summer dress approaches me and says with a tiny, weak-spirited voice: "Excuse me, can you help me, I got a flat tire." (Adapted Child)

My first reaction was to roll up my sleeves in my mind. But then I remembered my suit and said: "I would like to help you, but I have to hold a speech today and don't want to get my clothes dirty." (Adult)

Even this answer out of the Adult ego state did not suffice, since she added weepily: "But I never did that before."(Adapted Child)

She nearly got me to help her, but in the last moment I considered my suit to be more important, and so I said: "I do have time and I can help you in a way that you can safely drive your car again, I just don't want to get dirt on my hands or on my suit."

The young woman looked me up and down and answered in a totally new tone: "I understand. But maybe I try somebody else first." Said it and went away. Yet before I climbed back into my car I heard her asking another driver with childish voice: "Can you help me, I got a flat tire?"

A totally different situation can be found with behaviour patterns that are named "conversation savers" and which will be introduced in chapter 9. With the previous examples it could be shown that we are not forced to react a certain way but that we can choose freely to act out of the Adult ego state. Here the "conversation savers" are especially useful. They all have in common that the dialogue partner is addressed in his Adult ego state and is able to react out of it correspondingly.

To practice distinction and identification of the different ego states you will find a list of statements on the following pages, which dependent on the tone stem from the Adult, Parent, or Child ego states.

Please, note behind each statement, which ego state you can hear. Subsequently you will find my proposed "solutions".

	Your answer
(1) "When will you finally get ready with the document?!"	
(2) "This is not my fault!"	
(3) "You behave clumsily."	
(4) "And what do I do now?"	
(5) "What might be the reason for the missing payment receipt?"	
(6) "In this case you are totally wrong!"	
(7) "One question ..."	
(8) "This won't work!"	
(9) "Are you sure you calculated correctly?"	
(10) "Do it yourself then!"	
(11) "He may be a nice guy, but you can't leave him unsupervised."	
(12) "I don't think I can make a decision before I have talked to the person in charge."	

(13) "Believe me, this is all for your best!"

(14) "I appreciate very much what you have achieved in this short period of time."

(15) "If only I could get a pay rise, all my problems would be solved!"

(16) "If you can't do it properly you should better stop doing it altogether!"

(17) "I don't know what to do any more."

(18) "Come on, let me do it for you!"

(19) "Can you please tell me more about it?"

(20) "I think your proposal does not work because of two points: on one hand we have only fourteen days left, and on the other we don't have the technical equipment available at the moment."

And now four dialogue examples:

Supervisor: "How late is it, Mrs. Miller?"
Assistant: "Nearly half past four."

Supervisor: "How late is it, Mrs. Miller?"
Assistant: "I am ready in a minute."

Supervisor: "How late is it, Mrs. Miller?"
Assistant: "Do you think I'm too slow?"

Supervisor: "How late is it, Mrs. Miller?"
Assistant: "You are anxious if we will get it ready on time."

On the next pages you will find the commented solutions.

(1) "When will you finally get ready with the document?!"

The Critical Parent cannot only be recognized from the tone, but also from the word "finally".

(2) "This is not my fault!"

If you read this sentence aloud, you may experience that your voice will sound higher and more pressed than with the first sentence, a typical sign of the Defiant Child.

(3) "You behave clumsily."

Here the word "clumsy" hints at the Critical Parent.

(4) "And what do I do now?"

Depending on how you pronounce this sentence, it may be either the rational Adult or the Adapted Child, asking for help. With the latter the sentence will sound correspondingly a bit uncertain.

(5) "What might be the reason for the missing payment receipt?"

Reviewing facts is one of the preferred tasks of the Adult ego state.

(6) "In this case you are totally wrong!"

The reproachful tone in combination with the disrespective formulation hints at the Critical Parent.

(7) "One question..."

Here the tone also plays a big role: said calmly in a fact-oriented manner this could qualify for an information request out of the Adult ego state. With a tiny bit of helplessness and a stress on the word 'question' in a high-pitched voice we can at once recognize the Adapted Child.

(8) "This won't work!"

Whether it sounds patronizing or harsh and authoritarian, this statement stems from the Critical Parent.

(9) "Are you sure you calculated correctly?"

If this is meant as an objective question in the sense of a check, this is the Adult speaking. However, if the question is only meant rhetorically, it is the Critical Parent, for which it is already clear that the other has 'of course' made a mistake.

(10) "Do it yourself then!"

This sentence sounds especially nice in a stroppy tone = Defiant Child.

(11) "He may be a nice guy, but you can't leave him unsupervised."

In the list of the previous sentences this Critical Parent statement is special since it does not address the Child ego state of the other but his Critical Parent, according to: "We are okay, but surrounded by losers."

(12) "I don't think I can make a decision before I have talked to the person in charge."

Normally this information sounds businesslike and hints at the Adult ego state.

(13) "Believe me, this is all for your best!"

With a persuasive voice the other is patronised = Nurturing Parent.

(14) "I appreciate very much what you have achieved in this short period of time."

A well-meant and maybe even well accepted praise out of a position of predominance, the Nurturing Parent.

(15) "If only I could get a pay rise, all my problems would be solved!"

In this sentence not only the wording is childlike, but also the tone is a hint at the Adapted Child.

(16) "If you can't do it properly you should better stop doing it altogether!"

Reproaches always come from the Critical Parent.

(17) "I don't know what to do any more."

Helplessness can be learned, and the Adapted Child is always a good choice when others need to be asked for assistance.

(18) “Come on, let me do it for you!”

Friendly Nurturing Parent.

(19) “Can you please tell me more about it?”

Request for Information means Adult ego state.

(20) “I think your proposal does not work because of two points: on one hand we have only fourteen days left, and on the other we don’t have the technical equipment available at the moment.”

This sentence includes a judgement, but the proposal has been analysed critically, and an analysis is an activity of our Adult ego state.

And now the four dialogues:

Supervisor: “How late is it, Mrs. Miller?”
Assistant: “Nearly half past four.”

Exchange of information between Adult and Adult.

Supervisor: “How late is it, Mrs. Miller?”
Assistant: “I am ready in a minute.”

Reproachful, impatient Critical Parent of the supervisor and a dutiful response of the subordinate’s Adapted Child.

Supervisor: “How late is it, Mrs. Miller?”
Assistant: “Do you think I’m too slow?”

The supervisor asking for patience (e. g. when a secretary has been asked to complete an urgent letter after closing time) in combination with the Critical Parent of the subordinate.

In reaction to the Parent ego state behaviour the supervisor will most probably not collect payback points since for him the letter is most important at the moment and since he has voluntarily acted out of the Adapted Child, which always bears the risk to be treated correspondingly.

Supervisor: “How late is it, Mrs. Miller?”
Assistant: “You are anxious if we will get it ready on time.”

Again the reproachful, impatient Parent ego state of the supervisor, but here the assistant reacts out of the Adult, by describing her supervisor's emotions.

In chapter 10, I will deal with possible reactions in detail.

8. Conversation Killers

In the following you will find a list of popular statements, which have in common that they all come **from our Parent ego state**. Sometimes the tone alone is enough to recognise the implied superiority. Reading through the list you may feel reminded of chapter 6, since these conversation killers cause opposition (reactance) within your dialogue partner. How different these statements may be in detail, they all seem to aim at bringing the conversation to an end as quickly as possible. This is why I have chosen the term **conversation killers**. I am of course aware that the term conversation **killer** in itself is a judgemental classification. The term conversation inhibitor would also fit. However, since I started to use the term conversation killer in a previous book I have decided to keep it

First of all I would like to give you one hint for reading. I have had difficulties in writing this chapter with the same objectivity as the previous ones. The use of conversation killers is very normal everyday behaviour. In order not to play the constant role of an upholder of moral standards, I have decided for an ironic description, in which I explicitly include myself. Who finds irony inappropriate in a book like this, may proceed to the following chapters.

Give orders

It makes sense that we give orders only when we are convinced that the other cannot behave in the "right" manner (for whom?) without our instructions and therefore is in need of our commands. This communicative pre-assumption reveals that **orders** are addressed from the Critical Parent to the Adapted Child. In everyday dialogue behaviour orders can be everything between unfriendly and rude or factual and precise.

"At the beginning of next year you will move to our agency in Hicksville!"
" Will you (please) pick up the children after work!"
"Please do write the letter again and distribute the six paragraphs evenly on two pages!"

"Don't speed!"
"You must not drink (or smoke) that much!"

At the same time we assume when giving orders that the other will obey, since otherwise we would risk looking silly. When you pay attention to your friends or colleagues, you will soon be able to find that orders are not mainly disobeyed because of their content but because of their patronising form. These **reactions** are related to the **Defiant Child**. Sometimes you will discover an instant defiance, but in other cases it will be the cashing of a whole collection of payback points, so that the reaction is correspondingly vehement.

Try to convince someone to do something

Similarly to giving orders with trying to **convince the other to do something** we want to make him behave in a way he (still) does not do by himself. In contrast to giving orders with convincing we try to endear ourselves to the other. It is an attempt to make the other "voluntarily do the right thing". However, the decision on what is right or wrong has been made by the one who tries to convince and who uses his Parent ego state to tell the Child the friendly way.

"Just consider the unique chance for you when you change to Hicksville. Nowhere else will you find so much room for your own ideas."
"You would make the children really happy if you could pick them up at your sister's. Moreover, we would all be here for dinner and you could be back early for the sports broadcasts."

While we use orders only when we believe that they will be followed, we have to take a much higher risk when trying to convince someone. Despite the friendly and endearing wrapping including wording and tone, the other may sense our intention to limit his freedom and may react mulishly, which is nothing else than **reactance** or a **reaction** out of the **Defiant Child**.

Warn and Threaten

If we cannot achieve our goals with "well-meant" convincing, there is still the option to **warn and threaten**, to make the other, not quite as friendly as before, behave "correctly". In contrast to an order the other is made to "finally understand" the possible consequences, which is nothing else than by using the Critical Parent make the other react "reasonably" out of the **Adapted Child**. Warning and threatening always follows the same pattern: "You will see, what you get from it."

"Okay, if you do not want to move to Hicksville, you can of course reject the offer. Nevertheless, I am in doubt whether I will be able to come up with such an opportunity again. So don't complain to me when you will not be promoted in the next years."

"If you don't like it, you don't have to pick up the children. But I don't want to hear a single word from you when you are late for the sports news, just because supper takes so long and the children are not in bed. Just to make it plain."

Skilful warning and threatening aims at the known weak points of the dialogue partner. Of course he can still react with defiance, but only by risking his own goal, since the warnings or threats promptly turn out to be true. This conversation killer provokes others to collect payback points out of the Defiant Child or as it has been expressed in chapter 6 ("Resistance with the Dialogue Partner"): they restore the lost freedom indirectly. As an example the employee could agree to moving to Hicksville, but at the same time start to look for what one could call other options. Alternatively, the husband could call from the office to report that unfortunately something had interfered with his plans.

Reproach

While the intention of previous conversation killers was to influence future behaviour, with a **reproach** the horse has already bolted. Even so this conversation killer is very useful, since in this way we can make clear that this would (of course) never have happened to us and that we are not to blame at all. The Parent ego state documents its superiority once more and is able to show the other who obviously has done something wrong what an unimportant nothing he is.

Reproaches can be formulated as an order, a question, or a comment, which all have in common a derogatory tone and the pattern “Everything could be so easy if you were different”.

“What do you have your head for?”
“You know very well that you would have had to ask me upfront.”
“Typical!”
“You should have known that!”
“Didn’t you notice anything?”

There is a favourite reproach I will address in particular: The question “Why not?” which seems to be harmless at first sight. With this question we ask for an explanation for something that cannot be altered anyway.

“Why didn’t you do it?”
“Why didn’t you come on time?”
“Why don’t you want this?”

There is hardly any other conversation killer with which we can worsen our dialogue partner’s mood so quickly. To respond to the “Why not”, the attention is focussed on the negative, on what is not. Before we even realize it we face an escalating conflict.

Reproaches hurt people’s pride and self-confidence. They gnaw away people’s self-respect. Depending on the conditions the reaction can reach from a hanging head to defiant protest and accusations. If you imagine how many people walk around with uncashed payback point collections, which have solely been justified by reproaches, you may be horrified.

Judge

Maybe you are surprised now. Does judgement count as a conversation killer? Definitely! In chapter 2 (“Recognising Your Own Conversational Manners”) judgement has already been discussed as one of six spontaneous reactions. There is hardly a more subtle way to demonstrate superiority than stating a **judgement**. Comparatively harmless when it is a common judgement about somebody absent, between Parent and Parent ego state in a talk at the regulars’ table.

However, the case is totally different when a Parent addresses the Child ego state of the other. Here behaviour patterns are rated as positive or negative. In addition, the Parent ego state idea of being almighty let ideology win so easily over expert knowledge. Since we can tell what is good or bad, while our dialogue partner is not capable of it by himself, he is dependent on our opinions, ideas, and assessments, from our judgement. When I relate this to chapter 5, stating a well-meant judgement can be classified as **disregard**. Maybe you have already observed that people who use this conversation killer frequently seem to act under duress to find each and everything good or bad. Using of course a very abstract benchmark. And of course one's own point of view is believed to be universally accepted. Who could be surprised to find that we try to fight against such arrogant and moralising statements. After all so much disregard requires a certain level of self-protection.

"I find, you take this a bit too easy."
"Superficially seen this may be a good solution, but if one thinks it over objectively, it doesn't help us at all."
"That's absolutely great and people will love it!"
"Someone who has such good ideas, gets my full support."
"This position is entirely outdated."

Praise or blame from children to grown-ups easily sounds precocious because the superiority of a child over a grown-up is not given at all.

I can still remember well that after a school lesson a twelve-year-old student approached me, stood in front of me, and complimented me as follows:
"You, professor, you really are a good teacher and I just wanted to let you know."
I think you can imagine that I smiled. Very different the acknowledging reaction out of the Adult ego state of one fellow pupil who accidentally stood beside us:
"I admit, in the sixth lesson I already wilt pretty much, but with you I am fully concentrated."

With **negative judgements**, the **Child ego state** reacts either in an adapted manner, meaning to remain silent and tolerating, what however in no way excludes the collection of payback points, or it comes at once to a defiant reaction in form of the emphasized insistance on the position attacked. This position will even be defended when it is already clear that it cannot be kept at all. However, the negative judgement is often perceived as an attack against the person and is therefore battled against with all means.

In the case of a **positive judgement** we can assume that first of all praise means something enjoyable and for many people something desired. Nevertheless praise can also be interpreted as an interference with other people's matters or even as a direct tutelage if, for example, a painter has to listen to unwanted estimations during his work process, like how felicitous the proportions would be, how pretty the sunset, how wonderful the colours etc. Someone who can paint will experience such statements as bold pretentiousness.

Even where we are professionally competent, the danger exists that the **positive estimation** makes the other in his Child ego state **dependent from or even addicted to our praise**. Instead of applying one's quality standards to one's achievements, it is trusted in the judgment of others. In the long run the positive evaluation can promote dependence, an effect that can hardly be the primary goal. In addition there is the difficulty of how to admit a weakness or a mistake in response to a positive estimation, as in the following example:

Mr. Peace had decided with a heavy heart to cancel the bowling date with his colleagues in order to keep a promise he gave in the morning. Actually he only says: "My colleagues would have liked to have me with them tonight but you and I had agreed to go to the movies."

His wife appreciates this: "I find it very good that one can rely on you."

How can Mr. Peace express after this statement how hard it was for him to tell his colleagues he could not come. Impossible for him to add now: " I had hoped a bit that you did not want to go any more. For in this case I would meet the colleagues right now."

Especially with praising estimations it is difficult to fend off the other's influence. This may be an explanation for why this conversation killer represents one of the most popular means of subtle control. In chapter 15, I will tell how we can show our appreciation through "positive expressions".

Play something down

A subgenus of the previous conversation killer is to **play something down**. In many cases encouraging or comforting someone belongs to it, too, since it often takes the form of playing something down. You may remember the description in chapter 2 ("Recognising Your Own Conversational Manners"). Based on our lifetime experience and our knowledge of human nature we can decide if something is of great or minor relevance. Since the other unfortunately has a by far too extreme view of the situation we have to get him back down on earth (whose?). Here our Nurturing Parent wants to assist the helpless Child. It is only rarely verified whether the other is in need of such assistance and if he is open to deal with another view right now.

"Don't worry, he has put down others before you," someone says to a colleague who comes back from the director's office completely deranged.

"Don't think too much about it, it will get right again, many children have that at that age," a neighbour returns to the worries of a mother about her bed-wetting six-year-old.

"That's not the end of the world, tomorrow the sun will be shining again," as a reaction to someone's deep disappointment, when his plans have just fallen through.

"Cheer up! There are always problems, and you don't let them buffalo you. Come on, you'll make it," a supervisor reacts to the doubts of an employee regarding a project timeline.

Maybe you know the saying that the opposite of "well" is "well-meant". This is exactly the problem with this conversation killer: It is well-meant but very rarely desired. I do not want to deny that there are situations where comfort and support are really appropriate. In this case we have to show empathy with the other. With quick hits we only cause distance and the impression that we do not really want to react to what the other has just told us. I am often told that one does not want to further exaggerate what the other already dramatises. This sentence, too, shows the Parent ego state position. If something is experienced as harmless or dramatic can only be told by the one who actually is in the situation. Who is lovesick for the first time, whose roof has just been brought down on his head. He does not only feel shattered and hurt but may also say that life has no meaning any more. To answer in such a situation

"Wait and see. In some days everything will look different. We all have been lovelorn at time, and the first cut is the deepest, like in *Rod Steward*'s song."

may be correct from an objective point of view, but is hardly what is required. On the contrary, the other is denied the singularity of his grief, since this happens to everyone at times.

Playing something down does not only address the Child ego state of the other to help him. One can also use this conversation killer when one wants to be left alone as quickly as possible. I cannot interpret the words of NOC president *Tröger* in another way who said after the terrorist attacks during the Olympic Games in Atlanta: "It could be worse".

If this causes hardly any defiant reaction the cause may be that the other is so troubled that he just lacks power for reactance. This does not exclude however the collection of payback points. The easiest reaction will be to end the conversation as soon as possible – with a forced smile, and to take care in further conversation not to mention any personal matters and problems.

Do not take seriously, use irony, make fun of somebody

Similar to playing something down this is a way to either seize the lead in a conversation or to end the conversation quickly. **Not to take the other seriously** with his concerns is a typical Parent ego state reaction. Our Parent ego knows rather well what is to be taken seriously, affects us or is important for us. A training course participant who was very involved in his job told me:

"During the last weeks my thirteen-year-old daughter had told me several times, that her knee gave her trouble. However, I had other things on my mind, so I didn't take care. On the weekend we had a presentation for the new *Rover*, and my daughter was to serve the coffee. Again she told me about her knee. Instead of listening and having a look, my answer was just a short and offending: Girl, listen, serve the coffee, and we deal with the rest later. Then I made her walk home because I wanted to give a pep talk to my team after the successful presentation. I got the receipt the next day: She had to go to the hospital and has had her leg in plaster for four weeks."

While when not taking someone seriously we do not acknowledge the importance of the other and his concerns, with **irony** we deal with what the other has said, but at his costs, again typical for the Parent addressing the Child ego state. Moreover, we expect at least a smile as a reaction to our ironic remark. However, this smile requires a good deal of a certain sense of humour. You may already have experienced that someone who does not feel like smiling at an ironic remark is blamed for his lack of humour.

"My dear Mr. Brown, since I can see that you do not react positively to my offer to send you to Hicksville, I have to assume that you have doubts whether you can cope with the urbanity and the vast extent of the location."

"It comes close to impertinence to give an overloaded father the time-consuming task to pick up his children with their aunt after work."

Making fun of somebody is also rather similar. Here we do not even try to hide the meaning and laugh shamelessly about the other, who may like this or not. If this is not the case this is again a proof for lack of humour. Here the bystanders take the not unimportant role of spectators and cheerleaders.

"O, look, the pet of the family has an idea."

"Caution, close your eyes, folks, Mrs. Jones has a flash of wit."

"With so much work you will be in need of a ladder soon to be able to overlook the outstanding tasks."

About a loose button: "Can't have been easy to sew on this button in complete darkness."

A colleague tries to start the new copier: "Before you accidentally kill yourself, you should ask an expert."

With all three forms of the conversation killer we expect from the other to grin and bear it. He will most probably react out of the Adapted Child and collect payback points, which will be cashed in later. In such a situation often the thought of taking revenge arises: "You wait..."

Tell sayings, maxims and worldly wisdom

Basically **telling sayings, maxims, and worldly wisdom** is a special form of not taking someone seriously. Instead of dealing with what the other said or meant he is fobbed off with a piece of "wisdom". Here the use of common sayings is to support one's own point of view. It is a kind of reference to an authority, since a truism is nothing else. The most favourite platitudes are those which generalise one's individual experiences:

"We never did it another way."
"This is how we always did it."
"Take my advice."

Also referring to Bible passages, well-known citations, or popular phrases helps to avoid having to deal with a statement. The Parent ego state has a position and wants to strengthen it and show how well informed and literate one is.

An employee who wants to redesign his job quickly gets the answer: "Always think of King Solomon who taught us: To every thing there is a season, and a time to every purpose under the heaven." Or: "Rome was not built in one day."

A rather depressed colleague who talks about problems he has at home gets the answer: "As Nietzsche said: 'You go to women. Don't forget the whip!'"

And even if it may sound constructed, the following reaction style becomes rather popular also with non-politicians: "This sounds like a release of your girl friend, and you are still looking for measures to cushion it a socially acceptable way."

And a business man formulates a layoff: "I have made the man available to the labour market again."

One risk of sayings and worldly wisdom can lie in the quick-wittedness of our dialogue partner, who can muzzle us with a well-aimed parry. For example, the employee could answer:

"On this I can only say: Charity begins at home."

Talk about oneself

This conversation killer may be familiar to you from your childhood the phase of life where adults, often the parents, very quickly turn to their own experiences. Whoever **talks about himself** to "enrich" the conversation with his own experiences has already decided that his own point of view and what he wants to tell is more important than everything else. I am often surprised how well people are able in a conversation to lead over to themselves after only one or two sentences.

A: "Our last vacations were really good, we had wonderful weather and great luck with the hotel. Most probably we'll return next year."
B: "O no, I wouldn't go back there for all the tea in China. Our hotel was that bad. The catalogue said: in a narrow street about 5 minutes from the beach and ten minutes from town centre. What nobody told us was that we would live in the approach path of the airport and that the beach was a cliff line. The next real beach was 7 miles away."

This conversation killer is not only typical for private conversation, as the following example will show:

Customer of an insurance company: "Now I have collected all the files and papers as you wrote me, but I haven't gotten my money yet. How long do I have to wait? See, the craftsmen want to be paid."
Insurance agent: "Yes, dear Mrs. Weaver, it's not that easy. See, I have to check the documents and just take a look at the piles on my desk. Everyone would want the money at once. But how do you fancy this? In addition, I have to make up for my colleague who has been on sick leave for two weeks. Do you think I had the chance to take a day off this year?"

How often did you have to listen to other people's stories and tried to figure out how to get out of the situation without causing too much displeasure. However, our well-behaved Adapted Child keeps silent and hopes for an early end. It is typical to indicate one's

defiance by not paying proper attention, looking about, or by a demonstratively suppressed yawn.

Point out causes and interpret possible background

This conversation killer has already been briefly discussed in chapter 2 ("Recognising Your Own Conversational Manners") and named interpretation there. To explain to the other the reasons for his behaviour is a wonderful opportunity to demonstrate one's knowledge of the human nature and one's psychological know how. To point out to the other which **causes** lie behind his ideas has not only something of a detective but it also indicates one's diagnostic competence, which we cannot withhold from the other who is not so experienced.

This conversation killer comes of course also from the Parent ego state and is normally used with the intention to help the other as quickly as possible. Nevertheless, there are again two drawbacks of this conversation killer:

Either we read too much in a single statement and therefore misinterpret it. Sometimes we even imply that we are right and that the other only is not (yet) ready to see it.

Alternatively, we are really skilful enough to identify and name the "real cause" and our interpretation is correct; the other does not necessarily admit that this is the case.

I remember well that in a conversation one of my very best friends said in return to my tale: "Gracious God, Christian, you must admit that you are only extremely jealous!" Without hesitating a single moment I blurted out: "Are you mad, me and jealous, I can really act my age",

although his statement had hit the bull's eye. My behaviour was triggered by nothing else but jealousy. Only I did not want to admit that frankly in that moment, not even to my friend.

To help someone understand something may be a well-meant intention, but does not assure success if the other is not open for our ideas.

"Your refusal to move to Hicksville is based on a strong fixation to our local office. Your lack of flexibility may have been caused by the fact that you never left this region."

"Your workload is just a false pretence. If you don't want to pick up the children it is only because you do not want to meet Helen since your relationship to your sister is problematic."

Some vehement protest to an interpretation turns out to be caused only by the fact that it was voiced too early. With some more patience the dialogue partner would have had the chance to think his situation over and to understand the background of his behaviour by himself. With the use of this conversation killer we also express our **impatience** and our **doubts** whether the dialogue partner will understand the problem without assistance.

Quiz, investigate

How coercing this conversation behaviour can be you can most probably remember well from your childhood, when you had trouble to fend off the many control questions:

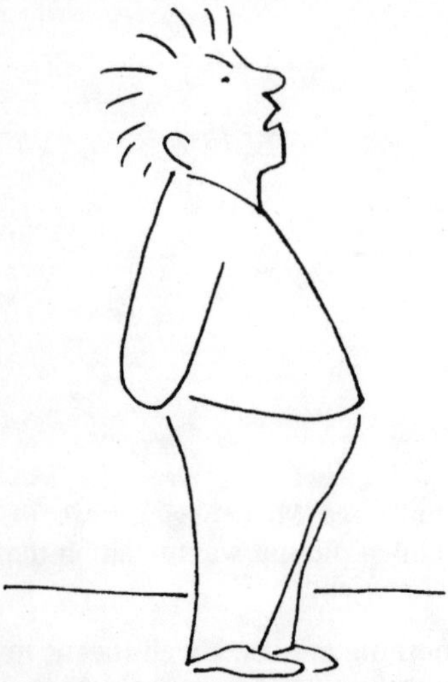

"Where have you been?"
"Did you do your homework?"
"Who is your playmate?"
"Why are you late?"
"What marks do the others have in the test?"

It is not without reason that in management literature questions are given a lot of attention, usually connected with the headline: When you want to lead, ask questions. This is the very chance that lies within asking questions. Whoever asks a question gives the respondent the horizon of the possible answer in addition. Yet, this also makes clear that this kind of **catechizing** is too often done out of the Parent ego state and that we do not aim at an exchange of information on the basis of questions, but at an **affirmation of what we have already expected**.

Questions of the yes/no type are especially popular. Here the interviewee is forced into a scheme that only allows him to agree or disagree. A comment is not desired.

Doctor: "Do you have pain when you wake up?"
Patient: "Yes."
"Is the pain more severe after breakfast?"
"No."
"Do you drink coffee in the morning?"
"Yes."
"Have you had these problems before?"
"Yes."
"In your family, do you often have cases of gastro-intestinal diseases?"

The benefit of this way of asking **narrow questions** lies in the strong **influence** on the conversation. The responsibility for the outcome is exclusively with the one who asks the questions; he decides what it is talked about. In addition you may agree that asking yes/no questions does not require too much thinking and can be done without deeper insight. In this context it is to be mentioned that such questions can transform into mere pseudo-questions. Through the suggestive formulation that includes or at least hints at the expected answer one has to be aware of the possibility that the interviewee does not tell what he knows but what he assumes the interviewer would like to hear. In the worst case he will believe the answers himself.

The other form of asking questions is the so-called w-question. Many interrogative pronouns begin with the letter "W". Here the question already includes an assumption that must not be challenged. When a waiter wants to know **what** the guest would like to drink it is already understood that in principle he is going to drink something, and that he is only allowed to choose between different beverages.

This type of questioning may satisfy one's curiosity, but it does not lead to a meaningful conversation.

"I feel absolutely shattered, I have just failed the exam."
"Who was your examiner?" or "Which subject?"
"Yesterday I survived a car crash, I am still very shocked."
"What happened?" or "What kind of car do you drive?"
"My dentist told me that she has to take out all four wisdom teeth."
"To whom do you go?" or "How often do you go to the dentist?"

Only too often questions are called legitimate since one wants to show one's interest in the other. I do not want to say anything against sympathy, but someone who **asks questions satisfies** mainly **his curiosity**. In addition, it may be very problematic if the response one gets collides with one's assessment standards, as the following example from a class about leadership in conversation may illustrate:

A participant had volunteered to reveal her problem and to ask the group for advice. She started: "I have really big problems to stop smoking. I've tried again and again, but after some days I slide back. It really makes me mad."
"How many cigarettes do you smoke per day?"
"Two, three, sometimes four per day."
"Well, that's not much. Some others would be glad if they could keep that level."

The following conversation was mainly influenced by the fact the young lady did not feel she was taken seriously, since she really had problems with the fact that she could not do without these two or three cigarettes per day; but the other switched from the conversation killer "question" to the conversation killer "play something down" and tried to explain to her that she did not have a problem at all.

Some readers may argue now: "One should be allowed to ask questions." I will assure: Yes, of course. Yet, even simple requests for information can be very artificial; be it that they help to avoid **personal involvement**, be it that they include indirect enforcement of a claim: **The interview replaces a dialogue**. The famous question "Do you love me?" is in fact a subtle way to replace the disclosure of feelings with a request to the other to reveal the extent of his or her affection. Via questions we are not only able to avoid personal statements – who asks does not tell anything – but asking questions is also a safeguard against taking actions. Every badly prepared student knows how one can hide one's lack of knowledge with a clever question. I rarely receive so many harmless organisational questions as in situations where participants are requested to be active.

Especially in conversations about decisions, problems, or conflicts, our questions can express that we **lack confidence** in our dialogue partner's ability to deal with his problems by himself. We are too impatient to believe in such an independent activity. This way of leading a conversation by means of questions may structure the process, but it is combined with a restriction of freedom regarding speed and direction of the conversation. The role allocation with the active structuring and the reactive following partner favours to ask for facts only, what easily makes the dialogue partner an object of diagnostic considerations. This becomes particularly clear in the pressing **why-questions**, since they ask the other for a reason and a justification for his actions. Either the other knows the cause for his current problems, and then we can assume that he has a good reason for not letting us know it. Or he does not know the cause, and in this case he will experience the Why as very embarrassing, because remaining silent makes his lack of competence obvious. It is not true that you have to know as much as possible about someone if you want to give him good advice. Gaining knowledge about someone very easily gives one the **feeling of superiority and authority** and thus is related to the **Parent** ego state. Whoever urges the other to answer further questions does not only steer the conversation but gains additional power. Several fairy tales but also the story of Oedipus show how someone who knows how to ask questions gains power over others. You do have to challenge the other and to prevent that he asks questions himself. In an extreme case questions can be used to subdue the other. Reality is only sought after when one wants it. So in many cases one only too easily sticks to an idea. Then questions are asked so that the answers support the idea, and be it through inquisition.

In this context I want to mention a phenomenon. Anyone who tries to structure a conversation via questions very easily gets into the situation to feel responsible for the further course of it. When you test this you will find that the other will give answers readily, but in a way he only consumes the questions without trying to give the conversation a direction himself. At the same time the one who has started to ask questions will have difficulties to leave this position again. The dialogue turns into an interview.

Offer ideas and solutions

Maybe you will be surprised that this behaviour is to be counted as a conversation killer and wonder if there are any remaining possibilities left to say anything. With this conversation killer the stress is on the **offer**, since most of the **recommendations** we give each other are well meant but usually given without being asked for it. With unwanted **proposals** and **solutions** we express from our Parent ego state that the other is in need of our assistance and will not make it alone, since being in the helpless Child ego state. How much the inferiority that is connected with the Child ego state is refused is often expressed in the typical reaction to unwanted advice: "Yes, but..." In other words we thank the advisor for his effort, which is contained in the "Yes", and subsequently we explain why especially this advice cannot be put into action. A typical form of dialogue develops:

"Since we have these new machines we face numerous bugs. I don't know what to do first any more."

"Before you start debugging you should restart the system program, usually the problems are solved then."
"Good idea, but this is what I've already done twice."
"Press repeat then. This may also help."
"I'm not that stupid."
"Sorry, in this case you'll have to look it up in the manual."
"Thanks, that would be the solution, but unfortunately the programmers didn't give an explanation for this exact problem."
"In this case the last chance is to call the system administrator."
"I've thought about that, but he is totally overworked and wouldn't have time anyway."
"If I were you I would go to my supervisor and ask her what to do."
"I think so, too. Unfortunately I still try to avoid her because of our argument the other week."

In the first place the unwanted advice conveys the other that we do not trust him to find an appropriate solution by himself. With our well-meant solution ideas we demonstrate again our **impatience** and **lack of confidence** in our dialogue partner's competence.

In many exercises on leading counselling conversations I was surprised to learn from the one who had asked for help how well the counsellor had dealt with the problem and that he had found a list of good proposals. Usually the proposals were especially praised. However, when I broached the subject again and asked when the proposals would be put into action I usually heard good explanations why this was impossible at the moment or what would hinder a realisation. In other words, innumerable recommendations are thankfully accepted and never carried out.

This does not mean that recommendations and solution ideas are to be abandoned in general, but before giving any kind of it, it is necessary to test to what extent the other is really in need of it.

With a simple phrase you can verify this:

"At the moment I am uncertain in how far you would like to hear my advice." Or:

"I am just asking myself whether you would be interested in a recommendation from my side." Or:
"I am just considering if you might be interested in what I would do."

These reflexive questions comparable to thinking aloud invite the dialogue partner indirectly to make his choice. Either the other is interested in my recommendations, in this case he will say so, look at me and wait. Far more often the answer will sound like this:

"Oh, definitely, I would like to hear your opinion, you know, the case is..."
Now the other talks and talks. And in most cases he will not come back to the offer.

It has to be admitted that in this case we have to keep our ideas under our hat. This has one big advantage: It is not our fault when the other makes a mistake. What I want to say is that an unwanted advice, especially when it is good, is only carried out half-heartedly leading to corresponding problems. In consequence we hear the typical reproach: "I will listen again to your advice..."

Recently a neighbour asked very concretely for my advice since she had educational problems with her daughter. After having given a detailed description of the circumstances she asked directly: "What would you recommend, I mean, you have studied this and ought to know what to do."
I do not know what the hell came over me but I actually let slip: "Sure. What would you like to hear?"
After all her descriptions about her cluelessness I was surprised to hear her answer: "See, you know, I think there is only one way and that is to be consequent and..." What followed sounded absolutely logical and would have never occurred to me as a recommendation. When she finally stopped I said: "Sounds reasonable." Whereon she returned: "You think so, too. Listen, I have to tell Carl immediately that you also think we'll get it under control this way."

What makes an unwanted advice so difficult to accept is the speed with which we conjure up a solution. Someone has pondered about the problem, turned it from one side to the other, and did not find a solution and now he tells us about his troubles. And like a magician draws a rabbit out of a hat we present a solution instantaneously. But with this (too) quick fix we let the other feel how incompetent, clueless, unrealistic we believe him to be since he was not able to think of this himself. In this Child-ego-state-assumption may be found one of the explanations for why so many people discard proposed solutions. From a certain point in the conversation the focus is no longer the problem that needs to be solved but the relationship between the dialogue partners and how they treat each other. In such a situation even very good solutions will be rejected only for not having to admit that one did not get there alone.

This conversation killer seems to be an ostensible attempt to find a solution and to help the other. However, in a deeper sense we demonstrate with this behaviour our quick-wittedness, competence, and our superiority. And this is not liked by anyone in the first place. It is a pity, but this is how people are.

At the end of this chapter you can practise to classify the conversation killers. Every statement of B contains at least one and sometimes even several statements out of the Parent ego state, which sadly enough do not lead to the desired reactions with A, forcing B to try with additional arguments to steer the conversations towards the goal, i. e. B's goal.

It is Saturday evening, around 6 pm. Albert (**A**) and Bridget (**B**) Grey have been invited by friends to a party.

A: "I think we should not go to the party. We do not even know the people."

B: "Don't worry. It will be nice for sure." (1)

A: "No, I am not really fond of going."

B: "I don't think it right to base an acceptance on like or dislike. And anyway the only reason for your dislike is that you feel shy when you meet people you do not know!" (2)

A: "This has got nothing to do with it. I only really do not know what I should go for."

B: "Ok, now listen, one has to keep one's promises." (3)

A: "You're only a stickler for principles."

B: "Now this is really nonsense, when you blame me just because you don't want to go any more." (4)

A: "Um"

B: "Now rather tell me, how come all of a sudden you do not like to go any more?" (5)

A: "I don't know. It will be boring for sure."

B: "On the contrary, it will be very entertaining" (6)

A: "Well, last time with the Schulze's it was more than stiff."
B: "I had a very good time, especially Mrs. Schulze, she was so funny. Her story about the goldfish still makes me laugh." (7)
A: "Yes, you and Mrs. Schulze..."
B: "Well, if I were you I would find a seat close to Mrs. Schulze, I am sure she will be there, and you will see, how nicely she will take care of you. And if people start telling jokes you can tell your newest one with Winnetou Koslowsky, I am sure nobody knows that one." (8)
A: "Somehow I do not like joke telling."
B: "That is not true. You just have to come out of your shell and you will see that everything looks quite different." (9)
A: "Um. I don't know..."
B: "And think of the excellent food. I am sure there will be a buffet with hundreds of dainties and with decent wines. And we will meet some interesting people. Maybe I can even fix a new order." (10)
A: "Um"
B: "Ok, if you really don't want, I will go without you, and you know what that means." (11)

Ideas for a solution:
(1) Play s.th. down
(2) Assess + Point out causes and interpret possible background
(3) Tell sayings, maxims and worldly wisdom
(4) Reproach
(5) Quiz
(6) (Claim)
(7) Talk about yourself
(8) Force ideas and solutions
(9) Force ideas and solutions
(10) Try to convince s. o. of doing s.th.
(11) Warn and threaten

This "harmless" dialogue does not only contain the entire panoply of conversation killers. Even from these very few sentences we can estimate with how much disregard Bridget Grey reacts to her husband's listlessness. Her conversation behaviour indeed provokes reactance. If we consider how Albert Grey will decide in the situation in question, it is easy to imagine that after the final warning the couple will go to the party together. But at what price? What are the payback points Mr. Grey could cash in?

In any case it will be difficult if not impossible for Albert Grey to enjoy the party and to admit this to his wife. Since this would make her say proudly: "See, I told you." In the easiest case Mr. Grey could let his wife feel on their way back home how much he was bored during the evening, and this does not necessarily have to be in the form of reproaches; subtler would be demonstrative silence.

Maybe he gets a migraine attack at the party and has to ask his wife to drive him back home at once.

Or he could behave so badly that his wife will be very embarrassed and regrets that she has taken him to the party at all, for example he could get drunk.

No matter which way Mr. Grey will choose this dialogue will turn out to be a Pyrrhic victory for Mrs. Grey. The final invoice will be presented to her much later. Viewed this way the short-term benefit from the use of conversation killers stands in no relation to the actual gain.

Avoidable mantraps

Quiz

Someone who asks questions tries to learn more about a subject and to lead a conversation in a certain direction that seems to be important to him. The main interest is to satisfy one's curiosity and not to facilitate a dialogue.

Questions of the yes/no type are especially popular. The one who is asked is forced to follow a certain pattern and is only allowed to agree or disagree. The advantage of such **narrow questions** lies in a strong leadership. The responsibility for the development of the conversation stays solely with the one who asks the questions; he decides what is talked about. The role allocation of the active interviewer and the reactive interviewee supports finding out about facts, which all too easily makes the interviewee the object of a diagnostic approach. The consequences are awkward feelings.

> Anyone who tries to structure a conversation with questions easily gets under pressure of feeling responsible for the further course of the conversation. It can be observed that the other is willing to answer questions but only in a passive way and that he abstains from trying to lead the conversation into a certain direction himself.

Another form of questions is open questions. Here the way to ask it already contains a presumption that must not be challenged any more.

"Where is the problem?" (Presumes that something is wrong.)

"Why do you agonise about the decision?" (Implies agony.)

"What do you want to drink?" (Thirst is assumed.)

Often questions are legitimated with wanting to show interest. Nothing against sympathy, but whoever asks questions mainly satisfies his curiosity.

In addition, the one who asks questions may have problems to leave this position. The dialogue turns into an interview with the character of an interrogation.

> **Hint:** Before you start asking questions the next time, check with the dialogue partner if he is willing to be questioned, like for example:

"I am uncertain if I can ask you some questions about xy."

You may be surprised when the other starts to splutter the whole story without you having been asked a single question. Maybe you will even find out that he talks about an aspect you would never have thought about but that is very important in that moment.

If you need to ask for facts you can try:

"If you agree I would like to ask you some questions about xyz."

You may be surprised that the other will talk about some things without further questions.

Offer solutions

Most recommendations are well meant but are given without being asked for.

Unwanted proposals and solution ideas express one's belief that the other is in need of support and cannot cope alone. The other suddenly finds himself in the position of the inferior and usually reacts with a negative answer: "Yes, but..."

With the hastily given solution we let the other feel for how incompetent, clueless, and unrealistic we hold him. It is implied that he is unable to solve the problem without assistance. This is why even good proposals are discarded, just to avoid having to admit that one did not find it oneself.

This conversation killer seems to be an **ostensible** attempt to find a solution and to help the other. However, **in fact** we demonstrate with this behaviour our quick-wittedness, competence, and superiority.

> Unwanted advice indicates impatience and lack of confidence in the dialogue partner's competence.

Before giving any kind of recommendations and solution ideas it is necessary to test if the other is really in need of it.

Hint: With a simple phrase you can verify this:

- "At the moment I am uncertain if you would like to hear my advice." Or
- "I am just asking myself whether you would be interested in a recommendation from my side." Or:
- "I am just considering if you might be interested in what I would do."

These reflexive questions comparable to thinking aloud invite the dialogue partner indirectly to make his choice. Either the other is interested in my recommendations, in this case he will say so, look at me and wait. Far more often the answer will sound like this:

"Oh, definitely, I would like to hear your opinion, you know, the case is..."

Now the other talks and talks. And in most cases he will not come back to the offer.

It has to be admitted that in this case we have to keep our ideas under our hat. This has one big advantage: It is not our fault when the other makes a mistake. What I want to say is that an unwanted advice, especially when it is good, is only carried out half-heartedly leading to corresponding problems. In consequence we hear the typical reproach: "*To your advice I will listen again...*"

9. Conversation Savers

The list of the conversation killers in the previous chapter may have led to the question, which possible communication behaviour is left for use. In the following I will give a list of possible reactions, which are apt to facilitate communication and which are therefore named **conversation savers**. With these behaviour patterns you can show your dialogue partner that you listen to him and are interested in his thoughts and emotions. The other will feel reassured and encouraged to go on talking. The message of the conversation savers reads:

> I would like to capture and understand what you mean.
> I am interested in what you are saying.
> Please, go on!

In contrast to the conversation killers, where one's own position is stressed, with the conversation savers you do **not** take a point of view. The essential thing in this behaviour pattern is that you concentrate on the dialogue partner **first** and abstain from well-meant advice, judgements, opinions, and disagreement.

Some reader may ask himself impatiently when he will finally learn how he can convince others and make them listen to him in return. Especially with the use of the conversation savers you will make the paradoxical discovery how quickly your dialogue partner starts thinking about your position when you concentrate on his.

While the conversation killers are typical Parent ego state behaviour patterns, the conversation savers have in common that they stem from the Adult ego state. They aim at exchanging and checking information to optimise understanding of the other's position.

Paraphrase, repeat with own words

This conversation saver you already know from chapter 3 ("Four Ways of Listening"). I often hear the remark that descriptive listening would slow a conversation down since no new aspects are added and since a repetition might come across to the other as being parroted. The following dialogue developed between a young lady and me in a training course:

Participant: "Well, I must say I don't like it at all, just to repeat what the other has said. What's the use of it?"

Weisbach: "For you it sounds like monkeying the other, you feel like a parrot, and this doesn't make any sense to you."

Participant: "Yeah, right, the other may think I make fun of him or he thinks I am stupid, if I don't have anything else to say than to repeat his statement."

Weisbach: "Such a stupid behaviour would make the other doubt your competence."

Participant: "Exactly. I wonder how it would be for me if someone would all the time just repeat my statements. I think I would find it somehow rather strange."

Weisbach: "If somebody would do that to you, you would feel like you are not taken seriously."

Participant: "Correct, I would think, I'm obviously not able to express clearly what I want to say. Since if the other had understood me, he would not have to repeat what I said in such an annoying way."

Weisbach: "Descriptive listening seems to you like criticism, like an offence to your ability to express your thoughts."

Participant: "Yes, I think that's what annoys me so."

The conversation was interrupted here, since the other participants were no longer able to refrain from laughing and the young lady looked about her very uncertainly.

Although this short dialogue gave me a very good chance to demonstrate the use of this conversation saver, I had really not understood at first why she had these big problems with "descriptive listening". Only after some time I realized that it was her fear of being criticized that was stopping her from making an effort. As an example I will show you how this dialogue would have sounded the "classical way":

A: "Well, I must say I don't like it at all, just to repeat what the other has said. What's the use of it?"
B: "The use of it? That's easy: You show the other how much you try to understand him. Try it out and you will see how helpful this is."
A: "What should be helpful in that? On the contrary, the other will think I am kidding. Me, I would interrupt such a conversation pretty quickly, if somebody repeats me non-stop."
B: "This is an answer I often get from people who judge about something they do not really know."
A: "You don't have to try every bit of rubbish yourself to be allowed to talk about it."
B: "As long as you disagree, this shows me that you haven't understood the concept."

You do not need much imagination to foresee how the dialogue would develop and how A and B would get along with each other in the future.

> Descriptive listening makes clear that you have understood your dialogue partner.

Summarize

A special form of descriptive listening is to give a summary. Some people have difficulties in voicing their thoughts briefly and precisely. *Heinrich von Kleist* has described, how thoughts develop during the process of talking, so that some people talk in a very peripatetic way and lose the thread of their thoughts. Here the abbreviating repetition can help. With this conversation saver you do not only prove that you have listened, but that you really captured the essence.

Anyway, I have to mention a temptation: summarizing is sometimes used to react to a statement, but in such a distorting way that the personal position is included in the abbreviated version. The following scene from a department meeting gives an example:

During a department meeting Mr. Adams says: "When I look at the numbers, this looks all very well. But in my view there are some important facts missing. For example we have fixed project closure for March 28th, and if I remember it correctly Mr. Stafford mentioned the month-end closing to be the reason. As far as I know internal auditing is due in May since the audit in BP&A usually takes longer than planned and they usually do the IT before us. Plus the schedule assumes that none of us will take vacation and nobody gets ill. This is more than unrealistic. And all the stress is only accepted since afterwards we will have advantages in second quarter. I mean, I wonder if there are better ways."
Mr. Stafford, department head: "If I understand you right, you are also interested in improving our position for the second quarter. You emphasize that we can only keep our schedule if everybody delays personal vacation plans during the next weeks. When I may also summarize your statement regarding the audit date, it can be very important for us to have our meeting earlier than the IT department. I think I will check that as soon as possible. And I repeat, Mr. Adams, that your concerns only regard March 28th and not the project objectives, you are also of the opinion that our numbers are excellent at the moment."

What sounds like a summary in pseudo-partnership style may impress rhetorically, but makes the department head look arrogant and as slippery as an eel. If Mr. Adams has already pre-experiences with Mr. Stafford, we will abstain from a correction and sulk in silence. And that is exactly the problem. Since someone who sulks in silence becomes very demotivated, he will reduce his engagement to the lowest acceptable level and in the case of a failure he can crow and say: "Didn't I say it? But nobody listens to me."

A true summary could have sounded like:

Mr. Stafford, department head: "If I understand you right, Mr. Adams, you believe the proposed end date March 28th to be unrealistic, since we do not have a time buffer for vacation and sick leaves. In addition you would like to discuss if we can make our goal for second quarter results with a lower stress level, when we better define the target."

The moderation of discussions requires practised experience with the conversation saver "summarize". Who does not want to hear that he is manipulative, will already strive during listening to distinguish between the other's statement and one's own opinion. The guiding principle reads:

What does the other want and what is important for him?

Clarify, put in a nutshell

With many statements a circumscription would be far too lengthy and a summary may be too complex. Here one can try to put the content in a nutshell. This conversation behaviour serves to clarify the dialogue partner's thoughts. With this conversation saver you can shorten a debate. In many cases statements will be embroidered, arguments listed and a long list of examples given. However, all these contain a common core idea. Anyone who can capture this is able to prove in a hardly to be beaten way that he has understood his dialogue partner.

In the previous example with the department meeting to put the content in a nutshell may have sounded like:

Mr. Stafford, department head: "Mr. Adams, you think we should not favour March 28th but test if we can meet the same objectives with less effort."

You may have noticed several times before that speech contributions are "decorated" with different arguments which still aim at supporting the same basic position. We can observe with ourselves that we often repeat our thoughts and describe all aspects until we get the impression that we have been understood. Yes, even it may sound paradoxical, we can only abandon a position without much resistance when we are sure that our thoughts have been heard. And in the reverse case you will have experienced that others defend their opinions the more stubbornly the less understanding is signalled.

To clarify and to put things in a nutshell in a conversation contributes to concentrating on the essentials.

To signal understanding does not include agreement. Maybe there is an explanation for why this conversation saver is so seldom used. It might be the existence of a latent fear that the dialogue partner may mix up understanding with agreement or approval and so one's own arguments are given at once instead of concentrating on the essential content of the other's statement.

Restricting repetition

Sometimes we are confronted with opinions which we do not like to repeat for fear of further fixing the point of view by it. In chapter 6 ("Resistance with the Dialogue Partner") you have learned to know phrases that help against a static description of a situation. The following list may help to increase variety in the use of this conversation saver:

- still
- at the moment
- now, right now
- just
- presently
- today

Normally your dialogue partner will agree spontaneously since he enjoys being understood. At the same time the agreement includes an acceptance of the time constraint.

With a car dealer a customer is asked whether he would be interested in taking a look at the new model of his present car, but he says:
"Well, thanks, but I'm rather satisfied with my car."
"That's great, and since you are satisfied a test drive is at the moment out of the question for you."
"Right."
"If you think about the entire year, when do you think will you be interested in a test drive? I am only asking today since I would like to

plan ahead and give you the car for an entire weekend."
"Oh, that's interesting..."

> With the conversation saver "restricting repetition" you can weaken rigid adherence to an opinion, when you add a time constraint to the repetition.

Overdone confirmation

In some situations you will have problems to react to your dialogue partner in a facilitating way because he has made his statement so absolute and final that he indeed proposes an end of the conversation. Here you can use the "overdone confirmation". Similar to the previous conversation saver the statement of the other is repeated, summarized and clarified. Yet, if you add a generalisation without stressing it especially, you will provoke disagreement. This is to be regarded as positive for the dialogue, since in nearly all cases it leads to further explanations. On one hand the dialogue partner feels understood, which is the effect of the circumscription and repetition, on the other he does not want your statement to remain this way, and he feels in need to give further explanations that usually contain thoughts with which you can further deepen the conversation.

Here I want to give you a list of ideas for phrases that may help you with "overdone confirmations":

- never, in no case
- unimaginable
- impossible
- excluded
- not at any time
- absolutely not
- under no/all circumstances
- in every case
- always
- forever
- constantly
- at all times
- everyday

In the previous example the car dealer could also react to the customer with an "overdone confirmation":

Dealer: "This means you do not want to test the new model at any time."
Or: "Testing the car for an entire weekend is absolutely unacceptable for you."
"No, I didn't mean it this way. Just that I don't want to buy a new car at the moment. I thought about next spring."

> You can resume a closed statement with the conversation saver "overdone confirmation" by adding a generalized statement to your repetition, thus making your dialogue partner further explain his point of view.

Relate aspects

While in the previous paragraphs it was illustrated that many statements can be reduced to a core argument, you will need the conversation saver "relate aspects" when several positions are voiced simultaneously.

With this conversation behaviour you can rearrange what you have heard according to the pattern:

- on one hand – on the other hand
- partly – partly
- ... as well as ...
- neither – nor

Anytime you hear words like **only, however, still,** and **though**, the statement consists of more than one thought. And the dialogue partner does not have to be aware of in which way his two thoughts are related. Sometimes one gets the impression that a certain wish is unconsciously opposed to with something that in a way creates a balance and which does not allow action, be it in one or the other direction. The purposeful use of this conversation saver can add to concentrating the conversation on the essence and to structure the respective statement parts so that one can achieve clarification.

A: "We have the chance to live in the countryside; they have offered us a house with a huge garden in Podung for rent. Our apartment has always been too small, so this offer comes just when we need it. But this also means that we lose all the contacts we have here and to start all over again."

B: "On one hand the offer to rent a house with a garden sounds very attractive, on the other you may lose touch with your friends and acquaintance."

You can imagine that B would have had no problems to express his opinion with a conversation killer, for example like:

B: "Me, I wouldn't go there for all the tea in China. Podung of all places." (Talk about oneself). Or:

B: "You are still young. It's not that difficult to find new friends. You definitely should accept that offer. If you hesitate the house will be gone and you will live to rue it." (Judge, Play sth down, Unwanted Advice, Warn and Threaten).

But of what help can B's comments be here. A has to make the decision and to find out what at the end is more important for him. In the Adult ego state he has the best chance to check possible consequences of his decision, and the conversation saver "relate aspects" can support him.

Ask for clarification

In contrast to investigative questions here the dialogue partner is invited to further explain his statement.

When you ask for clarification you refer only to aspects the other has already mentioned and which you have difficulties to fully understand. Typical phrases are:

- "Could you give me an example of...?"
- "What do you mean by...?"
- "What does... mean?"
- "At the moment I cannot really imagine this."
- "I did not get that."

Asking for clarification fosters understanding.

A: "Since we had to move to the barracks we are almost cut off from all insider knowledge. If we do not have a good idea, we are in trouble."

B: "What do you mean with insider knowledge?"

With this answer **A** is asked to express his thoughts more clearly. The course of the conversation would have been a totally different one if **B** had chosen a why-question:

B: "Why did your department have to move to the barracks?"

The typical legitimisation given for **investigations** is: "I only want to better understand the other". With **asking for clarification** the point is only to understand a **single statement** much better.

In a training course the following dialogue started which seems fit to further explain the difference between investigative and clarifying questions. **A** had started the dialogue and **B** was only allowed to use conversation savers, **C** was the "referee" and was asked to name the conversation savers or killers.

A: "Now it's nearly Christmas and we have discussed if this year we won't have the conventional Christmas tree but a bouquet of flowers instead."
B: "What problems do you have with a Christmas tree?"
C: "Stop! This is quizzing. Now **A** has to give her reasons."
B: "But I want to understand **A**, and so I wanted to use the conversation saver 'ask for clarification'."
C: "This may only refer to what **A** has just said."
B: "Okay, second try: What does your husband think about it?"
C: "Stop! This is investigative again. Now **A** has to report her conversation with her husband."
B: "Well, and how should I ask questions? If I ask: and what do you expect from a bouquet? it will be questioning again?"
A: "Indeed."
C: "I don't know if this is helpful, but I can think of the following way to ask for clarification: You say 'we' have discussed, whom does this include? Or: What do you mean with 'conventional Christmas tree'? Or: At the moment I cannot really imagine how a bouquet would look."

You see it is easier to satisfy one's curiosity than to ask the other for a more understandable expression of his thoughts.

At the end of this paragraph I want to print a longer part of a conversation from which you can see that asking for clarification does not necessarily have to be done in the form of questions. Using statements instead, also aims at getting further explanations but due to the tone it does not feel so pressing. Since questions are indicated with a raised voice at the end of the sentence, chains of questions can feel coercing. In the following dialogue you will be able to observe that sometimes the repetition of a single word is enough to make the other go on talking.

In my consultation-hour a student showed up who had some questions regarding a presentation. In the course of the conversation she finally revealed her real concern:

Student: "Well, actually this is not all I have come for. I'm at a loss there."

Weisbach: "What do you mean by 'there'?"

Student: "Yes, well, with my diploma thesis. The problem is, each time I think I can make it somehow, there are those doubts and also self-doubt."

Weisbach: "Who is in doubt?"

Student: "Well, first of all the others, but in a way me, too."

Weisbach: "The others."

Student: "The folks from my study group. They say things like: You cannot make it, or: How do you think you can do it in six months?"

Weisbach: "You said before that you are also in doubt, what exactly do you mean by this?"

Student: "Well – (looks out of the window) – mhm – I don't know, the thing is when I have stayed at my desk the whole day and have written some pages I am rather satisfied. And then I take up some book and suddenly I could burn the whole thing."

Weisbach: "As soon as you look at other books you are totally frustrated and the satisfaction has vanished."

Student: "Yeah, right. They can express everything so much better. They treat things briefly and precisely. Why should I bother with all the effort?"

Weisbach: "After all your theme has already been dealt with much better elsewhere."
Student: "No, not like this. They write about many different themes. But I will never be able to match them."
Weisbach: "I am not sure with whom you want to match."
Student: (remains silent, looks down on the floor) "Yes –whom? There are these requirements, for form and style, and somehow I cannot comply."
Weisbach: "I am wondering whose requirements you mean."
Student: "Hm, well (looks up a bit puzzled and then down on her hands), I mean, I think there are just the requirements for a thesis."
Weisbach: "And who has set these requirements?"
Student: (starts to laugh) "Yeah, who? That's a good question. Maybe you, Mr. Weisbach."
Weisbach: "You say 'maybe'."
Student: "Well, – maybe they are my own requirements, to be better in a way and thus to make more of an effort."
Weisbach: "When you say you want to be better, I am thinking about at what aspect you want to be better."
Student: (long silence) "Hm – I think, better than the others."
Weisbach: "In your study group?"
Student: "Mhm. Maybe I want to be better than Fred and Debbie from our group."
Weisbach: "I notice that you say 'maybe'."
Student: "I don't know. I think – mhm – well, I want to be better than Debbie."
Weisbach: "This does not make clear where you want to be better than Debbie."
Student: "Where? (silence) Well, from the whole make-up it has to be convincing."
Weisbach: "It has to be convincing."
Student: "The style and so."
Weisbach: "Can you give me an example for 'and so'."
Student: "The train of thoughts has to be coherent in style, not a word too much, and especially not a word missing."
Weisbach: "I just try to imagine whom this is meant to convince."
Student: "You!"
Weisbach: "And nobody else?"
Student: "I see, – well, it's probably Debbie I want to convince in the first place."
Weisbach: "You say 'probably'."
Student: "Well, half a year ago or so she said that I was not as good at it."

Weisbach: "As who?"
Student: "I think as she. Not to be able to write as well as she does. And somehow she is very arrogant since sometimes she writes a lot of garbage."
Weisbach: "I am just trying to imagine how Debbie will look when your thesis is completed."
Student: (long reconsidering) "This may sound silly, but I want her to go green with envy."
Weisbach: "In other words, you struggle for six months with your thesis, so that Debbie admits to your study group that she did not trust you to complete such a piece of work."
Student: "Alas – sounds like I'm a bit cuckoo."
Weisbach: "If you imagine just for a moment that Debbie would not exist. Would this have any consequences for your work?"
Student: (thinks it over) "I think I would complete it now. You know the content. I would assume I'll get a B mark. And then I would assign for the final tests."
Weisbach: "Okay, now I am only curious if I will get your draft in one or in two weeks."

Set someone thinking

Some questions in the previous text went beyond mere clarification. In this way you have already gotten to know the conversation saver 'set someone thinking'. This is also formulated as a question. Yet, here the dialogue partner is asked to broaden his horizon of thoughts. These questions are not asked to obtain an expected answer but they are formulated acting as a deputy of the other in order to start a reflexive thought process.

The thought-provoking impulse lies in crossing the in many cases self-set boundaries. Typical impulses can be:

- What if...?
- Which consequences would... have?
- How would it look like if...?
- What would happen if...?
- In the worst case what would happen if...?

You will be able to observe that especially in difficult situations people think about all aspects of a problem without making any progress. From a certain moment they merely think in circles; there is one point which is not thought beyond. The conversation saver **set someone thinking** makes the other consider the problem out of the Adult ego state and to test possible consequences of a decision. We tend to help people who seek for assistance by giving them advice; often it turns out that the conscious choice of a negation, the opposite opinion or the negative case leads to the point much more quickly. With the following questions your dialogue partner will find out where he stands:

- Imagine you would not do it...
- ... not today...
- ... not tomorrow...
- ... never!
- How do you feel about this?

Suddenly your dialogue partner finds out whether he has enough willpower and energy to achieve his aim. Let's look at the Podung example again:

A: "We have the chance to live in the countryside; they have offered us a house with a huge garden in Podung for rent. Our apartment has always been too small, so this offer comes just when we need it. But this also means that we lose all the contacts we have here and to start all over again."

B: "Assuming you would make up your mind for Podung. What would be the most positive concomitants?" Or:

B: "To lose your contacts here, what would it mean in the worst case?" Or:

B: "When you say 'start all over again', what would be the consequences for you?" Or:

B: "If you imagine to stay in your apartment in the beginning which problems do you see?"

Perhaps you are surprised how persistently these continuing questions regard the negative. Yes, one may even object that people are already too much focussed on the negative and that therefore one does not want to confront the other with the adversities. The thought-provoking impulse contained in the continuing questions requests to imagine the existing fears as concretely as possible. In addition, with the following questions, your dialogue partner can be made aware of his internal resistance:

- What would be the worst case?
- And what the second-worst?
- And which case do you deal with in your thoughts?

It can be found rather often that behind a negative restriction you can find an unreflected generalisation which can be detected with repeated questions. Not the well-meant advice is what really helps but a conscious assessment of the feared consequences. Even the best advice will be answered with a "Yes, but…", if the one who receives it somewhere deep in his mind has hidden an image of the negative consequences.

The following example may explain how someone can remain unable to take action because he imagines possible consequences in the darkest colours. This is also named 'to catastrophise'.

During a coaching session a female client asked for my advice regarding the following situation:

Client: "You know I'm in this department for only three months and I really like the job. Last week I made the horrible discovery that a colleague has handed construction plans to our competitor. I learned about that by chance without him noticing. I would like best to go to my boss immediately and let him know. But that's impossible. I have thought it over again and again, but I don't see a way."

Weisbach: "What would happen if you go to your supervisor tomorrow and talk to him about your observation?"

Client: "Not for the life of me! I'd rather move to another department again. No, under no circumstances."

Weisbach: "In other words, your boss will give you a piece of his mind and ask you to quit."

Client: "No, it will not be that bad. But anyway."

Weisbach: "I just try to imagine this: you are downright in panic to go to your boss. And you don't expect to be fired. This means there's something else that troubles you. My first thought is that your boss is choleric and may assault you."

Client: "What do you think, the man is calmness in person."

Weisbach: "Okay, so he doesn't fire you, will not assault you, what would be the worst consequence then?"

Client: "Hm, if I only knew. (Thinks it over) I don't know."

Weisbach: "We can try to imagine that together. At the moment you don't have to fear any consequences. With which reaction of your boss would you be unable to cope?"

Client: (Thinks it over.) "I believe it's if he doesn't say anything at all and smiles at me and nods his head and says 'Aha' and then shows me to the door. That would be really bad."

Weisbach: "If I try to imagine the situation, what would be then? I mean, you won't get a heart attack because of that."

Client: "Yes, what would be then? I would return to my desk. What else."

Weisbach: "I am sure that you would not be able to go on working in a relaxed manner like..."

Client interrupts: "Of course not! I would think, such an idiot. You sod."

Weisbach: "This sounds really resolute and self-confident. If you think it over now, how realistic do you believe such a reaction of your boss to be?"

Client: "If you ask me that way, entirely unrealistic. I think I have fooled myself all the time. – I'll tell you in an hour how my boss reacted."

With this example I wanted to show you that this type of question and these thought-provoking impulses do not aim at getting a concrete answer but at gaining deeper insight. With this conversation saver not the direct answer is relevant but what is induced by it in the dialogue partner.

Thought-provoking questions set the other thinking.

Work out wishes

In the previous paragraph it was pointed out that in difficult situations people think their problem over, but do not make any progress. From a certain moment they merely think in circles. And there is a certain point they do not think beyond. Yet, in addition you can find that even with the worst problems we have an idea of the optimal solution. I admit that this solution does not have to be conscious to us in every situation. And even if we are aware of it this does not mean that we openly confess it. Otherwise we would have to allow to be asked why we did not pout this into action long ago. Some solutions conflict with other positions and would only cause further trouble.

In a management training course a participant described the others his troubles with a certain employee and asked them for ideas and recommendations for how to solve that problem. What he did not mention in about twenty minutes was his idea of an optimal solution, which was to terminate the employee's contract.

With the conversation saver **work out wishes** the other gets the chance to understand his desires without the need to justify them.

In the example with Podung **A** had stated that moving to Podung would necessarily be related to losing all contacts. Maybe **A** does really believe that. Yet, which concrete fears does he relate to moving? Does he visualise himself sitting at the town entrance isolated and lonely without any friends and acquaintance? Or does he not have any ideas at all but is still caught in the thoughts of the current situation? Whatever, **A** has already made up his mind for or against Podung, even if he is not aware of it. This could be addressed most directly with a question for his goals:

B: "What would be the ideal solution in your eyes?"
A: "It would be best if we could make new contacts in Podung rather soon and if the others would come from time to time to visit us so that we do not lose all existing contacts at once. And we would probably come here sometimes, too."

With this statement **A** shows that he favours the moving and that only how to part from the old friends and to say good-bye is not defined yet. Very different it would be with the following answer:

B: "What would be the ideal solution in your eyes?"
A: "It would be best if we could find a house with a garden near-by. Does not have to be for rent, although this would of course be great."

Here **A** seems to favour the current location, so that he for example does not lose existing contacts. To make **A** find out about his secret solution he needs to deal with what sounds like understood in his first statement, but on second thoughts turns out to be an **unreflected limitation**. This sounds easier than it is. If we for example imagine that **A**'s family has been dreaming of a cottage in the countryside for quite a while, how the apartment turns smaller with each newborn child and how this offer to move to Podung has made an impact. In such a situation, to state one's doubts does not only require to be aware of them but also a significant amount of courage. So one would not wonder why **A** will hardly be willing to express the following statement:

"See, everybody is so happy about moving to Podung. And I am in doubt, whether it's really good. On one hand it's at the end of the world. It's twenty miles to the next town. I could never visit the movies or a theatre play, not to speak of concerts. On the other hand we have such good friends here that I would really have problems with reducing this to mail or telephone contacts. As far as I am concerned I would stay here and keep searching for an opportunity near-by, like we were able to do all these years."

> When using the conversation saver "Work out wishes" you give your dialogue partner the chance to find out about his real desires.

Even if it may sound unbelievable: stating a wish clearly does not mean that the one who has voiced it will now strive to make it become reality. However, clarity will help to distinguish between pretended and real wishes. To what extent the decision is really open you can find out with the following question:

- What would indicate that you already made your decision?
- For it?
- Against it?

In a seminar on counselling a participant asked for advice regarding the following problem:

"Well, I got a problem, since we will have a baby soon and then we will need a new car. The one we own currently may be too small, one would probably not be able to take a pram. Now I don't know what makes more sense, to buy the car right now or to wait until the baby has been born. What do I do?"

In total, four counsellors tried to find a helpful solution. How great was the astonishment when in the last turn it became clear that the one who had asked for advice did not really want to buy a new car. His final statement sounded like this:

"I think I know now where the problem is. In fact it's my wife who wants the new car because my brother-in-law also bought a new car when her sister had a baby. But for me this is too uncertain at the moment. I have no idea of what additional costs I'll have to pay up for. A baby costs a lot in the first year, and if I buy the car now we might lack money in another place later. During this conversation I understood for the first time under what pressure I put myself. I think I'll have to talk to my wife about it."

There is a little trick I want to reveal to you here: When you use the conversation saver "work out wishes" you ask the other to imagine that he has already achieved his goal and to describe how it would be then. Anyone who does not want anything else but what he has just stated will with bright eyes talk about his goal. It is very different when the stated goal does not have first priority but is overlaid by a secret competing desire. Here your dialogue partner will hesitate, frown, his face will not look happy and you do not get the impression that it is desirable to achieve the mentioned aim.

The following example may illustrate this:

One of my postgraduates did not make any progress with his doctoral thesis. The text so far made sense, was well structured and all in all very promising. Even so, the revision took longer and longer. At the end in one of our many conversations I asked him very directly: "We talk all the time about how you can solve this and that problem, Now I have a very different question: Please describe what will happen when you have completed your dissertation." Had I expected something like "then I'll cut a caper", I was even more surprised when my dialogue partner's face dropped and he answered in a rather suppressed voice: "Well, then I'll have to see how I get along." In the further discussion it turned out that the thesis was to be completed, but that not completing it would have the advantage to be allowed to stay at the university. Deep inside the candidate had the idea he was unprepared for a life afterwards and to fail on the job market. To avoid this he protracted the end of his studies without being aware of his funny tactics.

The following questions aim in the same direction:

- If you knew how this would end what would you do or not do?
  or:
- Imagine the point of time when you will be ready, how will you feel?
- What will be your next step now?

As soon as your dialogue partner will deal with these questions he will cross the boundaries he has unconsciously created. You will find that he will all of a sudden gain a lot of energy. Instead of the paralysing present he will imagine to achieve the goal and from there plan the next actions backwards. The sentence "What will be your next step?" is meant to be ambiguous: It focuses attention not only on the next step but also leads to what will come after the goal has been achieved. This works so well because at the moment of goal achievement we feel extremely well, energetic and strong. In answering this question we turn ourselves and our dialogue partner into a powerful state of mind. It turns out that this imagined power frees unexpected energies in the present to accomplish the next step.

Who uses the conversation saver **work out wishes** will not only listen to what the other says but also try to read between the lines where one can find even the opposite of what the other has just said.

> When you work out wishes you read between the lines.

The tunnelling effect

With this approach you ask your dialogue partner to imagine that the problem has already been overcome. In this way the other will approach his individual boundaries from backwards.

Principle: Imagine you have achieved the goal

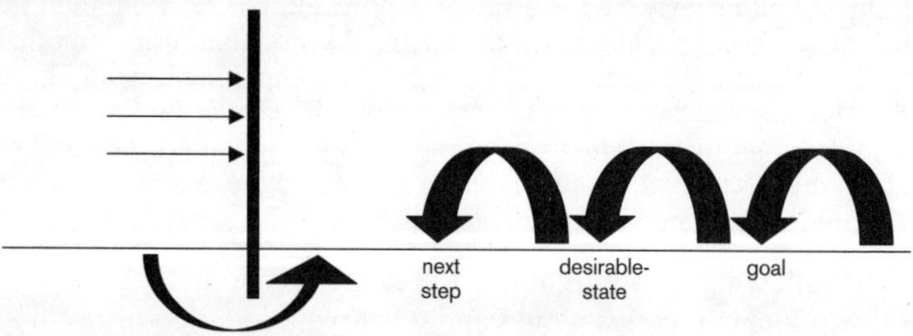

Address emotions

In chapter 3 **active listening** was described in detail. The point was to **address** the hidden **emotions** which our dialogue partner will hardly ever express directly. This conversation saver also represents a typical Adult ego state conversation behaviour, which also addresses the dialogue partner in this ego state, independent of his momentary emotional state. As soon as we have found words to express the hidden emotions the other will have to verify if and how far we got the point. And verifying is an Adult ego state function.

By addressing emotions you show that you can understand how your dialogue partner feels.

In chapter 3 it was also discussed that one goal of professional leadership in conversation is to create an atmosphere in which the other **feels understood**.

At the end of this chapter I want to show how you can react to the same statement with different conversation savers. Which one you pick is both a question of your personal style and of your relationship to the other.

"The cooperation with Mr. Mean is getting worse every day. Sometimes I get the impression he does only what he wants now and takes no notice of me. Or he is cheeky and impolite. Especially when I have a question. I don't know how to behave any more."

- **Address emotions:**
"You are clueless." Or:
"You feel like you are at his mercy."

- **Paraphrase, repeat with own words:**
"You don't approve of your colleague's behaviour, only you don't know what to do against it."

- **Clarify, put in a nutshell:**
"If I understand you right you find Mr. Mean's behaviour entirely uncooperative." Or:
"Your relationship has reached absolute zero."

- **Relate aspects:**
"One time he acts as if you were not there, another time he uses your questions to be abusive."

- **Ask for clarification:**

"You say it's getting worse every day, what does this mean?" Or:
"You say he is cheeky and impolite when you have a question, can you give me an example."

- **Set someone thinking:**

"You say that you don't know how to behave any more. What else needs to happen before you will do something against it?" Or in combination with addressing emotions:
"Leaving everything as it is, may probably be unbearable. But you seem to fear significant consequences if you take the initiative."

- **Work out wishes:**

"When you say that your colleague only does what he wants *now*, your relationship seems to have been better in the past. I don't see if you want to get back to that state or which other goal would be more desirable for you."

At this point I will come back to an example from the previous chapter:

It is Saturday evening, around 6 pm. Albert (A) and Bridget (B) Grey have been invited by friends to a party.
A: "I think we should not go to the party. We do not even know the people."
B: "Don't worry. It be nice for sure will."

We can only speculate about how the conversation would have developed if Bridget Grey had voted for a conversation saver reaction such as:

B: "You would prefer to cancel it."

Almost certainly her husband will agree to that. Although her description only states something, we can assume that Mr. Grey will in some way explain what he does not like with this invitation. In any case he gets the chance to talk about his problems. If he makes use of this offer and talks frankly about his concerns or rather avoids that and just asks for a cancellation, will in the first place depend on his pre-experiences with his wife and on the general conversation atmosphere.

I have "composed" an alternative dialogue, using conversation savers:

B: "You would prefer to cancel it."
A: "Yes. The more I think of it the more strange it seems to me."
B: "What do you mean by strange?"
A: "Well, first we had not been invited together, but only you. And now somehow I feel funny."
B: "And now you feel like a stopgap."
A: "I don't want to say that, although ... You know what, in the beginning I thought I might not be wanted there. And then I asked myself who might have an interest in you coming alone."
B: "You have pictured to yourself what might happen on the party."
A: "Yes. And I did not need too much fantasy. Please excuse me when I bring this up, but it is not so long ago that we had this row because of your affair with Carl."
B: "For you this invitation poses a new threat."
A: "To be honest, yes. When I think of you meeting Carl, I feel horrible."
B: "You cannot look forward to the party, because the whole time you are afraid I could meet Carl and take up something with him again."
A: "True. Now that you say it so clearly, I realize that we never really talked about it."

How you can weaken fixed opinions

Restricting repetition

With descriptive or active listening you concentrate on WHAT and HOW. Yet, in some cases you do not want to repeat a position since you fear to encourage the other to further reinforce his opinion.

Instead of taking the bait of bringing the other to terms you will rather want to make use of active listening in this situation. The knack is to add a time restriction to the repetition. If this is done **without stressing it,** it is normally not recognised and **subconsciously** acts against a reinforcement of the point of view.

Out of the desire to be understood the other will mainly take care that his position, his objective, or his negative answer will be accepted. With a spontaneous "Yes" he will let you know promptly.

At the same time your dialogue partner agrees that this is true "at the moment". His agreement includes becoming open for new points of view.

> With the conversation saver "restricting repetition" you answer the desire to be understood. In addition you give the other the chance to think his point of view over again.

The following list is useful for a "**restricting repetition**":

- still, not yet
- at first
- at the moment, momentarily
- now
- just now
- at this time
- at present
- today
- currently
- temporarily
- in the beginning
- in this situation
- for the time being

Tip: If you expect resistance or objections you can prepare for the conversation so that you have pre-formulated some statements like:

"At the moment you are (still) of a different opinion."
"This does not convince you now."
"At present you do not like my idea."
"You do not see a window of opportunity right now."

Overdone confirmation

If your dialogue partner has made his statement so absolute and final that he indeed proposes an end of the conversation, you may be tempted to oppose. Especially when you do not agree with a statement this may provoke your resistance, but thus lead to an escalation.

Instead it helps to repeat the statement, to ask for clarification or to give a summary.

As soon as you **add** (without stressing it) a generalisation you will provoke the other's resistance.

This will facilitate the conversation since it usually leads to further explanations.

On one hand your dialogue partner will feel understood, which is the effect of the repetition.

On the other hand he does not want your statement to remain this way and feels the need to give further explanations which often contain thoughts which you can use to make the conversation more profound.

With an "overdone confirmation" you can resume a closed statement by adding a generalisation to your repetition. This will make your dialogue partner further explain his point of view.

The following phrases are apt for "overdone confirmation":

- never
- unimaginable
- cannot be done
- impossible
- absolutely excluded

- neither now nor ever
- definitely not
- under no circumstances/under all circumstances
- in every case
- always
- constantly
- uninterrupted
- every time
- every day

> **Tip:** When preparing for a conversation you can pre-formulate some statements like:

"You won't consider this under any circumstances."
Or: "You don't want to try this out neither now nor ever."
Or: "You will agree (disagree) in every case."

10. Four Ways to React

Maybe you shook your head several times when reading chapter 8 on conversation killers and maybe you asked yourself whether people really need to be that touchy.

To say it in advance: we do not **have to** react that way; on the contrary, we do have a wide range of possibilities. Yet, it requires quite a lot of practice to leave the normal track of Defiant Child behaviour and to stand one's ground the Adult way.

This chapter will show that in a given situation there are always four ways to react, and how best to make use of them.

In a conversation, not only the *literal* content of a statement is important. The idea that a message can have more than one "side" has already been part of the "language theory" of *Karl Bühler*, which he developed in the thirties. *Bühler's* communication model was seized, extended, and spread in the seventies by the philosopher *Paul Watzlawick*, and finally further consolidated by the communication scientist *Friedemann Schulz von Thun*. The latter used a descriptive model to indicate that each message we receive consists of four aspects of information:

(1) **Factual Aspect**: The facts and circumstances are given. This part of communication is directly available.

(2) **Appellative Aspect**: We communicate to achieve something. We try to meet, consciously or unconsciously, a certain objective. Be it plea, recommendation, appeal, warning, or order, in each case we – either openly or secretly – want to make the dialogue partner behave in a certain way.

(3) **Relational Aspect**: Our relationship to the dialogue partner and our opinion of him is expressed in the way we talk to him.

(4) **Aspect of Self-Disclosure**: With everything we say we also say something about ourselves. We express our emotions, preferences, opinions, and attitudes both verbally and non-verbally.

This model will become more clear with the following example:

When a co-driver says to the driver: "It's green", this statement includes the following pieces of information:

Facts	Appeal	Relationship	Self-Disclosure
The traffic light is green.	Go on! Make us pass the crossing this time.	You need my assistance. You cannot make it without.	I am in a hurry. I doubt that we will make it on time.

Since every message contains these four aspects, the responsibility for what is understood is not only with the one who talks but also with the one who listens. The listener can always choose freely to refer to the aspect that seemed to be most relevant for him. Anyone who until now perceived listening as something passive may be surprised now to be confronted with the "**listener's responsibility**". The attractiveness of the following thoughts lies in the freedom we have when listening to choose between four totally different ways to react. Independent of what the other intended with his statement, the responsibility for the reaction lies with us.

> The course of communication is mainly influenced by which aspect of a statement we react to.

In the example "It's green" the driver can choose, which aspect of the message he wants to answer to:

Facts	Appeal	Relationship	Self-Disclosure
Talk about traffic lights	React to the appeal	To feel patronised and offended	Active listening
"The new progressive signal system is very comfortable." Or: "It's the pedestrian light."	Speed up Or: "Thanks."	"I've seen that." Or: "Do you want to drive?!" Or: Sulk in silence.	"You are getting nervous." Or: "You want to be home for the News."

Depending on how the driver reacts, not only the conversation itself but also the atmosphere in the car will be influenced.

Many of our reactions happen automatically, i. e. without being thought over, and it may seem to be a hair-raising thought to forego confided answer patterns. Maybe you will gain unexpected benefit from the content of this chapter.

For clarification I make again use of the dialogue examples from the end of chapter 7:

Supervisor: "How late is it, Mrs. Miller?"

Does the assistant understand the question in the sense of request for information, here the exact time, she will answer:

Assistant: "Nearly half past four."

But by far not every assistant will understand the "harmless"

"How late is it, Mrs. Miller?"

as an objective question. She can also assume that the words in this question include an order to speed up. And her reaction will sound accordingly:

"I am ready in a minute."

In the third example the assistant interprets the

"How late is it, Mrs. Miller?"
as criticism. She feels attacked on the relationship level, which explains her shirty answer:

"I can't do more than hurry."
"I told you I can't make it."
"If you think I'm too slow, you can do it yourself!"
"Instead of making me nervous, you'd better help me."

But there was a fourth way to react to this short question. In the fourth version the assistant tries to capture what at the moment is important for her supervisor. Having sufficient practice in **active listening** she reacts with sensitivity:

"You are anxious we will not get it ready on time."

The following answers would also be appropriate:

"Meeting the timeline is very important for you, and if we don't make it it will have horrible consequences."
"You have the impression this develops pretty slowly."
"You are nervous about the timeline."

> When listening we always have the free choice of what we want to hear, i. e. which aspect of a statement we regard as important.

Whether we can make use of our freedom of choice depends on how experienced we are in changing our perception filters. Figuratively said: As we put on or take off our sunglasses we can also use our perception selectively and test in every case which aspect of a message we want to concentrate on. Sometimes this can be different from our dialogue partner's intention. This will help us especially if our interlocutor tries to manipulate us or to fool us into actions which we will regret later.

Maybe it is easy for you to switch between the given opportunities, others may have problems with it. With the following drawing I want to demonstrate the process:

- **Look at the drawing for a while. What do you see?**

Before you turn the page please check, disregarding what you have seen, whether there is something additional or something totally different to be seen.

Some find at once an old woman with a big nose, the chin hidden in a fur collar, others see the left cheek of a young woman.

If after a while you do not manage to "switch", i. e. to give up the existing image to be able to recognize the other one, the following explanation may help you: the long bow that forms the nose of the old woman is the cheek of the young one. The left eye of the old is the left ear of the young. The mouth of the old woman is the necklace of the young, her right eye a piece of the young woman's nose etc.

No matter which woman you have seen first, it is never the only figure that can be found in the picture. If you transfer this to everyday experiences it can be said that what we see is right but it is not necessarily the one and only correct and possible way to see things.

At the end of chapter 8 Albert and Bridget Grey had a struggle about an invitation to a party. Let's take a look at them the next morning:

Albert Grey is watching TV, silently and with furrowed brows, shaking his head from time to time. Since he has been very monosyllabic the whole morning and has only picked at his food at breakfast, his wife wonders what has happened. Is he pouting for whatever reason? She walks up to him and wants to know what the problem is.
Bridget: "Why are you looking so shirty?!" Albert: "I'm not shirty." He snatches the TV newspaper and demonstrates that he is not willing to talk about it under any circumstances.
Now she is angry because of his moodiness, slams the door shut behind her and leaves to see a friend, complaining bitterly to her.

Bridget Grey meant well, but what was the use of it? Her husband did definitely not feel understood by the question "Why are you looking so shirty!", on the contrary: he perceived it as a reproach or attack: He was asked to look different!

To show the opportunities in a "four-sided" message, let us imagine Albert Grey would have one ear for each aspect:

His wife says – in a special tone: "Why are you looking so shirty?!"

Now he has the following ways to make use of his "four ears":

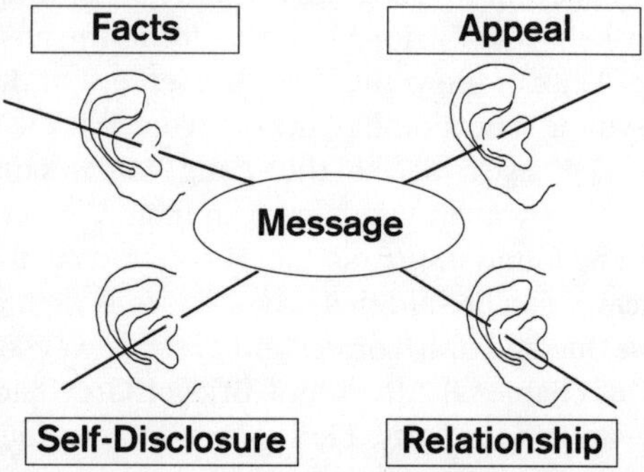

- He listens to the **factual** aspect: His face gives a shirty expression.
- He notices the **appeal**: She wants to get an explanation. She would like him to talk to her about it or at least to change his behaviour.
- He takes care of the **relationship** aspect and listens to how she is talking to him. Her reproachful tone expresses that she does not take him seriously and blames him for the tensed atmosphere on that Sunday morning.
- He understands the self-disclosure: Bridget Grey is annoyed because she does not understand why he is "again" in bad mood.

Obviously, Albert Grey has three deaf ears:

The **appeal** was unmistakable. For instance he could explain that the discussion about the party they had had the previous evening is not yet forgotten. Yet, since it is not what one says but the way one says it that counts, he may not intend to answer to his wife.

Many everyday arguments start as a reaction on the **relationship** level. Typical would be a reaction according to the pattern: "You of all people has to ask this!" Or: "This is the first time you take interest in my mood."

Albert Grey does also not react to his wife's **self-disclosure**. Although her tone tells a tale about her mood and attitude, he misses the opportunity to address that. I agree that this requires quite a bit of independence from one's emotions to be able to say for example: "It annoys you to see me sitting here this way." Or: "You are irritated when you don't know what is the problem with me."

But he chooses to ignore her annoyed tone and the appellative aspects when he reacts stating a **fact**: "I'm not shirty."

Now we could start all over again and analyse what Mr. Grey expresses beyond the mere facts:

Picking up the newspaper can be interpreted as a non-verbal **appeal** to please leave him alone. And this is exactly what Mrs. Grey reacts to when she leaves the house and him "as requested".

He also **reveals** that at the moment he does not intend to give an explanation. We can only assume that he interprets her question as a reproach – which does not alter his mood at all. If Mrs. Grey would want to address that she could answer: "You want to be left alone." Or: "It annoys you that I'm asking."

On the **relationship** level we can detect the unspoken disparaging message: "Who are you that I have to explain my behaviour to you." For someone with a big relationship "ear" this would present a premium chance to start a fight, maybe like: " This is the way you can address your subordinates, but not me." Or: "You seem to believe you can get away with everything."

Anyone who decides to listen to the facts only, may conclude that Albert Grey is talking about his mood which – according to his words – is quite alright. Typical reactions to this aspect sound like: "Fine, then we can go and visit my parents later." Or: "In this case please take a look in the mirror and tell me how you would name your facial expression."

In the following I will show some of the chances and the limitations of each of the four aspects of a message:

Facts

Since the factual side of a message is laid open it is always tempting to try one's luck and rely on **fact-based** communication. This is always successful if the point is indeed exchange of information or clarification of circumstances.

> Testing a message under the aspect of "correct/incorrect" is a task for the Adult ego state and makes use of the facts in the available pieces of information.

But a statement sounding fact-based often includes an **appellative** aspect. In this case a reaction to the factual side may be totally misplaced, especially when one could conclude from the context that the statement has never been meant this way.

A visitor holds up her empty cup and says: "Your tea is very good."
The hostess relates to the fact part and says: "Yes, it's from *Fortnum & Mason's*."
A supervisor talks to two assistants: "Unfortunately your colleague, Mr. Baker, is sick and his desk is piled with papers."
One assistant smiles: "Well, yes, this doesn't make it different from mine." In addition he glances at his colleague, but the other also ignores the appeal and answers addressing the facts: "That's funny. Yesterday evening we met in the swimming pool."

While we can deal with this side of a factual-sounding statement rather quickly, now comes the interesting part: Ever so often a formal discussion about correct or incorrect is only a camouflage for a struggle about who is right. And this is only widely related to the subject discussed; instead we can observe a **relationship** struggle. Many discussions in work life seem to be solely fact-based at first sight, but at a closer look it becomes clear that it is an undercover fight for bonus points in relationship hierarchies, like for example:

"The proposal may sound reasonable, but when one takes a rational view..."

These "pseudo-factual" statements are usually voiced in a very calm manner, so that it is difficult to defend oneself against them. Nevertheless, the message strikes on the relationship level, since it contains:

"Someone who has thought things over before saying something, would never state such nonsense."

Recently I had the chance to read from the shocked faces what effect such "factual" statements can have:

"When I look back to our discussion, I am glad that we as board members decided to talk to you again, so that you get the chance to join our opinion."

Since none of the addressed said anything against this clumsy demand, I tried during the next break to find out what everybody felt about it. Everyone I talked to felt funny, misunderstood, and treated with disregard. Yet, nobody was able to tell the exact moment on time when these feelings had come up. In other words: This way to talk is a very subtle way of claiming predominance, which to withstand requires the highest level of concentration on what is said. Children are easily able to blind out any criticism that may be included into a factual statement and to react to another part of the message:

A father asks his child who returns home late: "Where did you hang around all the time?"
To which the child answers fact-based: "Between four and five I was in the schoolyard, and then I joined the others collecting chestnuts."

But even statements that sound truly factual can include a very clear self-disclosure. Not to react to this is a way to keep the other at a distance and to stay uninvolved to a certain extent.

"If only I didn't have this migraine headache. I can hardly look at the screen."
"Yes, the weather is really stressing."
"I failed to pass the test to become a certified revisionist."
"This happened to 48 % of the others, which is the average failure rate per term."

Appeal

When a plea is stated openly and clearly it is easy to deal with it. Yet, many requests are stated in a well-disguised way. The dialogue partner hopes to be understood in the right way, but does not dare to voice his request directly. This may be a kind of self-protection, since many people avoid being turned down by never stating their wishes clearly. In the dating stereotype the famous stamp collection is mentioned instead of saying directly: "I would like to spend the rest of the evening with you."

Most people listen to the hidden appeal and react accordingly: the other has not stated what he wants but has made it clear anyway. Yet, there is one hitch in this way to react: however kind we may seem to be, we take over responsibility for the other who got what he wanted despite his indifferent way of expressing himself. There is a way to avoid this and to leave the responsibility with the other: We confront the other with our interpretation of his statement. In the example with the traffic light the driver can directly react to the hidden appeal, for example by accelerating but also by stating what he has just understood, like: "You want me to drive faster." Now it is time for the other to state clearly what he was aiming at.

Anyone has enough practice in **active listening** will be repeatedly surprised by the usefulness of this proceeding. Even a directly stated appeal can turn out to be meant in another way, as I often experience myself.

As a professor I am often asked for an opinion, like when one of my students addressed me after a lesson and asked: "Mr. Weisbach, do you know the new *Sprenger: Trust – The best way to manage*?" – Instead of answering this precise question with a clear "yes" or "no", I said without giving it much thought: "You would like to know what I think about it." To my astonishment she said "yes", but then I was not able to get a word in edgewise. Instead she explained to me in great detail the differences she had detected between this book and the previous ones written by the same author.

Who states the hidden appeal, adds to open communication and goal clarity. The responsibility remains with the dialogue partner. The final decision to act according to the appeal remains open.

Maybe you have already made the experience that you can achieve an increase in popularity by satisfying the unspoken requests of others. Yet, sometimes this can lead to grotesque scenes if an appeal is searched for in each and every statement.

A guest asks for a piece of information: "Where did you buy this tea?"
Whereupon the hostess gets to her feet and says: "I'll go quickly and make us another pot."
"For vacation we'll go to Rome."
"In this case I can lend you our city map and the Baedeker."
In the office: "How do you open the new table format?"
"Leave this to me, I'll do it for you."

On the other hand it will become equally grotesque when in a clear appeal the hidden **self-disclosure** is addressed.

One of my students was a guest in the house of a famous psychotherapist. On her question: "Could you hand me the salt, please," she got the answer: "You don't like the taste, do you?"

Equally ludicrous seems the following reaction on the **relational level**.

In the example above the host could address the expected criticism: "And I took such care about seasoning."

Even if it seems to be far-fetched, some people are able to react to a clear appeal the **factual** way:

"I could spend the whole night dancing with you."
"Getting to bed before midnight is said to be very healthy."

Relationship

In chapter 5, I explained that each statement contains an aspect of the quality of our **relationship** to our dialogue partner. The degree of esteem, acknowledgement, and respect is not only expressed by our words but also in tone, body language, and facial expression. And it does not play a role if we are aware of **how** we are talking. Yet, our dialogue partner will diagnose our current disposition towards him via a kind of **reception filter**.

We can observe that many people use this filter to check every statement for:

- How does he/she talk to me altogether?
- Whom does he/she think he/she is talking to?

These questions are often linked to the following reactions:

- I'm not a little child.
- I don't have to tolerate that.
- Don't treat me like that.

But who has already such a reaction in mind is ready to defend himself or to start a counter-attack. And before you can say knife, the conversation develops into an argument while the original purpose vanishes and gives way to the struggle over who is allowed to address whom in which way. If you just imagine the atmosphere in the car when the driver answers to "It's green!" in an acrid tone "Next time it's your turn to drive!".

When dealing with the "conversation killers" I explained that they all stem from the Parent ego state and bear the risk that the dialogue partner starts to defend himself against being addressed in a Child ego state kind of relationship.

This may be illustrated by the following scene:

During a break in a training session, I find myself standing side by side with a participant looking out into the November rain. So as not to appear silent I say: "Today it's really raining cats and dogs." To my astonishment she confronts me with the following answer: "All you can come up with to talk to me about is the weather." –
At that time this seemed to me to be a typical case of biased reception, but later this episode turned out to have an aftermath:
When my wife asked me how the training course had been going, I reported the scene and let slip the snide remark that this young lady had

a distorted relationship filter. Promptly my wife asked: "In other words, you had said the very same sentence about the weather to everybody else in the group?" I briefly thought this over and blushed. I had to recognise that I would have been able to talk to the other participants about many other things, but with her I could not establish contact and could not come up with a more profound remark. Viewed this way the participant was right: The content of what I had said was absolutely irrelevant (I did not care of neither cats nor dogs that moment) – but I had revealed my attitude, which was – I had to admit it – hardly flattering.

This example makes clear how listening to the relationship aspects may influence the content aspects. Even if nearly every statement contains a personal aspect, this does not force us to agree to the included definition of the current relationship.

Another way to react on the relationship level can be to verbalise what was to be transported subliminally.

If the driver detects in "It's green!" the message:

"I don't trust you to get along without my assistance."

this does not require him to return "Is it me who drives or you?". He can just as well react calmly to the unwanted hint and address the relationship aspect, maybe like:

"You want to help me." Or:
"You don't think I can handle that at the moment." Or:
"You think I'm not paying attention."

I admit that this is new to most people and may seem strange. For many people it is a kind of taboo to address the interaction and to clarify the relationship. Whoever is willing to practise this will soon experience a decrease in the number of everyday frictions and conflicts.

Here, too, the question arises:

- How does he/she talk to me?

But before one reacts, another step is being inserted:

- How do I feel treated by him/her.

Out of the gained distance, the other can be confronted with our perception, which at this early stage – before emotions start playing the main role – allows for the chance to climb down. In the example with the car, the reaction to "You don't think I can handle this" could read:

"O, I'm sorry, I didn't mean it this way."

and so this would be settled. Another possible reaction can also be:

"If you really want to know it: yes, in my eyes you drive like a maniac."

Maybe this answer will alienate us. Yet, now we know the odds. Instead of feeling insulted we now have the chance to talk about the relationship in general or to express astonishment.

"In this case I wonder why you are coming with me in spite of this."

Whoever openly addresses the hidden relationship aspects of a statement does not only contribute to clarification, but also maintains a kind of emotional distance that keeps him from overreaction emotionally.

Even if listening solely to the relationship aspects is rather common, it is nevertheless not binding. We can also listen to another aspect.

Self-Disclosure

It requires quite an amount of practice to concentrate on the parts of a statement in which the dialogue partner expresses something **about himself**. Imagine the atmosphere in the car, if the driver reacts to "It's green!" with a calm: "You are anxious to be on time".

In chapter 3, I talked about **active listening** and that it helps us to make the other go on talking. Ever so often we lack the important background information that would allow us to understand how a statement was meant, what its context is and what it is aiming at. Anyone who takes a stand at once can be compared to someone who sets off before knowing directions.

Many people are used to feel offended by negative statements and will react to the following sentence with anger:

"Concerning the current financial situation, your proposal is entirely unrealistic."
"Do you have a better idea?"
Or: "On the contrary, if you would take the trouble to recalculate, you could see immediately, ..."
Or: "Of course it's realistic, because ..."
Some may even retreat and feel offended, remaining silent and imagining to pay back one day ...

It is not hard to imagine the further course of the discussion. At the end, there will be one winner and one loser (this will be further addressed in chapter 12).

Whoever takes care of the other's interests will respond to what the other has revealed about himself:

"You don't like the idea at all." Or:
"You think it's absurd." Or:
"You have concerns regarding our financial situation."

There is a high probability that the other will add another explanation to his first answer. And this is exactly the advantage of this proceeding: you give your own statement only when you have learned more about the other's intentions. It can happen that we find out during this process that it might be advisable not to reveal our own point of view because the other intends to start an argument.

A woman who came to me for counselling told me about her mother who – having just arrived in her apartment – said:
"Your curtains definitely don't match the furniture."
She reported that she nearly had let slip a snappish remark like: "*I* like it!" But this would only have resulted in a critical reaction like "Well, everyone to his taste, but maybe you should talk to somebody who knows about this ..."
Instead, the daughter merely said: "You don't like it."
And in return the mother started to talk lengthily about her troubles in arranging her own apartment.
Following this pattern, the daughter managed to leave each of her mother's critical remarks on the level of self-disclosure. Used to reaction on

the relationship level she found to her surprise that she could meet her mother without ending up in quarrels and arguments.

> Whoever develops the ability to verify what the other has just revealed about himself before giving a statement can free himself from the emotional reactions that all too often lead to a conflict.

As helpful as this proceeding may be, there has to be a warning of possible misuse: anyone who always leaves the active part with the other does not only avoid a personal statement but does in addition never become involved in a situation. This can end up in a power struggle, if a requested opinion is that decidedly avoided:

One partner arrives very late and the other is outraged: "Tell me, what do you think when you make me wait like this?" Whereupon the other calmly states: "You cannot cope with such a situation."

The first one feels inferior and flares up: "Don't start on me the psychological way!"

But even now the other stays relaxed and returns: "Now you feel very helpless." Etc.

What this "cool" dialogue partner stated was correct; the self-disclosure was indeed part of the message.

But instead of reacting with sympathy or dealing with the statement, he hides behind a mask made of diagnostic skills. The one-sided concentration on the self-disclosure is used to demonstrate one's psychological superiority. Carried to the extremes this can lead to dialogues with the following pattern:

"It's a scandal how I'm treated here."

"Did you ever think about what this might have to do with yourself?"

"How long do you think you'll need to make a decision. You make everybody wait!"

"Does this occur frequently, that you burst out without being able to control yourself?"

What can be hidden behind a statement you test with the smallest pieces of everyday conversation. And maybe you will notice that we run into special habits here.

> Depending on which relationship you have with the other, you will interpret the contained information in different ways. And you will always find: we only hear what we want to hear and only see what we want to see.

Whoever concentrated mainly until now on the relational side of a message and checked for hidden criticism is now able to deal with another layer.

"You were the only one who did not visit me in hospital."
Maybe this statement is meant to criticize. However, we are still responsible for which reaction to choose. Instead of giving our reasons, we may as well change aspect like with:
"You are really disappointed." Or:
"I just realise how important this would have been for you."

This can be especially useful if the other tries in a subtle way to put us under pressure like for example:

"For the christening of our youngest we expect more than 30 guests. You cannot imagine what this means for me. I have to do all the preparations alone and have no idea, how to manage this."
Instead of the expected "You can count on me" we can also address the hidden expectation:
"You count on my help."
"This sounds like you rely on my support."

Even reproachful and accusing remarks offer the chance to find a new perspective when focusing on another aspect.

"One really cannot trust you with anything."

Normal reactions will vary between counterattack ("You are the right one to say that") or excuses ("I'm really sorry, I couldn't know... "). We can also switch to active listening and find out how the other feels, which leads to a very different reaction:

"It was really embarrassing for you that I talked about it." Or:
"I brought you into a very unpleasant situation."

It is obvious that the other will explain what was so embarrassing for him. Knowing the background, an excuse can be much more authentic.

It requires quite an amount of training to recognize the different aspects and to switch between them with ease.

When doing the following exercise you can test how quickly you can recognize what may be hidden in a message.

▶ **Please note down in direct speech**

- **what** is hidden in the statement
- **which answer** would be appropriate.

(1) A colleague stands in front of the copier and says to you: "There is no more paper."

Facts

Which fact is the colleague stating?
Possible answer:

Relationship

Which role does the colleague think you have?
Possible answer:

Appeal

What does the colleague want to achieve?
Possible reaction:

Self-disclosure

What does the colleague say about himself?
Possible answer:

(2) During dinner you are addressed: “I think there is not enough water in the windscreen washer system.”

Facts

What does the other say from an objective point of view??
Possible answer:

Relationship

How does the other treat you?
Possible reaction:

Appeal

What does he/she want to achieve?
Possible answer:

Self-disclosure

What do you learn about the other?
Possible answer:

(3) You enter your office with a new hairstyle. Your colleague's comment is: "What do you look like?"

Facts

What is the factual statement?
Possible answer:

Relationship

How does your colleague treat you?
Possible answer?

Appeal

What is he/she aiming at?
Possible reaction:

Self-disclosure

What do you learn about the colleague?
Possible answer:

Proposed solutions

(1) A colleague stands in front of the copier and says to you: "There is no more paper."

Facts:

- "The paper container is empty."
- If you want to answer to this you merely say: "Right".

Relationship:

- "I want you to take care of it. If I make a statement like this I just want you to react accordingly without me saying clearly what I want. In our department people are either more or less important. You can take care of the less difficult things."
- If you want to talk about the relational aspects you could say: "In your eyes I am responsible for paper supply."

Appeal:

- "Please take care of it. Please make sure I can take copies whenever I want. Understand that I do not take care of it myself."
- React according to the hidden appeal, get new paper and refrain from giving any comment.
- Or you verify if you have interpreted the hidden appeal correctly: "You want me to take care of it."

Self-disclosure:

- "I am annoyed when I cannot complete a task. I expect to always find the copier ready for use. As a colleague with an important role I expect to get what I need. It is the easiest way to just state what I see. I don't need to ask for something."
- If you want to verify this you could say: "You are annoyed that the copier doesn't work."

(2) During dinner you are addressed: "I think there is not enough water in the windscreen washer system

Facts:

- "The windscreen washer system does not work. The water tank is empty."
- If you listen with your factual ear you may say: "It's always amazing how small these tanks are."

Relationship:
- "You are responsible for taking care of the car. Please assure proper maintenance. And take care of this problem."
- If you want to verify the relational message you can address it directly: "I get the impression that in your eyes I'm the "WWR", the windshield washer responsible."

Appeal:
- "Please, refill the water tank. Please, understand that I don't want to do it myself. Feel responsible!"
- Obey to the unspoken order and refill the water tank.
- If you do not want to take over responsibility for your dialogue partner's goals you can circumscribe: "You would want that I feel responsible for it."

Self-disclosure:
- "I'm not a technical person. I just want the windshield washer to work. I find it annoying if I find out during driving that it does not work."
- If you want to address this you could say: "You don't trust yourself to do it." Or: "You don't want to do it yourself."

(3) You enter your office with a new hairstyle. Your colleague's comment is: "What do you look like?"

Facts:
- "You look different."
- A reaction on this level could be: "Yes, I wanted a new hairstyle for the summer."

Relationship:
- "You are someone to whom I can state my comments rather frankly. You change your hairstyle without having asked me before. Anyway, I am the one who knows what suits you best."
- You can switch to the relationship level when saying: "You are surprised that I did not ask you beforehand."

Appeal:
- "Please, explain what made you have your hair cut that short."
- Now you can report how you came to the idea, to which hairdresser you went, what ways of styling the new hair-do offers etc.

- And you can address the hidden appeal: “You want to know what made me change my hairstyle.”

Self-disclosure:

- “I don’t like your new hairstyle. I am so shocked that I cannot refrain from giving a comment. I would never think about walking around with a hair-do like that.”
- You can answer your colleague like: “You think it looks horrible.”

Your four ways to react

The following typical phrases may help you to make use of all possible ways to react to a statement:

Facts	**Appeal**	**Relationship**	**Self-Disclosure**
Address the facts that can be drawn from the wording	Address the unspoken wishes	Address how you feel treated at the moment	Try to understand the situation and address the other's emotions
Stress on **"It is"**	Stress on **"You want"**	Stress on **"You-to-me"**	Stress on **"You about yourself"**
"It is . . ." "Right." "Yes." "No" "Correct."	"You want . . ." "You would like to . . ." (see also descriptive listening)	"You think I am . . ." "In your eyes I am . . ." "You treat me as if . . ."	"You are . . ." "This makes you . . ." "You feel . . ." (see also active listening)

It depends mostly on your behaviour regarding the relationship level, how you are perceived and if you manage to create trust and credibility.

In the following you find a list of common statements from everyday communication and how they can come across to the dialogue partner. When trying them out, you can compare which ones help you achieve your goal most easily.

Statements on the relationship level	**Possible interlocutor reaction**	**Alternative**
"Wrong!"	I am viewed as stupid.	"I have a different opinion."
"I don' want to repeat..."	Are we at school here?	Leave out entirely
"That's not what I meant"	That would never have occurred to me.	"What I meant was..."
"You have to bear the following in mind..."	I don't have to!	"Please consider..."
"You are totally wrong!"	You too!	Drop it
"This is impossible."	Oh, sure? Wait and see...	"I see another way."
"You have misunderstood me."	Am I this thick?	"I'm sorry I did not express this the right way."
"I have to correct you."	Oh, really? And what did I do wrong?	"In my opinion..."

11. From Cause Analysis to Purpose Finding

Whoever tries to explain his behaviour often starts in the past. There he looks for root causes of and explanations for the current situation. If one looks back the question reads: "Why?" And the answer will give a reason: "Because ... ".

With this approach, it is assumed that one's own behaviour is merely an answer, a reaction to something that happened previously. With this simple way to find an explanation according to the principle of action and reaction, the responsibility for one's own behaviour is assigned to the impulse. Who claims to be only reacting to somebody else tends to blame him also for an escalation according to the motto: "It's always the other's fault." Typical for partnership conflicts are scenes like the following:

He returns home tired from a long day in the office and first of all wants to relax. He drops into the cosiest armchair and reaches out for the newspaper.

She has been busy all day with housework and their toddler and looks forward to a chat, and a chat with an adult for a change.

She sits down close by him and starts to talk about her day, takes the newspaper out of his hand and huddles against him.

That is too much for him. At the moment he would just like to relax. So he says:

"I'll go down to the cellar and paint the cupboard before dinner."

But a short while after he believed to have found some peace in the cellar, she turns up, watches him painting and starts again "to pester him". Since even in his workshop he is not left alone, he decides to leave the house. While washing the brushes he says:

"I have just remembered that today is the meeting of the jubilee preparation team. They are waiting in the 'Rose' for me. I'll see you later."

At first she is disappointed and clueless. Yet, who will be surprised that some time later she turns up in the pub and joins the team.

Characteristic for this striking example is the mode of explanation which explains one's own behaviour solely as the necessary consequence of somebody else's actions. He flees because she strangles him, and she clings to him like a limpet because he tries to avoid her.

In her perspective the situation looks like:

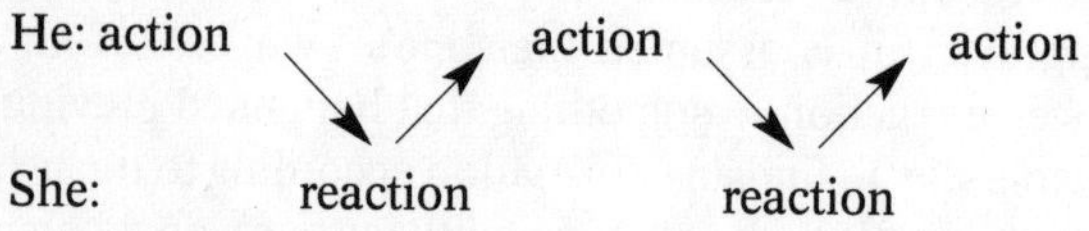

In return he will insist that his flight is nothing but a necessary reaction. If she would not cling to him like that he could as well stay at home.

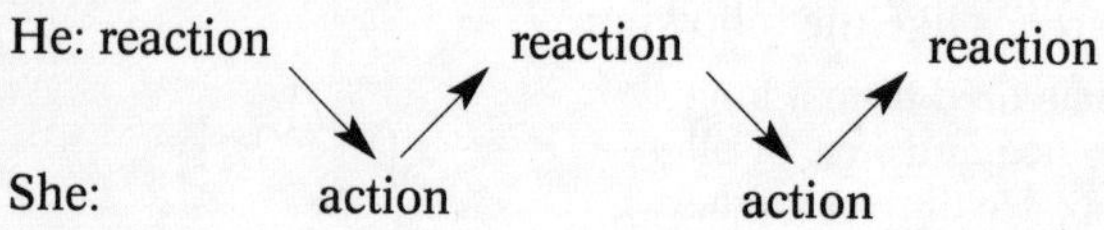

What both have overlooked: Any respective reaction is at the same time an impulse for the other. It is useless to think about what came first: chicken or egg. When looking back with the familiar cause-finding approach, we go the easy way to explain causal connections.

But present behaviour can also be deduced from the future, when we look at the purpose of somebody's actions and the direction of his intentions. Looking forward we ask: "What for?" And the answer is either: so that… or: in order to…

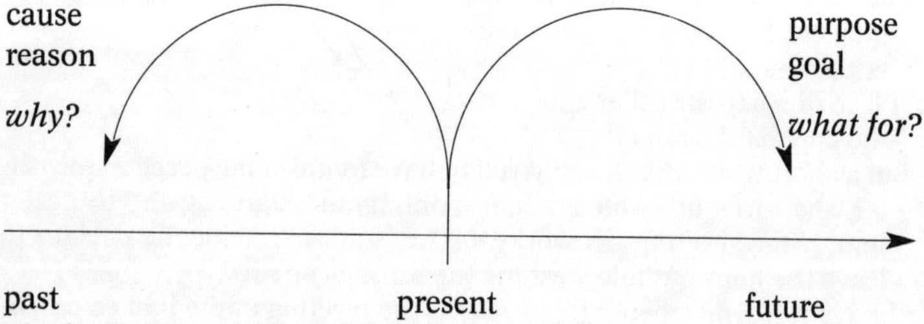

Explaining reality as a connection of cause and effect is so familiar that another approach than that with the Why-question does hardly ever come to our mind. Whoever for example hits his thumb with a hammer usually cries "Ouch!" Why does one scream that loudly? Because the hammer has hit the thumb and now the thumb hurts. Yet, from experience we know that the volume of the "Ouch!" is dependent on who will hear it and is to come. Being looked at this way, the cry does not only have a causal but also a consecutive aspect. What does one scream so loudly for? To call for help (or comfort). This behaviour is perfectly common for both children and adults.

In the example mentioned above he flees to be alone and she follows him to be near him. This approach focuses on the respective goals for which it has to be determined how they can be achieved. If the goal is relaxation or nearness, the behaviour expressed is only a second-class way to achieve it. It is very likely that being in his workshop is not the way of being near to him she dreamed of all day long, and in return his visit in the "Rose" does not mean the calmness he would have desired after an exhausting day

Whoever understands his own behaviour as purpose-driven is able to check whether another way is as well or maybe even better apt to achieve the respective goal.

Behaviour is goal-oriented.

The example would end in harmony if he could master himself to say:

"See, I have just sat down to relax after a long and strenuous day. Let me read the newspaper for half an hour, then I'll feel fit again."

Her intention can also be voiced unmistakably:

"I've spent my whole day with the child. Except from in the supermarket nobody talked to me since breakfast. Now I want to lie in your arms, snuggle up to you and have a chat."

It is still open after the **revelation of the goals,** who will get what he or she wants. Maybe she allows him half an hour, or he sets his relaxation aside, or she cuddles in his arms while he reads the newspaper.

Not only in partnership and family, goal orientation and purpose-finding contribute to conflict solution, also on the job possible mistakes, violations of rules, or failures can be treated this way.

It has to be admitted that it is much easier to react to the repeated late arrival of an employee with a question for the cause, like:

"Why are you late again?" or
"Why couldn't you come on time for this meeting once?"

than to look for possible intentions:

"What are you late for?"

The latter sounds almost absurd, and even so the answers will sound rather different. In the first case we get answers that sound logical and that explain being late as the unavoidable consequence of prior causes:

"Unfortunately the bus was late again."
"Because there was a traffic jam on the highway."
"Because I had to take my child to the kindergarten."

In the case of the what-for-question the addressee will have problems with the answer, since the question assumes that being late is a purposeful and goal-oriented behaviour. Who would like to admit that? And even so, it could be that the employee aims at something, for example to make clear:

"I'm special."
"With my qualification (my qualities) I am in no need to stick to the rules that are made for the average."
"I'm the oldest in the team and I can get away with this."
"With my workload I am entitled to be late." Or entirely different:

"It doesn't play a role if I'm on time or not. I get so little attention that nobody will notice anyway when I arrive."
"In the eyes of my boss I'm a loser anyway, what does it alter if I'm late?"

Instead of the unfamiliar what-for-question I use:
- What do you intend?
- What do you expect from it?
- What are you aiming at?
- Which benefit do you have in mind?

Even without having a conversation you can speculate about possible answers. This may lead to a totally new evaluation of the situation.

After a seminar a sales manager sent me a letter in which he had written a report on how a goal-oriented assessment had helped him to solve a long-lasting conflict:
"Mr. Benwick, you know that I have talked to you several times because you are always late. Until now without any success. Now I have considered what you may intend with coming five to ten minutes late for each sales meeting. (Mr. Benwick is getting nervous and tries to interrupt.) Please, let me finish this. You have been with us now for four years and during this time you have proven what you are capable of. You know that I value your talent as a salesman. Maybe I did not expresse this often enough in front of the team. I have realised that for difficult customers I tend to ask you, but I never mentioned this in front of your colleagues. Your colleagues Leland, Palmer, and Newman may be much older than you are, but they have not been in the team as long as you. Maybe I can help you directly to achieve your aim. This is why I want to ask you today to think about what I can do to treat you appropriately. Maybe you have one or the other idea, and if you agree you'll come back tomorrow after lunch."
Without waiting for a reaction I stood up and signalled the end of the conversation.

Mr. Benwick came to my office the next day and swore that his being late did not have to do with any kind of purpose. Yet, subsequently he asked if it would be possible to hand him a master key, because he would frequently stay after closing hours. He would agree to lock up the office building when he left last.

What until then had seemed impossible became true. Since three months Mr. Benwick has turned up on time for our morning routine and is very cautious to mind meeting agreements to the minute.

Goal-oriented behaviour does not only imply purpose but also conscious action. Here it has to be admitted that we usually do not think things over if we want to avoid something. Maybe you know scenes like the following:

Just before closing hours some colleagues spontaneously agree to meet for bowling that evening. Unfortunately, Alan Friend has promised his wife to go to the movies with her. He returns home a bit moody and during dinner he lets slip: "What the hell did you brew together tonight?" Already a bit pissed off because of the atmosphere in general, his wife bursts out: "If you don't like it here, why don't you eat someplace else." Promptly Mr. Friend gets to his feet and says in a cool manner: "As you like it." He fetches his coat and makes his way to the bowling centre with a clear conscience, since it was his wife who wanted him out of the house.

Maybe the remark about the dinner "brewed together" was a conscious one, but usually those scenes have a hidden dynamic which makes goals somehow be achieved "automatically".

If the task is to understand one's behaviour asking "What for", even if it is unfamiliar, often helps; even in the explanation of one or the other indisposition or illness. The cause of having caught a cold may be bad weather, an infected neighbour, or cold feet. When looking for a possible goal, maybe an aspect of avoiding something may emerge like:

With this cough nobody will expect me to...
As long as I am ill, I don't have to...
"Unfortunately" I'll have to cancel the date with...

With professional conversation leadership a "Why" gets only limited attention, since the answer will only explain an event from the past, which cannot be altered anyway. Asking "What for" you direct the attention towards goals and intentions, which can still be influenced in a conversation.

> "What for" asks for goals and intentions.

In this book you will often read about the images we create in our minds. There is quite a number of people who are convinced that they do not think in images, but when I confront them with the story of the crossing of the river Rhine from chapter 1, they usually realize how much they let their thinking be influenced by their spontaneous imaginations.

When explaining human behaviour out of people's goals and intentions, the following thought may help: The outcome of a future event is already imagined previously. The "real" reality only confirms one's own ideas. It is significant that often an event is, aloud or in one's mind, commented: "Didn't I know it?!" And even it may again sound paradoxical, this need for getting a **confirmation** of one's

imagination is so big that even negative events are almost happily commented. Typical self-affirmations sound like:

"This had to happen."
"I could have told you before."
"No wonder that this has happened."
"I thought so at once."
"Typical!"

For many people the confirmation of a negative imagination seems to be more desirable than a positive but unexpected event. As soon as our dialogue partner has an idea of a future event, he will – and of course unknowingly – strive to make the real reality and his imagined reality match. You may remember the example from chapter 1, about my colleague who stumbled and fell when climbing the podium. When I asked him about this later, he admitted that while falling the thought "I *knew* it!" had flashed across his mind. Also the confirmation of a negative event, and be it a catastrophe, will be experienced as satisfactory, since this is a repeated proof of how "realistic" and appropriate the future had been foretold. It may be a sign of competence to adapt one's behaviour to future events in a way that bad surprises are avoided, but it is often overlooked that via our expectations of future events we have significant influence on them. This is also called a "**self-fulfilling prophecy**". The "prophet" has an idea of the future and makes a prediction. In a second step, from that point on he unknowingly makes sure that this prediction will come true...

When I was sixteen I got a new English teacher. After the first lesson I told my friend "She doesn't like me. I bet next term I'll get an E" as a practical consequence I reduced my commitment during lessons and homework significantly. Why bother if I would get an E anyway? When the teacher asked me a question it happened ever so often that I did not know the answer. For me a proof of her dislike. Why else should she always ask me if I did not know the answer? After some time she asked me less and less often, another proof of her dislike. And indeed, I got "my" E at the end of the term. Not without pride I showed it around and said: "Didn't I say it, she doesn't like me and I'm bound to get an E."
It took me another ten years to realize that I actually had contributed to that mark.

For professional conversation leadership this has practical consequences. Our tendency to influence somebody will soon meet obstacles if we have a totally different idea of a future situation than our dialogue partner. In this context we can explain in another way why people react to our well-meant advice, recommendations, and suggestions so reluctantly or even openly negative. It is not the advice as such that is not good, it just does not fit into the other's imagination; and in this sense it is indeed out of place.

As long as the secret goal is the affirmation of an existing image, each recommendation – however skilfully formulated – will meet resistance.

So before you start to influence someone, to win him for an idea, or to convince him, you will have to find out which idea the other has of his goal. Until you know that, all success is merely based on chance.

> When leading professional conversation you concentrate on the "target image" of your dialogue partner.

I know that the conversation saver "work out wishes" is not familiar to everyone, but I am always surprised how readily resistance is answered with advice: Promptly another proposal is added, then a third, and a fourth follows soon. You can observe that advisors insist in the rejected recommendations and explain their use and purpose, without having the slightest idea of the other's goals.

In a travel agency, a **C**ustomer says: "We would like to make a journey with our two children during the Christmas holidays.

Travel agent: "How about the mountains? I have a very interesting offer for the Dolomites. Absolute guarantee for snow at that time of the year."

C: "Nay, we thought about something in the South. With really warm water."

T: "I see, in this case the Maldives are an option . . ."

C: "No, no long distance travel. The flight takes so long."

T: "Then what about the Canary Isles. Four hours flight, eternal spring, comfortable water temperature, and excellent animation."

C: "Sounds horrible."

T: "Yes, this is the name for the extensive entertainment programme offered there. You said you will take two children. You will be thankful for the programme offered for children. Many parents have assured me how happy they were that somebody took care of their children and they could relax in peace.

C: "This is not at all what I had in mind for my vacation."

T: flips though some prospects: "It's difficult to imagine how wonderful this is for children. Look, here you can see on the photos what is for example offered in the *Ocean View Hotel.*"

Even with people whose main channel of perception are either listening to someone or touching things, you will find imaginative thinking. Just notice how often our language uses expressions out of the world of vision and imagination:

- to see = to understand, to look through, to point out, to describe, to figure out
- apparently, insight, foresight, oversight etc.

The phrase "I cannot imagine that" seems to tell you unmistakably that for a certain context there is no image available. Far from that! The complete and more laborious statement would be: "I cannot imagine it the way you describe it. My imagination is entirely different." In other words: Although the other claims to have no image, which in an ideal case would result in open-mindedness and receptiveness, he grimly clings to his already existing idea. If you manage to understand the other's image, you meet the prerequisite for possible influence and change.

Nothing else is meant with the often cited statement of *Henry Ford*:

> "If there is a secret of success, it is to understand the other's point and to see things with his eyes."

This sounds easier than it is. If people have problems in admitting that they have a concrete, visual idea of future situations, they will hardly be able to talk about it. And this is exactly the problem: What is stated as a goal does not necessarily have to correspond with the other's real image. Most sales people can tell a tale of woe about it:

A salesman welcomes a customer and asks "What can I do for you?"
Customer: "I'm looking for a coat."
Salesman: "Are you looking for something specific?"
Customer: "No, I have not yet made up my mind."

Salesman: "This means, in principle every type of coat could be considered."
Customer: "No way. No leather coat, and nothing heavy anyway. And no hood. Rather something lightweight with a lining that can be unbuttoned. Light colour, too. No waist belt and other bits and pieces."

Consider how much of the urge to buy a coat may have been extinguished if the salesman had taken the customer at his word "I have not yet made up my mind" and had led him to the fashionable leather coats. Since in that case automatically a negative atmosphere would have been created because the customer had been confronted with something that did not at all meet his expectations.

If you take care you may be surprised how often a goal statement hints at that the idea the other has in mind is the direct opposite of what he has just said, like in the following example:

One day a friend of mine who is an attorney talked to me about vacation time and the determining conditions for self-employed people. He named his goal very concretely:
"Next year we will try to take six weeks off. It will not be easy, but I'll make it somehow."

What amazed me was the phrase "We will try . . .". The "somehow" in the next sentence made me assume that he did not have an imagination of his vacation and was influenced far more by the idea of which problems might hinder the realisation. To verify my assumption I said:

"This sounds as if six weeks of vacation cannot be realised at all."
And like a shot came in return: "You say it. What do you think my desk will look like when I come home. One might say that I pay back for every single day with extra work later."

This statement indicated that he was well able to imagine how his desk would look like, but had no idea of his "non-work" time, i. e. his vacation. So as not to offend him I stated in general:

"This would mean that as a lawyer one cannot afford to take vacation."
Without hesitation he continued: "Basically spoken, yes. The liberties of your profession do not apply for lawyers."

This statement made me assume that he had no intention to change his situation. The strategic withdrawal towards the job of a lawyer in general seemed to me like a permit to object to every proposal. Even so, it made me test his resistance.

"You know that I have given training courses on time management for lawyers. I know many attorneys who were able to use my ideas rather successfully."

The refusal followed immediately: "Yes, in normal offices there may be several ways to make more efficient use of one's time, but with our focus and our personnel structure there is no opportunity to save more time."

The last sentence made clear: Who does not see any way does not have an imagination of goal achievement. However precisely the goal may be stated, at the end the existing image will win.

This chapter deals with purpose finding, and therefore I am not going to ask why the lawyer tried so vehemently to defend himself against a change in his work conditions and vacation plans. What I am going to ask instead is which (hidden) goal he tried to achieve with this behaviour. Since it can be expected that there is one. Now I did not want to ask "What do you do this for?" Such a question usually meets violent resistance, since it implies acting consciously on a certain purpose, which is usually not the case. You can think over for yourself which advantages an overloaded desk may have. The "desk-pilers" among the readers may feel caught, so the list of possible explanations is incomplete on purpose...

- A desk covered in paperwork looks like a lot of work.
- One is to see that I do not only work a lot but also bear a lot of responsibility.
- Nobody will expect me to find anything in that chaos.
- With this workload, mistakes are to be expected, and nobody can blame me for them.
- If I cannot manage this, nobody will expect me to take over anything in addition.
- As long as I have these many tasks I can have a clear conscience when I let other things wait.

The last statement incorporates recognisable benefits. With emphasised engagement in a well-accepted area one can steal away from other more disagreeable duties. Who for example has problems with his partner or his children, in today's society will find an excellent excuse when returning home late because of work overload and has to back out during the weekend to complete one or the other task. The possible accusation to be constantly unavailable can be answered with "But I do this only for you!"

> When dealing with goals and purposes, you ask for the goal behind the goal.

Many people have a negative idea of intimacy and close relationships. In their imagination they view themselves as contained, controlled, dependent, at someone's mercy, helpless and speechless, and much more. Not at all a worthwhile goal. So to prevent this feared vision from becoming reality, another image is developed. A vision of how the "horror" is banished. An evident image may include job career, workload, or duties for the XYZ club, responsibility for projects and tasks no one else can master that well, or anything similar. In other words: The purpose behind many an altruistic engagement is just avoidance behaviour. That this is much more often the case than you would assume at first, may become more obvious to you when considering the fact that most people are able to describe without any problems what they do not want, but get deep into trouble when asked to state what they want. This can only be explained by the fact that negative imagination is difficult to avoid. These visions in a way lead a life of their own without being conscious to us. Our negative imagination holds a kind of magical power which makes us ascertain that we were right with our negative images. In the example with the negative idea of intimacy we try to get close to the other in spite of our anxiety. And in the way of a self-fulfilling prophecy, situations arise, or better: situations are created in a way that what we have known before will really happen. This is how you can explain why people make the same experience again and again.

This is how it becomes understandable why people in all their trouble are ready to give self-congratulatory and dogmatic comments.

If you want to understand somebody and follow his goals and purposes, the approach may help you to search for the advantages of a certain behaviour. Purpose-finding this way becomes a search for the benefits.

Look out for the benefits of a behaviour.

Maybe you shake your head spontaneously and argue that there is a kind of "real" misbehaviour, that one behaves sometimes in a way one would like to shed, like blushing or crying easily or the inability to say "no". Even if this may seem absurd at first sight, these behaviour patterns some time in the past were part of an optimised solution and guarantee goal achievement. Maybe you had the chance to observe how adults react to a little girl blushing. You will hear sentences like:

"Look, how cute."
"Isn't it charming."
"Look, how nice she looks."

In addition the little girl will soon find out that adults not only welcome blushing because they find it so "natural" but that is a way to fulfil ones needs and wishes much easier. The same way every child learns that it gets the grown-ups' attention through crying. A crying child needs support which is immediately given. Viewed this way, helplessness can be learned. There is hardly another behaviour with which a child gets positive attention so instantaneously like with silent tears, trembling lips, and openly demonstrated helplessness. As long as this behaviour, acquired in early childhood, leads to the desired results, this strategy inhibits the development of new and more successful strategies.

Rather similar circumstances you will find with the inability to say "no". You can also express this as the ability to say "not-no", a skill that many a child needs to acquire early in life to get by with father or mother. Often the firstborn are in the awkward position that their parents' affection is connected with the accomplishment of certain tasks. To maintain attention and appreciation, the child will suppress its spontaneous "no". The acknowledgement often coupled with this helps to stabilise the ability to say "yes" in any case. Who as an adult answers "yes" all too easily to the pleads and requests of others tries to gain regard and attention in the adopted way. Yet, this sometimes useful behaviour inhibits the development of new behaviour patterns that are equally helpful in maintaining other people's appreciation.

Before you judge somebody else's behaviour, you best try to understand his goal(s). If you know which objectives he follows and which "good intentions" move him, you may be able to show him that he can achieve the same goal in another way, through another behaviour much easier, more directly, or with less effort.

Some readers may object that this sounds very idealistic and that the general concept of "good intentions" mismatches reality. If something is viewed as positive or negative depends on subjective factors. We may wish to have an objective measurement but until now mankind has not been able to establish an absolute idea of value. Even the value of a human life, viewed as the highest good, may be treated differently in wartimes, depending on the side one is on.

The former slave and roman stoic philosopher *Epictetus* stated accurately:

> "Men are disturbed, not by things, but by the principles and notions which they form concerning things."

Our opinions let us often get caught by interpretations. If we assume that people use their behaviour to follow certain objectives, independent of being aware of them or not, and if we understand that their behaviour is only the expression of their ways of a practical solution, we will stop judging others and start dealing with their interests.

If you want to modify behaviour, start with the question, what possible benefit from this problematic behaviour might have resulted for your dialogue partner.

People are easily to be influenced if we can show them how to fulfil their needs in a better way. I often experience in training courses, that participants ask especially for negative feedback. And the same participants become very resistant when I indicate which mistakes they need to avoid. Yet, if I manage to show them how they can become more successful and fulfil their needs in another way, the same participants become very studious.

How to achieve your goals more easily

Ask the right questions

Using a "why" question is the common way to clarify cause-effect-relations. Behind this is hidden the idea that if one knows the reason for a decision it might be influenced correspondingly.

But what is common and often useful in science and engineering, the way to deal with the present defects by analysing their past causes, cannot be transferred to social life.

Even if it is familiar to perceive reality as a result of cause and effect, human behaviour in the present can as well be deducted from the future. In contrast to a machine, human beings act for **purposes** and strive for **goals**.

Instead of only asking "What for", the following phrases may be useful:

- What do you want to achieve?
- What do you expect from it?
- What is this aiming at?
- What do you think you can gain?
- What would be different, if...

> If you manage to capture the others idea, you have built a foundation for possible changes and influence.

Goal orientation

To deal with a problem induces a different emotional disposition than thinking about a goal. Whoever acts **problem-oriented**, tends to ask the following questions:

- "What is your problem?"
- "Why do you have this problem?"
- "What exactly is stopping you?"
- "Where are the difficulties and what is causing them?"
- "What are your concerns?"

To be able to answer these questions, the dialogue partner has to become aware again of the entire significance of his problem. And of the negative feelings involved.

But instead of concentrating on the past, it may be helpful to realize that the past is gone and cannot be influenced any more. Only the future can be changed. When communicating goal-oriented you create a positive disposition in your dialogue partner through asking:

- "What is your goal?"
- "What do you need to achieve this?"
- "What will be different when you have achieved your goal?"
- "Which hopes do you connect with your goal?"
- "What support do you expect from my side?"

These questions take a lookout into the future. They are emotionally connected with hope, confidence, and relief.

12. Behaviour is Goal-Oriented

Imagine that for the completion of a job you need the help of an assistant or a colleague. After having explained in detail what it is all about and why it is so urgent you get the answer:

"That's impossible. I've more than enough to do."

You can go on reading now, but maybe you have more fun with the coming paragraphs if you stop for a moment to think about how you would react to this. You can note down your reaction to compare it with other possible answers subsequently.

Your answer:

In the following you will find a selection of typical answers in training courses:

"But this is more important and must be done at once."
"You haven't understood me, I'll explain again why this job so important..."
"Why, what else do you have to do?"
"Of course it's possible, if you really want it."
"I'll show it to you and you'll see how easy it is."
"Why is it impossible?"
"What if you try with actually working for once?"
Not to say anything and to ask somebody else.
Keep silent and try to do it alone.

I do not know how your answer sounded. All answers cited here have in common that no reaction addresses the dialogue partner and his goals. I admit that this is not easy. If we are brushed off so abruptly when addressing someone with our request, it suggests itself to give it another try with more effort. But what is the purpose?

In chapter 1, I made a distinction between efficient, i. e. action-oriented, and effective, i. e. goal-oriented, formulations. In this chapter I will again deal with goals and purposes. Our entire behaviour is goal-oriented:

We want to be taken seriously, we wish to receive attention and to be respected by others. We strive for making our opinions not only heard but accepted, and we feel well when we experience regard and acceptance and a feeling of belonging; in other words:

> We want to receive other people's regard.

Even if I assume that all my dialogue partners strive for this, it does not mean that people are generally aware of it.

In the first example the dialogue partner who has been asked for help blocks any action from his side in short words:

"That's impossible. I've got enough to do."

What makes this reaction so unpleasant is not the lack of support but the disregard expressed by the shortness of the answer. With these few words the other fobs us off showing disrespect and lack of acceptance for our request. In other words: we do not feel taken seriously. This disregard is in contrast to our own wish for esteem. And this has consequences!

A three-stage escalation plan is put into action, and each of these steps has only one goal which is to regain regard and respect.

Stage I: Demonstration of power

According to the motto "Excuse me while I laugh" a struggle for power is started like with the first example answer:

"But this is more important and must be done at once."

Many a power struggle is acted out openly; maybe you know the statements of crammers and grinders: “If they don’t love me, they will at least fear me.” This is nothing less than the desperate attempt to gain respect via power and threatening gestures. Sometimes this struggle is also well hidden and subtle, like in the following examples:

“You didn’t understand me. I’ll explain again how urgent this is…”
“Of course it is possible. If you really want it will work out.”
“I’ll show you how I do it, and you’ll see it will be very easy.”

As ostensible as these three examples may be formulated, their only purpose is to let the other know that he is merely lacking the right insight, that he is “thick in the head”, but that one is willing to nobly help him on the way.

Power struggles are based on an either-or disposition: Either I will win or the other. And if, rather me. It is because a power struggle knows only one winner, that there has always to be someone who loses. And this loser will in no way feel respected and gets the impression:

- I got a raw deal
- I could not achieve acceptance
- I pay extra
- The other is more powerful
- I feel discriminated

It is one of the very common but paradoxical ideas that one has to put down somebody or get him in a bad position in another way to make him behave with respect and, indeed, friendliness.

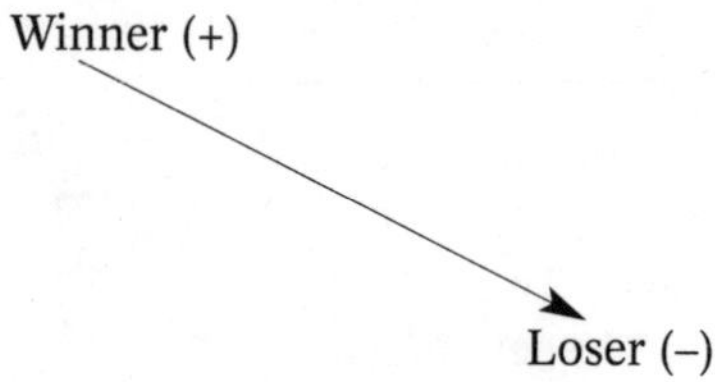

This has consequences! Escalation reaches the next step:

Step II: Revenge

While in a power struggle there is at least one winner, revenge knows only losers, following the motto: “If I don’t get what I want, you will not get it either.” **Revenge is** always and only **destructive**. It may be, that a well-aimed reply creates a feeling of satisfaction, but these retaliations build on the erroneous belief, of being able to gain back the lost appreciation in this way. Let us take another look at the first statement from the first example:

“But this is more important and must be done at once.”

A supervisor may enforce compliance with this phrase, but at what price? Of course the employee will obey since he will not risk his job. However, one does not need much imagination to foresee how the result will look, how engaged the employee will be on this task and later takes up the interrupted work again. If taking a closer look the everyday struggles and the spanners thrown in the works of many companies turn out to be escalation step II: **revenge as an answer to a lost power struggle**. This answer to a suffered defeat can be given in a subtle or in an aggressive way: In one case there will be only passive resistance, for example decisions may be misinterpreted, undermined or even manipulated, or an order is carried out verbatim or overdone, in the other case there is open mutiny and rebellion, for instance via strike, sabotage or disobedience. This way the victory turns out to be dearly purchased:

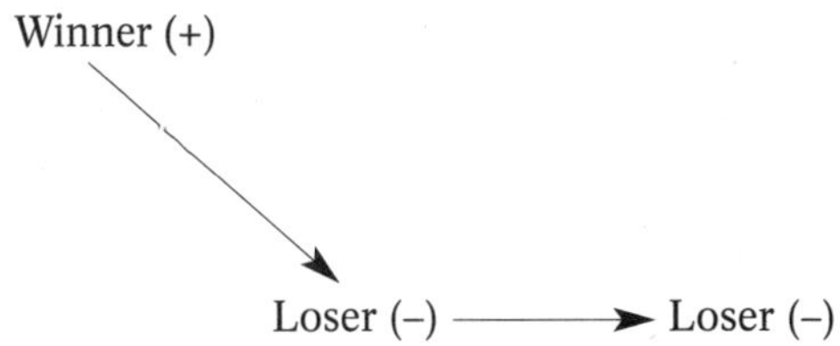

Unfortunately, instead of the desired appreciation the only thing that follows is:

Step III: Demonstrated helplessness

Since all attempts to regain respect have gone wrong, on this step one **gives up demonstratively**, which is usually coupled with the hope for being let alone at last. Yet, at the end, this leads to doubled helplessness, because it makes both conflict partners incapable of action. I am always surprised how many people in many companies have "settled" permanently on this step of helplessness. According to the motto: "I'm a sucker anyway", they only accomplish the most necessary tasks and seem to be overloaded and distressed when the slightest deviations from the normal procedures occur. It may sound cynical to claim success for these employees, but usually they are left in peace by their co-workers and superiors. The latter often admit their inability to change something. A department head once admitted: "I've tried so much. Until now all measures failed. There's nothing one can do about it. One can only wait until he goes into retirement."

Objections and the dangers in dealing with them

There is no attempt to convince someone without objections and critical questions from the other side. The various ways of handling these objections can have very different effects on the dialogue partner. One may wake resistance, others seem "dishonest" and are only the means to an end, while one could ask to what end, indeed? Is the primary goal to react to objections in a way (i. e. tactical, using special "techniques") so that one is right or "wins" at the end?

This starts with the often used term of **handling** of objections, which sounds as if the goal has to be to rebut the objections and make them collapse. As an "objection handler" one may forget that it is of limited importance in the process of convincing someone of something if an objection is correct or not. It is all too easy to miss taking the "subjective character" of many objectives into account. This may lead to a situation in which a rhetorically trained "handling" of an objection creates an attitude towards the dialogue partner, that makes the other often feel not taken seriously but only "handled".

Many objections are a spontaneous **reaction to lack of appreciation**. With opposing points of view the value for one's own view is usually combined with a devaluation of the other position. And one can observe that people the more vehemently attack the opposing view the more rickety their own arguments are. Sometimes the impression may come up that a different view is perceived as an attack on one's own position, even on one's identity and has to be counter fought decisively.

This discourse makes clear which influence disregardful behaviour will have on the willingness of the other to open up for a different or a new point of view.

However, someone who listens carefully and expresses appreciation will establish a basis for a rational examination of different interests, with which the dialogue partner may change or abandon his point of view **voluntarily**.

Let us come back to the first example. A colleague or assistant was asked for help and blocked that with the following words:

"That's impossible. I've got enough to do."

That this is an especially disregardful reply, we have already stated. Yet, we can ask ourselves what makes the other react in such a repulsing manner. If we want to take the easy way out we may tend to believe that this is the way he is and that he has no manners.

Yet, one can assume that this answer is only a **reaction to** previously expressed **disregard**. It is a way you can view this pattern in all areas of life. This may seem to be like the hen and egg problem, asking for: Who started it? But later, when analysing a conflict we can often observe:

Every conflict has a history that started with lack of appreciation.

How often do struggle and anger begin with someone not feeling respected. I will try to illustrate this with some seemingly harmless everyday situations. Many problems in a neighbourhood that end up in court start with a bagatelle, but one which expresses how one thinks of the other.

Anyone who moves into a new apartment, can introduce himself to the neighbours and demonstrate, that he is interested in the community. Or one can abstain from it and show that the neighbours are of little importance.
Who plans to have a party that might not only be noisy but even noisy until late at night, can inform the neighbours beforehand and ask for tolerance and understanding to show that he is aware of their presumably reduced well-being. Or one can forget about that and claim that one pays a rent and has the right to have a party from time to time. All too often the neighbours answer this powerful demonstration of disregard with satisfying their desire for revenge by calling the police.
Family music, which is to the neighbours' displeasure and according to *Wilhelm Busch* combined with noise, will quickly become the bone of contention when forcing the legal point of view instead of verifying with the "audience" to what extent they may be disturbed by trumpet or clarinet exercises.
Hedges, fences, and other borderlines offend some neighbours because instead of communication they face an offending demarcation, which can hardly be understood as the expression of appreciation and respect And many a dispute has its origin in someone parking his car on the neighbours' car park without having asked, which the other may understand as a sign of disrespect for his rights and his property.

If we get back to the example with the request for help, we have to test first how **respectful** the chosen **introduction** phrase has been. Supervisors often do not think about how to address subordinates who are occupied with a task. Often this sounds like:

"Could you please just come with me..."
"I need you now..."
"Now listen,..."
"I have gotten the following..."
"Could you just pay attention..."
"Could you just..."

You can imagine how you would react if one of your employees would step into your office and tell you about his request with the same introductory phrases. One department head once told me: “There have to be certain differences.” And exactly here lies the disregard for the employee. He feels and hears day after day that he is “only” a subordinate whose work procedures can be interrupted by the superior at any time, because he has more important things to do than to take care of the momentary well-being of his employees.

A customer service member of a car dealer told me that he finds it especially strenuous when some customers with unnerving arrogance treat him like an errand boy. As an example he related one situation when he was busy writing a repair order when a customer commanded him from several yards away:

“Come out with me! Something’s rattling.”

Of course he went out with the customer to look at the car. Looked under it to find out what was rattling. Yet, instead of fixing the loose clamp himself, he explained to the customer that he would take care of having it fixed at once. He filled in another repair order, the car was brought into the workshop and a mechanic instructed. Summary comment: “Revenge tastes sweet. I’ve taught that guy.” I was interested in how the customer service guy would have reacted if the customer had treated him with respect, like for example:

“I see that you are writing something. Maybe I can show you something on my car later. Something’s rattling.”

Without hesitation I got the answer:

“Most probably I ’d have interrupted my work at once, and gone outside with him, had fixed the clamp and said ’Have a good trip!’”

You can ask yourself how readily you are prepared to react to someone's request if he interrupts you with bold implicitness and signals that right then he and his problem are more important than your current task.

The common phrase

"May I interrupt you?"

in no way expresses appreciation and is sometimes – who will wonder – answered with the words:

"You are already doing it."

Very different the question:

"When do you have some time for me?" Or more precise:
"When could I talk to you for ten minutes?"

Now the one who is addressed in this way can act as he sees fit and name a point of time that suits him well. Of course this decision can be made easier if the plain question is added with a reason:

"When can I talk to you for five minutes? It's about the date for the training course next week."

But this is by far not the desirable degree of appreciation. We feel taken really seriously only, if the one who interrupts us waits at least until we signal through eye contact that we are ready to listen. Not only is it an act of courtesy to wait for the "Come in!" after having knocked at a door, it is also a sign of respect and regard when approaching somebody's desk to wait for being invited by eye contact before addressing the other. And this is not only true for employees!

I can very well hear the hoarse cry of some supervisors: "Where would this get us if I had to wait every time until my subordinate allows graciously to give him an order." But any time I rate my time more important than that of others and myself more important than my dialogue partners I express my attitude towards them. And this reveals the degree of disregard and lack of respect. In this context I want to add some typical examples, in which the disregard is expressed in the fact that they could never happen the other way round:

When supervisors step very close to an employee's desk, lean against it or even sit on it; take paper or a pencil from the employee's desk without asking; step behind the employee, watch his work progress over his shoulder and control him; write directly into the files or papers of an employee; keep one or even two hands in the pocket when talking to an employee; tap him or especially her on the shoulder or approach them in another physical way.

The behaviour itself does not seem to be problematic to me at all. Yet, I have hardly ever met a supervisor who could imagine to be treated likewise by his employees.

Maybe the following examples sound a bit laborious for you in the beginning:

"I assume that you are still rather busy with the final report. When could I talk to you for five minutes? I need your support with the new project and I would like to clarify when and how you could take part."
Or:
"I can see that I'm interrupting you. Could you please come to my office when you are ready, I need your assistance with the closing report."
Or:
"I know I'm messing up your schedule. Can you interrupt this work? I need your help with a process documentation."

You will start using this uncommon and therefore seemingly long-winded proceeding as soon as you have experienced that you achieve your goals much quicker this way.

> We want to express regard for our dialogue partner while keeping our own goals in mind.

The entire last paragraph indicated how much energy we need if our dialogue partner has already said 'No'. Whether we decide for pressure or for eating chalk, it usually takes a second and in most cases a third attempt to make the other change his mind, if this is possible at all, and we do not have to give up entirely. I am always surprised that especially people who fight vehemently against respectful, but in their eyes time-consuming, manners will never get tired of trying to convince others of the importance of their desires again and again. Strange to see, that time and energy consumption of this way of pursuing one's goals is not taken into account.

The title of this chapter reads "Behaviour is Goal-Oriented". The further explanations are based on the following assumption:

> People undertake all their activities only to produce pleasant emotions. People want to feel good.

However different people may be and how different they have organised their lives, at the end they all strive solely for well-being. And everyone is doing this his individual way:

Some work hard to earn a lot of money to be able to afford what contributes to their well-being: be it a sports car, a big house, exciting trips to exotic places, or expensive sports.

Others work a lot because they can be sure of the pleasing appreciation of others. School grades alone do not stimulate good performance; this is only formed by positive reactions of parents and teachers.

For others the consequent compliance with instructions, rules, and regulations creates a comfortable security, while there are people who on the contrary feel well when experiencing the thrill of doing something forbidden, when violating these instructions, rules, and regulations.

And many social action is not only undertaken to help but also to feel needed or as a sacrifice. This can result in a clear conscience or in the delightful feeling of being morally superior.

These examples can show that all our effort serves mainly to achieve well-being.

A different way to contribute to this well-being is to show our appreciation for people before they have returned something, just by paying them respect and attention. You can test how big your will to cooperate, your commitment, your readiness to give in, and your generosity become, when you feel respected and taken seriously.

Please, do also answer the opposite question, how low your willingness to cooperate is, how fussy and even finicking you can be if you feel uncomfortable when sensing that you are not taken seriously and are treated disrespectfully and without regard.

Every well-trained waitress knows that she can influence the tip by making, in a discreet way, the guest's stay as comfortable as possible.

In holyday resorts it is well-known that a tourist is willing to fork out money when he feels fine.

Shop assistants know that buying a new shirt and tie in addition to the new suit depends on the customers "disposition". To influence that is part of their professional skills.

And clever kids pick the time to ask for an increase in pocket money when having good marks at school or when their parents are in a good mood.

Many more examples could be added to that list. They all have in common that one's goals are achieved via showing respect for the other. And who will be bothered by the fact that others achieve their goals, if at the same time one feels fine. I will try to summarise this:

Behaviour is mainly influenced by the present state of well-being. HOW is often more important as WHAT.

Imagine you plan to dine out. Since it is a special occasion, you choose a very fancy restaurant and order an especially extravagant and expensive meal. The food exceeds your expectations. It is seasoned with refinement and tastes extraordinarily well. On the other hand the waiter is short-spoken and lets you wait for the menu quite a while, forgets the beverages, but manages to bring the check unwanted immediately after having removed the plates. What will your impression be of this evening?

Let us now turn the example around and access another restaurant: the extravagant meal turns out to be quite plain and bourgeois, you even need salt and pepper. On the other hand, the waiter takes care of you in a very friendly and undemonstrative manner. Without having to turn your head to him to order another drink, he comes to your table, is quick without pacing, and even with the check he deals very discreetly. What is your impression of the evening this time?

For whom the 'how', i. e. treatment and atmosphere, are unimportant, will have no problem in revisiting the first restaurant, since the food was excellent. Yet, whoever felt offended by the waiter will not only tend to avoid the restaurant in the future but also advise others not to go there, too. Even after some years one may recall the bad overall impression if one passes by the restaurant occasionally.

Whoever values the 'what' will give the second restaurant no other chance and avoid it in the future. Whoever is influenced by the 'how' will in the second case rate the atmosphere higher than the disappointing food, since the overall impression was positive. Maybe this restaurant gets a second chance, trying out another dish this time.

We know the typical background music in shopping centres with which the customers should be put into a good mood. Behind this you can find the realisation that "happy" and good-humoured customers develop a greater desire to buy something. Increasingly activities are started to make the customer feel well:

While you wait for an oil change, many car dealers offer coffee and tea, and you can choose between several newspapers.

Like in America, customers of a hair dresser will be offered a variety of beverages.

While a guest waits for his dinner he will be served a small appetizer that prepares him for the coming courses.

A flight may be very short, but the airline may offer candies, champagne, and other treats.

But all these marketing measures cannot replace communication and the personal encounter of people. This is the only way to experience respect. No "good mood measure" will ever be able to replace missing regard. Yet, conversely, the natural form of respect and attention can contribute to making real inconveniences overlooked with generosity. Only **prerequisite**: we need to feel really accepted and take the **appreciation** demonstrated to us for **real**.

I go back again to the examples from the neighbourhood, and you can make up your mind on how your reaction might look like.

The new neighbours who moved in last week ring your doorbell on Friday at six o'clock: "Good evening. We have just come over to introduce ourselves. Maybe we are disturbing you at the moment (pause). We would like to invite you to our housewarming party next Saturday."

Wednesday evening one of your neighbours knocks at your door: "Excuse me for disturbing you. Next Saturday I plan to celebrate my birthday. I have invited twenty people and I fear it may be pretty noisy. I wanted to ask if it would be very problematic for you if we dance until midnight?"

One day your neighbour addresses you: "I live in the apartment above yours. Now I have inherited a piano and I don't know how much it would disturb you if I practice regularly. I thought, before you get annoyed I ask you directly how you view this?"

In your garden, you are addressed like this: "Our grounds lay very open. Now we would like to plant a hedge. We are not sure if this may offend you. Maybe this looks as if we don't want any contact with you."

One neighbour addresses you in front of your house: "I have noticed that you do not use your parking space. Would you allow me to park my car there? Only as long as it is okay for you, of course."

This proceeding does not guarantee to achieve every goal in interpersonal contact. On the other hand, I believe it to be very improbable that acting with regard is bound to cause classical reactions in form of power struggle and revenge.

> When pursuing your goal, keep the other's well-being in mind, and you will be successful.

Or as *Alfred Adler*, a scholar of *Sigmund Freud*, stated in the twenties:

> "The successful deals mainly with other people's interests, the unsuccessful and ordinary mainly with his own."

At the end of this chapter, I will come back to the first example to show how you can pursue your goals when reacting with regard even to a negative answer and show the other that you respect him.

The easiest way is **descriptive listening**, for example:

"You can't help me, because you don't have time at the moment." Or: "You have such a lot on your plate that you can't support me at the moment."

According to experience descriptive listening leads to the dialogue partner giving further explanations. Yet, this time the dialogue continues on a voluntary basis which leads to an entirely different atmosphere than it would have been possible with a direct question ("Why is it impossible?").

For whom the **relationship** with the dialogue partner is important can decide to tell the other **how his negative answer comes across**:

"I'm surprised by your reaction." Or:
"You say that so strictly. That makes me wonder."

There is a high likelihood that the other will feel the urge to explain and give additional reasons for why he cannot help you.

Whoever listens carefully may also **question** the vague **excuse** ("I've got enough to do"), without being aggressive, maybe like:

"If you did not have that much to do you would help me at once." Or:
"At the moment this is just due to your extraordinary workload."

Here, too, you will find that spontaneous acceptance is usually followed by another reason or explanation.

Another possibility is to use the energies that are focussed on "No, it's impossible" in a constrictive way by directing them towards **opportunities and solutions**:

"Under which condition could you help me?" Or:
"What could I do to get your support?"

This proceeding assures continuation; the conversation, started the negative way, can now turn positive; it is the turn of the dialogue partner to name conditions, that allow cooperation and instant support. To what extent these conditions are acceptable and you are willing to fulfil them can only be decided when they are discussed openly. Experience shows that respectful reactions generally lead to turning in and to good cooperation, which at the end was the main goal.

Win-Win Strategies

Anyone who regards negotiations as a power struggle overlooks the danger of an escalation. The loser will be provoked to taking revenge.

> Anyone who tries to win at somebody else's costs will always risk ending up as a loser.

Successful negotiators never criticise their dialogue partner. Even in difficult arguments it is important to view the other as a partner together with whom one tries to find a satisfactory result.

> **Hint:** Accept, that your dialogue partner has the right to have a different (even if sometimes wrong) opinion, and avoid arguments. They are time-consuming and lead to loss of sympathy.
>
> You can minimize energy consumption and maximize success when following one rule consequently:
>
> Value **each** of the other's statements.

Most conflicts on a personal level result from lack of appreciation. Often this happens unknowingly. One concentrates too much on stating one's own opinion and forgets to value the other's point of view.

> **Hint:** It is unnecessary to concede a point to someone, but only to signal that the others opinion has "reached" you.

Consider the other's interests

Defensive Give up	**Offensive** Balance of interests
Regressive Retreat to "neither – nor"	**Aggressive** Enforce at any price

Consider one's own interests

Aggressive and **defensive** positions are both based on the same prerequisite of an "either – or". This attitude will always lead to a win-lose-strategy.

While the regressive "neither – nor" position includes negligence of both one's own and of the other's view, the offensive "as well as" proceeding expresses mutual appreciation.

As long as your dialogue partner feels that his opinions are treated with respect and that he is allowed to view the things the way he wants them to view, he will be relaxed. This will support creative processes when solutions have to be checked that go beyond a usually dissatisfying trade-off.

This is the paradox of a win-win strategy: As long as you do not accept the other's point of view he will even more tend to insist and defend than deal with a point of view that is new to him.

13. To Take Someone at His Word

The previous chapter dealt with situations in which the other confronted us with statements that knock us off our feet. Understandably many people react with fierce opposition when shocked emotionally, and promptly an argument arises. Yet, we can leave what the other has just told us with him for further clarification, if we concentrate on the included self-disclosure. This is to add to chapter 10, in which I have shown the variety of possible reactions.

The following will deal again with postponing our own reaction, but now the focus lies on **the responsibility of our dialogue partner**. With this way to react the other has to check whether we really have to take him at his word. This will seem new and strange to most of your dialogue partners; many will feel under pressure when confronted with the responsibility for their own statements, which is normally not done in a more conventional conversation.

The following example was told to me by a participant who had the chance to test this proceeding the day after the training course:

She came back from the supermarket and found her sixteen-year-old daughter in the living room reading the newspaper. On her request: "Please, help me to carry the mineral water, I want to empty the car," she got the answer: "Is it always me?" And the daughter opened the newpaper again. The mother was just about to say as usually: "Everyone in the family has to help. With cooking, ironing, shopping, I don't say 'Why always me?' and now come on!" A conflict would have been unavoidable.

Instead, the mother made up her mind for confronting her daughter with the meaning of her own words when saying: "You have decided that you will not help me now."
At once the daughter looked up and said: "I'm coming."

It makes a difference whether one makes a conscious decision for or against something and says so or whether one tries to avoid a decision and states it indirectly. The latter is very common, indeed. How often a clear 'No' is hidden behind a reluctant:

"Always me."
"Must that be now?"
"I have so much to do."
"I don't want to."
"Is there nobody else to do that?"
"Is that really necessary?" Etc.

Let's state the four ways to react with the example "Does that have to be now?":

Facts	**Appeal**	**Relation-ship**	**Self-Disclosure**
Give facts for why it has to be now. Address the rational side.	Leave the other alone and look for somebody else.	To take it personally and talk about moral standards.	Talk about the other's decision and the hidden 'No'.
⇘ You can win this lap if you have the better arguments.	⇘ The buck was passed. Results in additional effort.	⇘ Whoever puts the other under pressure tries to convince the other this way.	⇘ The other can verify if he is willing to bear the consequences of his reaction.

Who concentrates on the **self-disclosure** avoids a spontaneous reaction. So valuable spontaneity can be, it usually leads us directly into an argument.

I admit that this proceeding can make the other rack his brain over it. On the other hand, I think it is legitimate to confront the other with the **consequences** of his statement and to assume in the first place that the other did not utter airy-fairy but has given a conscious answer.

A short while ago, I was told that this confrontation would be unfair, because everybody would know what was really meant with statements of this kind. True, everybody knows how to interpret such a statement and acts accordingly. Yet, this is exactly the point where the responsibility is transferred: Not the Must-that-be-sayer but the Cotton-wool-means-no-interpreter takes over responsibility, when following the appeal considerately and leaving the other alone. This turns out to be annoying when afterwards you get to hear reproachfully: "I didn't know it was that important". Or: "You'd better say that more clearly. I didn't understand you really need me." Etc.

> Anyone who when confronted with a hidden No concentrates on the self-disclosure does not block a negative answer, but gives the other the chance to verify his statement.

You do not need much imagination to guess, what the matter-of-fact question "Must that be now?" is really aiming at: "Leave me alone!" Or: "Don't disturb me now." But this is exactly what the other tries to hide. Instead, he is hiding the appeal in a question. So he has to reckon with our addressing this aspect of his statement. And instead of in a kind of cockfight struggle for the better arguments, it is useful to ask the other for a clear **decision**.

Even when this comes close to an imputation, we merely confront the other with the assumption that his statement followed a serious decision.

Maybe our dialogue partner will be perplexed when on his moody "Must that be now?" we react like that:

"At the moment you do not want to help me." Or:
"You decided against it." Or:
"My wish comes untimely." Or:
"Your question makes me think you don't want to help now..." Or:
"Correct me when I'm wrong, I understand your question as a No."

In an analogous way the sentence "Is there nobody else?" or "Why always me?" reflects like this:

"You want me to ask somebody else." Or:
"It's very inconvenient for you that I am asking you (of all people)." Or:
"You are annoyed that I have asked you."

And according to the same pattern we can also react to the following statement:

"Is it really necessary?"
"You only want to do it if you understand why it has to be done." Or:
"Before you start you want to know what it's good for."

Whoever hides his refusal or rebuff behind common phrases does normally not think about how to formulate them the most canny way. These figures of speech are part of everyday communication and are normally used without thinking. Yet, whoever listens carefully will discover aspects to deal with in further conversation.

In chapter 11 ("From Cause Analysis to Purpose Finding") I talked about the fact that we think in **images** and strive for making these images become reality. The point was to find out about the other's image and thus to find a base for possible changes and for further interaction. In this context I come back to *Henry Ford*:

> "If there is a secret of success, it is to understand the other's point and to see things with his eyes."

I had hinted that most people are not aware of the fact that they constantly produce images, but it is their language that "gives them away".

The statement "Does that have to be now?" could have been meant as a brusque rejection. However, the word 'now' includes a time constraint and can also mean: "In general yes, but another time would suit me better." In other words: the dialogue partner feels that the 'inconvenient' request does not go along with his idea of reality. And at the same time we can assume that he has an idea of when the request will not be inconvenient. And this is when conversation leadership comes into place: Who knows that now is not an appropriate point of time is able to tell us when such an appropriate point of time might be.

"Does it have to be now?"
"This sounds like you would prefer another time. What would you propose?" Or:
"You will agree as soon as we found an appropriate time." Or very directly:
"Tell me when it would suit you."

By the question when it would suit the other better, the focus is moved to the future and an image of an appropriate point of time can form.

The common phrase: "I can't imagine that" indicates that we think in **images** all the time. It always strikes me how many people do not take care for that. Yet, before we know the other's ideas, we can only influence him by a fluke.

The statement "This is too expensive" people often interpret as an unmistakably negative answer and draw their consequences. One may offer a cheaper product, another one tries to justify the price, and a third one feels personally offended.

But the statement "This is too expensive" is only one part of an unspoken **comparison**, which in its complete form would read: "In comparison to xy this is too expensive." And this xy may be real but may also exist in the other's imagination. Anyway, he has an idea of it.

> Only when we know the image the other has in mind can we lead the conversation towards success.

I talk about an incomplete comparison when two things are compared but the base for comparison is not stated. Not only experiences, people, or objects are compared, but most often we meet a comparison between imagination and reality.

But we can always ask for the missing piece of information:

- In comparison to whom or what?
- In relation to whom or what?
- Under what aspect is it too ...?

If a teacher says to a class: "You are too noisy" this can mean a lot of things:

"When compared to other pupils you are too noisy."
"Compared to yesterday you are too noisy."
"When I think of today's goal you are too noisy."
"You are too noisy to read out a story to you."

But probably behind the statement is hidden a certain image:

"When I prepared for this lesson I had a totally different idea of how you would behave. Compared to that you are too noisy."

In everyday communication the incomplete comparison is not an exception, but the rule. Since it remains open what something is compared to, one can either guess what would be an appropriate reaction or ask for the missing part:

"This is too expensive"
"If compared with what?" Or:
"You have a certain idea of how much this may cost you." Or:
"You have fixed how much you want to pay (for it)."

When during the next days you pay attention to it you may be surprised to find how often something is rejected with an incomplete comparison. For example:

"This seems to be too complex."
"The time is much too short."
"This is too eccentric for me."
"You are too pushy."
"You are too early."

Instead of listing arguments against it we can also take the other at his word to make him reveal the image that made him make this statement.

Anybody for whom something is "too complex" has a certain idea of cost and benefit and an imagination of the result, and thus it makes sense to ask:

"Too complex for what?" Or
"What do you have in mind when you say it is not worth it?"
"Too complex if compared to what?" Or
"What do you compare the complexity with?"
"Too complex regarding what aspect?" Or
"When would the complexity be justified?" Or
"What is the outcome you have in mind?"

Even if people think in images all the time, this does not necessarily mean that they are aware of it. Yet, leading a conversation can contribute to making them aware. We can even direct the dialogue partner's attention towards his imagination which may have been somewhat blurred or totally unconscious to him.

The following letter I received from a participant who had noted down from his memory how “leading with regard” in combination with “taking someone at his word” had helped him to make an unpleasant management decision:

Four members of my department had been picked to present our newest product at the *CEBIT* fair. The preparations had started six weeks before. In the afternoon before our flight to Hanover, an employee whom I met by accident in the hall addressed me as follows:

Employee: “I hope you don’t expect me to come to the *CEBIT* in our company dress.”

Supervisor: “You have a clear idea of how you would feel well. And I am unhappy when I think of what our customers will think of it.”

E: (with a low voice): “That’s so middle-class, to believe we can only market our products in a costume. Plus you make a mock of me. If I meet an acquaintance I’ll hear ‘Hi, Hanna, looking respectable today?!’ I don’t want that.”

S: “You worry about meeting an acquaintance and how your look will effect that, and I am concerned about the conclusions our customers might draw from our appearance.”

E: “I don’t get that.”

S: “We only managed to get the product ready in such a short time because everyone in the department abstained from receiving special treatment for quite a while. You for example have postponed your skiing in February to allow for better progress. And this unity must be visible to the customer. If everyone dresses as it pleases him some customers may draw the unreflected conclusion that with us everyone can do what he wants.”

E: “Okay, But this doesn’t mean it has to be this donnish dress.”

S: “Good, I just understand that you agree to my view on a corporate identity.”

E: “But we could just as well all dress in jeans and t-shirt, which fit our smart product much better.”

S: “You have a clear idea of how you like to be dressed. All I’m asking is how you will achieve that all colleagues are dressed alike. You know that Mrs. Bell and Mr. Cords have already departed.”

E: “Mhm.”

We can imagine how the conversation and the fair visit would have ended up if the supervisor had reacted in a typical authoritarian way:

“Of course I expect it. You know the rules for fairs very well.” Or:

"Do you really want to discuss the dress code now? I ask you . . ." (walks away). Or:

"My dear Mrs. Roth, if I had known how you look in a costume I 'd have talked about this question with you earlier."

If it is important for you to leave the responsibility where it belongs, the iron rule is not to accept the responsibility without being asked. In the example above, the employee names a wish and without saying it makes her further reactions dependent on the supervisor's answer. If for example, he answers in the authoritarian style, she can take over the role of a martyr and blame her impossible supervisor for all problems. At the same time she formulates her request in a way that she pushes him to make a decision. Yet, he can make clear to her what her responsibilities are:

Employee: "I hope you don't expect me to come to the *CEBIT* in our company dress."

Supervisor: "You say this so decidedly that I assume it's very important to you."

E: "Yes, sure, this costume can't be beaten in stiffness."

S: "I am only surprised that you address me at the evening of our departure in the hallway." Or:

E: "You expect a decision from me and for this important question you have picked the last possible moment. That surprises me."

I admit that this is a rather direct proceeding. However, in this case the responsibility stays with the employee, and she can only be angry about her clumsiness. Or she can blame her supervisor for not taking part in her game.

If you make it a habit to concentrate in negative answers on the special and not on the general content, you can break new ground. It is your own decision if you accept a demur with the included disagreement or to view a reasonable objection as a conditional agreement.

> Facing a 'No' you can deal with the reasons behind it and test with your dialogue partner if under changed conditions you can achieve a 'Yes'.

Most objections are constructed according to the following pattern:

- No, because of x.
- Yes, but x.

No matter if the rejection comes in form of the 'No, because' or the 'Yes, but', our dialogue partner suggests that there is only one, i. e. the mentioned, reason for his objection. Instead of dealing with this context of reason it can lead further much more quickly to be sceptical about this one reason and to ask for others:

- "Is there another reason why you don't..."

This proceeding is always appropriate if you suspect that the objection is only a false pretence. As soon as you have found out by this question that there is really only this one reason, you can verify its importance by making it negative and ask:

- If x would **not** be, would this also mean you **don't** say No but Yes?

The following phrases are typical "killer arguments" used to muzzle the dialogue partner. These phrases are especially used to disguise the true motives and attitude towards the subject in discussion. The examples are put up in a way that you can try to formulate an answer before reading my proposed ones.

	Your answer
(1) "That's impossible because the costs are too high."	
(2) "We can't do that, the headquarter would never approve."	
(3) "This sounds very nice in theory, but the praxis is somewhat different."	
(4) "I cannot allow that, the costs are higher than my budget."	
(5) "Sounds nice, but it takes too much time."	
(6) "I don't know, it looks rather sensitive."	
(7) "I don't mind, but my boss doesn't approve. Forget about it."	

	Your answer
(8) "I would like to help you but I can't take over responsibility alone."	
(9) "Until now our customers always liked that, and I don't see why we should change anything."	

I came up with the following answers:

(1) "That's impossible because the costs are too high."

"When we have found a sufficient solution for the costs you will agree." Or:
"You worry about increasing costs. And you can only agree if this point has been clarified." Or:
"You have a clear idea of how high the maximum costs may be."

(2) "We can't do that, the headquarter would never approve."

"Are there other reasons why we cannot do it?" Or:
"If the headquarter agrees you are in the game." Or:
"You can well imagine how the headquarter will react."

(3) "This sounds very nice in theory, but the praxis is somewhat different."

"Are there additional reasons why it does not suit?" Or:
"If praxis would be different the solution would convince." Or:
"This doesn't meet your understanding of the praxis."

(4) "I cannot allow that, the costs are higher than my budget."

"What in addition to the costs stands against it?" Or:
"I get your approval if the costs remain in budget." Or:
"You imagine what will happen if you exceed your budget."

(5) "Sounds nice, but it takes too much time."

"It will be more interesting when we have more time." Or:

"If we can free enough time you will approve." Or:
"It takes too much time compared to what?"

(6) "I don't know, it looks rather sensitive."

"Maybe there are other aspects that stand against it?" Or:
"If it would look less sensitive you would . . ." Or:
"You have an idea of the sensitivity of this machinery."

(7) "I don't mind, but my boss doesn't approve. Forget about it."

"What else hinders you?" Or:
"As soon as the boss signals approval you will agree, too." Or:
"You try to imagine the reaction of your supervisor."

(8) "I would like to help you but I can't take over responsibility alone."

"This is a just cause. Are there other reasons why it is impossible?" Or:
"If you were sure not to be held responsible you would not hesitate a single second to help me." Or:
"You imagine you may be called to account for it."

(9) "Until now our customers always liked that, and I don't see why we should change anything."

"Are there other reasons for not making any changes at the moment?" Or:
"When our customers do not like it any more you would be willing to talk about a change." Or:
"You have an idea of when changes are appropriate."

When reading it for the first time you may have asked yourself reluctantly what the advantage is to make the other answer our reformulated statement with a 'yes'. First we can assume that with a very high likelihood this 'yes' is followed by further explanations, that helps us to see the whole picture. Or the other realizes that with a 'yes' he is skating on thin ice, and that his objection that was only a false pretence is threatened to disintegrate, which usually leads to a new objection. No matter how the dialogue partner reacts we can go on taking him at his word, which I will do as an example for the last statement:

A: "Until now our customers always liked that, and I don't see why we should change anything."

B: "When our customers do not like it any more you would be willing to talk about a change."
A: "Yes, of course! We live from our customers, and fortunately they are very satisfied with us."
B: "In consequence this means we start with the changes, when we have already felt the dissatisfaction of our customers."
A: "No, not this way. But I will not give up anything time-tested just like that."
B: "You would give it up when the customers criticised it."
A: "Yes, of course, after all we are a service provider."
B: "And now if we want to start the change before our customers voice problems, when exactly shall we start?"
Etc.

This way of leading a conversation may seem very tough to you, since one drills down further again and again. At the same time we have to reckon with unnerving our dialogue partners with this style because they are asked for a decision that they either do not want to make or for which they do not want to take over responsibility.

This is also true if our dialogue partner tries to camouflage his intentions. It is a difference to say "I will do it" or "I can do it" or even "I will try to do it". The other tries to give the illusion that something will be done and at the same time makes it a mere possibility. Confronted with the disappointment of the others it is answered: "But I only told you I will try." Even here you can take the other at his word and make him understand his responsibility for his action when asking:

- "What has to happen so that...?"
- "What do you need to..."
- "Under which circumstances could you really..."

Sometimes it helps to puzzle the other on purpose:

- "What has to come true so that you do **not** ...?"
- "What has to happen so that you will **not** ...?"
- "What could make it go **wrong**?"

You can assume that your dialogue partner will hesitate and then rethink what he can and really will agree to.

If you want to be proactive and confront the other with his responsibility you can talk about the decision that is to be made:

- "Either you do it or you don't. But I don't want you to **try**."
- "Will you or could you? Please **make up your mind**!"
- "I ask you to find out what you want. **Make** your **decision** for Yes or No."

As a warning remark I can add that this style can make us very unpopular if we use it too one-sidedly and take the other at his word while lacking the necessary regard. Yet, who knows our way now will in the future better think about what to say to us.

Attitudes, interests, and actions are much more steered by emotions than by our intellect. To convince instead of to persuade it is always necessary to make the dialogue partner agree **emotionally**. Whoever wants to convince others needs to win them on the emotional side.

Many people do not like to admit that their emotions play a bigger role in the decisions than their intellect. They like to explain, using rational arguments, why an (emotion-based) decision made sense. By this way of rationalisation it shall be concealed that a decision has been made mostly because of emotions. Here it is hidden a very common fear of the unpredictability of one's emotions and also worries that one's wishes and feelings might be influenced by others. To avoid being manipulated, logic and reason are emphasized very much.

Professional conversation leadership takes care of the emotional side and can be proven not by relying on the 'better arguments' but by addressing the dialogue partner's emotions, his wishes, and his current problems.

The success formula

Everyone gives us an idea of **his** reality by what he or she is saying. And who wants to change something has to learn and use the dialogue partner's language. The way the other expresses his thoughts is relevant. I get much better along when I talk about difficult or sensitive points in the other's language instead of mine. This is not at all an invention of me – it was Aristotle who said that first. He said: If you want to convince someone use his arguments.

Success (S) in communication can be viewed as a product of **Goal Clarity (G)** and **Orientation towards the Other (O)**, which leads to the following formula:

$$\mathbf{S = G \times O.}$$

Is one of the factors approaching zero, the result will as well approach zero – no matter what the other factor is.

You can carry the orientation towards the other to the extremes when at the end of a negotiation or discussion you ask openly:

- "Which points are still open?"
- "What are you still missing?"
- "Is there something you are still worrying about?"

Of course the last questions require a certain sovereignty. Some readers may shake their heads and decide that they will under no circumstances threaten the achievements with so critical questions. Whether a discussion or negotiation was successful will always be proven afterwards when the other is also satisfied with the results.

Orientation towards the other

The following checklist may help to systematically build up an orientation towards the dialogue partner:

- What does your dialogue partner value most?
- What are his interests and his preferences?
- Where are his problems?

- Which situation is he in?
- Which solutions have been tried out until now?
- How does your dialogue partner react to proposals?
- What are his usual objections?
- In which way does he make decisions?
- What is his development background?
- How honest and reliable is he?
- How generous – how just?
- How discreet?
- What will his future look like?
- What is his relationship to his supervisor, his colleagues, and his subordinates?
- What are his competences?
- Which people is he dependent on? And what is their attitude?
- What is his relation to other competitors?
- What are the minimum results he needs to obtain?
- What does he have to achieve or prevent to secure his future?
- What is important for his status?
- What are his special interests?
- What does he already know – and what not?
- What does he believe – and what not?
- What does he like – what not?
- What annoys him?
- What does he fear?

14. From Persuasion to Conviction

Convincing somebody has a lot to do with selling something. As well as selling has a lot to do with convincing. Who sells a product usually knows how important it is to indicate the benefit for the customer. Since only what is of use for the customer will in the long run be of use for the vendor. A professional salesperson is aware that buying something is an entirely egotistic procedure, from the customer's point of view and not, as one may sometimes deduct from sales negotiations, from the vendor's. A professional sale means problem solving.

This is also true for the "selling" of ideas. Since someone who has an idea and cannot put it into action alone, needs partners who "buy" his ideas. Nothing else means the quotation from *Alfred Adler* I mentioned above:

> "The successful deals mainly with other people's interests, the unsuccessful and ordinary mainly with his own."

The following dialogue may show how unsuccessfully some people try to "sell" their ideas:

Mid November, an assistant addresses her supervisor in the following way:

"I have just done a cash check. We still have € 1948.70 left. Corporate Administration says that we need to complete annual accounts by November 30th. I propose that we order a new high-speed scanner. We can then store printed texts and other originals directly in the computer, and I don't have to file all that stuff in paper. I've already asked, and we can get a cheap model starting from around eighteen hundred Euros. Since we have gotten the money, it would make sense to buy a scanner."

Supervisor: "No, no, no. There are more important things to buy."

Assistant: (in a shirty tone) "And what would that be? If I may ask."

Supervisor: (Now a bit angrily, too) "You will get to know that soon enough."

Assistant: (offended) "It was just a question."

Only very few people are aware that **motivation**, **presentation**, and **causing interest** are not only the three important arts every good salesperson has to be capable of, but which are relevant in all processes of convincing. Basis is a fundamental knowledge of the use, which the product or idea may have for the dialogue partner, but it is also requiring the ability to present this use in a way that causes the other's interest.

> Convincing in a dialogue builds on the ability to create images, which the other adopts as his own and regards as desirable.

When we analyse the assistant's desire for workload reduction through a scanner, we find, at first, that regard is missing. She has done a cash check, and this is why her supervisor independent of his own interests has to deal with this at once. Maybe the supervisor would have taken the time if the decision about it would have been his, like for example with the following start phrase:

"When do you think we can talk about what to do with the remaining budget? I have already done a cash check."

The assistant's unexpected proposal is alienating. Of course qualified proposals of employees are welcome. Yet, in this case the decision about when these ideas may be voiced is left to the supervisor, who feels respected and less restricted in his freedom, if asked in another way, for example:

"In how far are you interested in my ideas? I have thought about workload reduction in our office."

With the unwanted explanation about what a scanner is good for the assistant assumes that her supervisor does not know anything about scanners. The disregard of the following sentence is hardly to be beaten: "File all that stuff." This way the work results of her supervisor are disqualified as "stuff". She could as well have stated the use for the supervisor:

"If filing could be automated with a scanner, I would be available for other tasks."

The disregard finds its climax in the statement: "Since we have gotten the money, it would **make sense** . . ." With this judgement the impression is created that only with a scanner could the money be spent in a meaningful way. Everything else would be **unreasonable**. When dealing with conversation killers I had talked about how easily unwanted judgement can lead dialogue partners into a conflict.

When we want to tell somebody something or win him for something, our main difficulty is caused by our discontinuous way of information processing. Our mind jumps back and forth between the information we hear and our own thoughts and is constantly creating images, no matter if we know all the details or not. How much we struggle with the slow sequence of words in a sentence has already been demonstrated with the example of the Rhine crossing. Delivering facts takes time – in the case of this text of six lines when read out aloud approximately 20 seconds. Yet, while you were reading and further important information was added, your brain had already created a vision. I admit, the first sentence "Near Coblenz two men wanted to cross the river Rhine." suggests an image in which both men stand on the riverbank side by side. With this image the problem could not be solved. The main barrier for solving this problem can be found in the fact that we seem to be "in love" with our images and are attached to them in a way that makes it difficult to abandon or replace them. With this Rhine riddle I regularly experience that either the facts of the story are altered (one is rowing and the other is swimming, for example, or one carries the other on his back) or aids are added like a rope a kilometre long or another ship, a ferry, or else. Some are so attached to their images once created that they absolutely insist that the problem cannot be solved.

I had promised on page 7 the solution for the nine points to be connected with four straight lines.

Who views the nine points as an entity, tends to accept the outer ones as a kind of border and strives to solve the problem within these self-defined system limitations.

But a solution is only possible when looking at the nine points and the page that surrounds them together. With this image in mind, one may ask where the problem is:

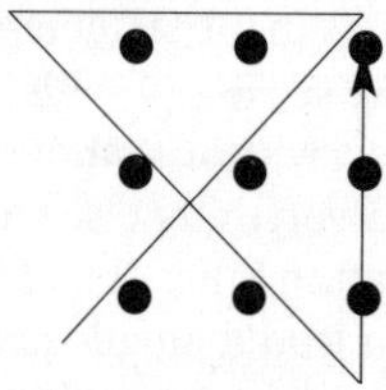

From optical illusions you know the human need for holistic perception. Although the full moon can be seen as a circle for one night only, many people add the missing parts some days before and after to full moon wholeness. Our perception tends to form something complete – a "shape" – out of incomplete images or information. Typically, you will add a meaning to the following pictures, even if I ask you not to look out for it:

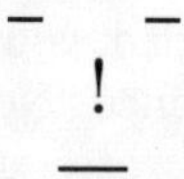

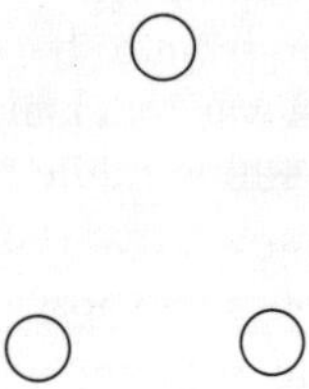

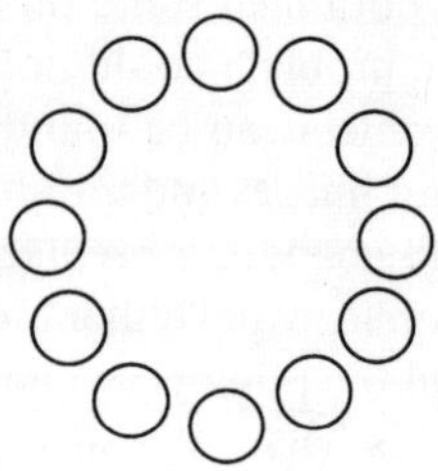

We constantly strive for understanding something's meaning, to understand what we are confronted with. And whether the meaning is "right", "correct", or makes sense form a "scientific" point of view, does not play a role. Who is for example superstitious will explain the reason for an accident by the fact that there is generally a higher risk of accidents on Friday thirteenth. You know the typical question after a stroke of fate: "Why me?" The search for an acceptable reason reflects our search for the meaning of life. It seems that we can bear the troubles in life much easier when finding a plausible explanation. Yet, since our perception is influenced by prior experiences, we interpret the new according to the pattern of the known. We try to connect our perception with something we are already used to. In the above illustration, a circle, a triangle, or a face are bound to be more familiar to you than a sample of single points, which do not seem to make sense and are therefore not viewed this way.

For professional conversation leadership this has consequences:

Your dialogue partner is constantly striving for obtaining wholeness, to get the whole picture. If you fail to deliver that picture, your dialogue partner will create an idea by himself and react according to his perception. And he will hardly understand that there is a difference between his and your idea.

> Provide your dialogue partner with an image, or he will create his own.

A common bad habit in conversation is to beat about the bush. Often the core of a request is approached by going the long way around, with the consequence that the other creates an image in his mind before even knowing what this is all about. This holds the danger that the other is blocking everything, just because in his mind he imagined something that creates uncomfortable feelings, in the worst case he even interrupts the conversation. The following example is to show how the dialogue partners forms a reaction in his mind, because he constantly imagines something:

Supervisor: During the last months I have observed you several times. I do this with all my employees, but you have attracted my attention.

(Employee is thinking: Oh God, what did I do wrong?)

Now there are several young team members, who regard our company more as a self-service shop, according to the motto: doesn't hit the poor.

(Employee is thinking: Now he is going to imply that I have nicked something. Dirty trick!)

This is not only true for equipment and materials, but also for time as such and personal engagement.
(Employee is thinking: That takes the biscuit, me and not engaged.)
Now, as I said, I have noticed that you are different from especially the younger colleagues in the best way. And this is why I want to ask you today, how we can best handle that problem.

If you want to prevent that your dialogue partner draws premature conclusions, you should address his desire for wholeness in the very beginning and let him know which benefits you can offer.

With what you want you will as a rule only get some polite attention from the other. Real interest is created when you can make clear to your dialogue partner of which use your desire, your idea, or your goal can be for him.

Communicate the "benefits" for your dialogue partner.

Even if we know from ourselves how difficult it is to concentrate for a long while and how easily we are distracted, we take the encouraging nods and the approving "Mhm" from our dialogue partners for the expression of pure attention. Yet, appearances are deceiving. Every child learns on elementary school how to make an interested face. For some it is extremely relevant to fake attention that is indeed non-existent. Interest flickering on and off is not an exception, but the rule.

Alfred **(A)** and Betty **(B)** Botch have a talk one Sunday in advent:
Albert Botch: "I think we should do something together with the kids during the holidays. If I take three days off, we can visit your parents from the 28th until New Year's eve."
Betty Botch: "Good idea. The kids will be happy. When would you propose. I think the 26th would be best. Maybe we can also call at your sister."
A: "When we are with your parents for four days and then go to Iris we cannot be back on New Year's eve. I think you will annoy the kids very much when they also have to go and visit Iris."
B: "Leave that to me. When I talk to the kids it will work out."
A: "No, this doesn't suit me. Now you are playing the kids off against me. If this is so, I have no desire to go on a trip."
B: "What's on now? The truth is, you don't want to visit my parents at all but are just looking for a good excuse to stay at home."

We can speculate about how this misunderstanding between Mr. and Mrs. Botch developed. In the beginning Alfred Botch talks about the holydays during which he would like to do something with his children. Probably an idea is forming in his wife's mind of the family doing something together during Christmas. The following information of Mr. Botch taking three additional days off fits into this, and results in the idea of a three days tour. The concrete date is ignored. Betty Botch's answer begins with "Good idea!" One could get the impression that both have the same idea. By no means! In return her husband ignores the proposed start on the 26th, since he has in mind to go on a tour between the 28th and the 31st. The suggestion to drop in with his sister is interpreted by him as a longer stay, in other words: Alfred Botch is imagining to stay with his sister after having spent three days with his parents-in-law, which interferes with his schedule. This causes his vehement rejection, which he hides behind the possibility of the children being upset. The next statement of Mrs. Botch indicates that she is not yet ready to abandon her idea. She can see them leave on the 26th, visit the sister on the 30th, to be back on time for New Year's Eve. Mrs. Botch has blinded out where her husband sees the difficulties. All she hears is the reproach of having voiced an idea that is disqualified because the children would not like it, and she plays it down at once. Her husband experiences the sentence "When I talk to the kids it will work out" as a reproach and reacts accordingly. The reaction can be even better understood when we realise that Mr. Botch believes to have to change his idea of New Year's eve he is so "fond" of, since he has understood that his wife and his children want to spend the night either with the parents-in-law or with the aunt. With her reaction, Betty Botch finally picks the fight. For her reaction she needs an explanation, and all she can come up with is the assumption that in reality he wants to stay at home.

Well, a painstaking analysis that at some points may have seemed to you like splitting hairs. Yet, everyday communication is full of misunderstandings. Especially since it is only an exception that we focus 100 % of our attention on the other. The term "divided attention" reveals the belief that we will understand the other even if we think about something else in addition. Another difficulty can be found in the latent ambiguity with which we express ourselves.

Especially when we have a very clear view of something the danger is very big that we neglect our language expressions. We forget about the possibility that our words may be interpreted by the interlocutor in a totally different way.

> The clearer something is to you, the more concentration you need to avoid inaccurate formulations.

What did Betty Botch mean with "Maybe we can also call at your sister"? I do not know which timeframe you connect with "call at somebody"; I imagine a visit of one to two hours. If I now find the effort too high for such short a visit, my resistance is unavoidable. I might let slip the following sentence: "That's not worth it". Or: "That's too much." And the next conflict is pre-assigned. In my imagination the visit was too short for the long time it would take to get there. And this clear idea ended up as the multi-purpose word "that". The other interprets my "That's too much" in relation to his own image and understands that two visits directly after another do not suit me.

What do you associate when I tell you somebody is active? Do you think he likes sports, or he is flexible, or he is engaged in a club? Or do you have something entirely different in mind?

How different images and ideas can be caused by the very same words and what a different meaning a word can have for different people, you will be able to experience with the following exercise. Maybe you have fun reading the text out to somebody aloud. Pause briefly for each "..." so that the other has time to think about his associations.

▶ **We have a weather ... I take a walk through a forest ... I walk on a pathway ... I find a cup ... I pass a water ... I go on walking and come to a house ... I take a look at the house ... and walk around it ... behind the house I see a bear ... I run back to the pathway, go on and come to a wall ... I take a closer look at the wall and find a gap ... and I peep through this gap ...**

How different the images caused by this text can be, is made clear by the following two examples, which students kindly left to me:

Under a bright blue sky I walked on a broad forest pathway, which was lined on both sides with tall old fir trees. Hardly any ray of light made its way past the branches. The ground I was walking on was soft and springy. The path was flat so that walking did not take any effort. All of a sudden a delicate collector's cup lay on the way. It was spotless white, with a gold rim and a small handle. It was lying there as if someone had put it there on purpose, upright and ready for a fill. It looked a bit mysterious. I walked on, along a narrow but happily whispering brook. The bank was steep and grown over by grass and buttercups. The water was not deep and very clear. I followed it for a while and then came to a hut, a log cabin. Very solidly built and stable it was sitting among the trees. The blinds were closed so that I assumed that nobody was at home. I had no interest in taking a look inside, but walked around the house, finding a little teddy bear on the ground children might have dropped there. I left it where it was and continued my way until I came to a wall made from fieldstones, which reached up to my knees; I could easily look over it. The landscape behind it seemed endless. Hilly meadows, meadows again, and blue sky, an inviting peacefulness was spread behind this wall.

On the opposite, the following example:

It was drizzling on a windy autumn day. I walked in deciduous woodland whose trees had already shed their leaves entirely. The trees looked bold and sticky. My way turned uphill; a narrow pathway full of stones and roots. I had to keep a constant lookout so as not to stumble and fall. I saw something white glittering and found an old cup made of thick porcelain, half burrowed into the ground, the handle lost. The saucer lay in halves by its side. I was not interested in the cup that much, so I walked on and reached a small, deep, black pool. The water was mouldy and the bank was grown over with reed. I walked on and came to an old, half-collapsed house, whose roof had been taken down by wind and weather. The wind was whistling through the broken windows. I felt a bit spooked. I shivered, this was weird. Even though I walked around the house. There, I saw a big bear, standing upright on its hind legs. I was shocked, it looked so wild and shaggy. I only calmed down when I realised that he was attached to a heavy chain. I left this unpleasant place and ran away. Some time later, I reached a high concrete wall with barbed wire fixed to the top. I found a hole big enough to put my head through. What I saw was a military camp with all types of weaponry and many soldiers. I was afraid of doing something forbidden and of being caught and punished. I went back and made up my mind to return home to my own comfortable place.

The formulation "This does not meet my ideas" proves that we switch between reality and the idea of how we would like reality to be. We are now aware that our mind constantly draws comparisons. Even in such a basic process like when estimating the size of objects from a greater distance we compare what we see to our experiences. Anthropologists found out that pygmies who solely live in the rain forest are unable to identify a herd of grazing buffalos as such. They were sure that this was a swarm of insects. Since they had never been on a wide plain before and long distances were not part of their experience they compared what they saw to what they knew, which led to the erroneous belief that these were insects.

A customer says, "This is too expensive". Even if this remark sounds absolute in the sense of independent, it contains a comparison: "The benefits stand in no comparison to the costs." Completed, the statement would read: "I have an idea of what I can expect for this amount of money. What I would get is far away from what I had in mind. This is why it is too expensive for me." Someone may argue that nobody thinks or actually talks this way. Yet, nothing else will happen when you walk over to the next takeaway and order fish and chips. If they would charge 10 pounds I assume that this would be by far "too expensive" in your opinion. Yet, too expensive only in relation to what you get. When you invite a business partner for dinner and are served a "clearly arranged" dish, which all in all will not satiate you more than the fish and chips, 10 pounds are far from being "too expensive".

Even our judgements include an unspoken comparison. Saying "I like it" becomes valid only with the background of with what it has been compared. "It's a great car," means that this car, compared under the aspects of equipment, engine power, and driving comfort to one's own previous car or to the car of the neighbour is "great".

Realising that perception always includes a comparison, professional conversation will make use of the chance to influence others and to avoid objections.

Normally, objections arise from a discrepancy between perception and idea. Due to the ongoing creation of images in one's mind it is possible to put facts into a new perspective by comparing them to something drastic.

The "clearly arranged" portion mentioned above seems to be expensive when the menu ends with £15. The same dish is rated differently when the range is 10 to £60.

A piece of clothing does not become attractive through the reduced price alone, but only through the difference between the new and the original price. With a leather jacket being reduced from £350.– to £250.–, the customer realises in the first place the savings of £100.–; that he still has to pay £250.– becomes unimportant.

It is not only easy to manipulate us with pricing, the same is true for dates which can be proposed in a way that the existing idea is replaced with a new one:

Instead of: "You would like me to come to you. In this case I would propose that we fix a date at once. But the first time I'm available is Monday morning."

Better: "I'm ready to come to see you. If you agree we can settle on end of next week. Only if it is very important for you that I come earlier. In this case I could make it next Monday morning."

Another example:

Instead of: "Payment order processing usually takes seven workdays. You'll have to wait until then."

You will achieve a different effect with the following formulation: "When you hear that some orders take a fortnight to be processed you may be shocked. Fortunately your payment order can be processed much quicker, so that you can count on an answer in seven days."

A participant in a training course told me about a successful request for a salary increase she proposed in the following way:

"When I hear from my colleagues that they would like to get €200.– more per month, I find that too much in our current situation. I'm only thinking about €100.–. And I'm fully aware that this increase would not become effective at once or even retroactively. Even if you can make it only from third quarter on, a corresponding agreement would be helpful for me."

Since we always perceive in a comparative way we can easily be influenced by images that put facts or opinions into a perspective. Compared to something horrible, the unpleasant seems to be harmless. And in return, the good is relativised when compared with the better.

> To compare professionally you need an addition to your original statement that fills your dialogue partner with relief that he can get away so easily.

When your dialogue partner says, "This does not meet my expectations" he does you a favour since he is admitting that he has an idea of reality. If you can manage to learn about his ideas you get closer to goal achievement and may even be able to meet his expectations entirely, which is real "sales success". The easiest way is a question, like for example:

"You say this doesn't meet your expectations. Can you describe to me in detail what you have in mind then. Maybe I can meet it exactly."

All too often we assume without asking, that our dialogue partner has the same idea we have, especially when he uses the same terms. It is evident that subsequently we expect the other to act accordingly, the same way we rate as appropriate in a given situation. Yet, from this assumption that the other has to view, judge, appreciate, or feel tings the way we do, everyday conflicts arise.

If we rate our arguments as reasonable, we tend to assume that our explanations will convince our dialogue partner. If this is not the case we believe the other to be pigheaded and therefore impossibly to be won over for our really good cause. During the discussion we focus solely on our own arguments and lose the dialogue partner figuratively out of sight.

When the other tries to get involved and voices doubts or objections we usually try to understand the cause of this rejection. Yet, instead of finding out with questions what he really wants to say, if his objections are caused by lack of information or lack of trust in our credibility, many people make their own assumptions about possible reasons. As long as we interpret the other's statements from our point of view, we deal more with our assumptions about the other than with the other himself. We develop ideas about possible explanations for our dialogue partner's objections, and then we state the counter-argument against our own interpretations. This may seem to be exaggerated, but many discussions are nothing else but two monologues in parallel.

At the end of a sales demonstration, the customer says: "I don't think that the new machine is as capable as what we have now."
The sales man reads his customer's thoughts and believes to understand the reasons for the rejection. Subsequently, he answers: "Our newest development is exactly made for your needs. Productivity increase by 20 %, new fields of application, much quicker, and it will open entirely new uses for you."
Customer: "Exactly! That's the very problem, that's much too complicated. Our people will be bewildered, and we need to invest more time into training. This is no use for us."

In this example the customer will hardly be aware that his rejection was caused by his imagination. The image in his mind most probably developed during the demonstration and was influenced by real pre-experiences, assumptions, emotions, and opinions. We do not need to care about how the negative answer has been formed. Yet, we can assume that the customer is sure to have carefully checked all pieces of information and that his rejection is based on rational arguments. As long as somebody is convinced to have all available information he might need for his decision, you stand no chance to influence him. This leads to the following useful rule:

> If you want to influence other people you first need to reduce their certainty.

In other words: your dialogue partner needs to understand that he is in no way in possession of all required pieces of information.

Every time you make him understand that he does not know enough about something to rate its benefits, you will increase his uncertainty. This will make him curious, and he will tend to ask you. When informing him now, you only provide him with what he has asked for. One and the same piece of information can have the opposite result, when you present it before or after being asked for it by your dialogue partner.

In my local pub, the following incident took place. At the neighbouring table, a man in his fifties announced: "I don't understand what this bloody roll of honour is good for. The Holocaust did not truly happen." Two young men at the next table were willing to join the discussion and to prove, that there had indeed been a persecution of Jews. Every argument re-bounced. For example, one of the young men said: "You can look up in every single history book what happened to the Jews."

"You can write a lot. As far as I am concerned, I don't believe a single word of what has been written. These are all atrocity tales dictated to us by the Allies."

"I've been in Dachau once. Anyone who has seen that will never have doubts again."

"Do I listen correctly? Dachau! Don't you know that the Yanks have built that up in spring 45. Every piece of it propaganda of the Allied forces."

"That's too much. There are even filmed documentations about how the concentration camp was freed."

"Very funny. These so-called documentations have been filmed in Hollywood. And do you know with what actors? German prisoners of war. You have to imagine that."

"But there are survivors. For the Schwammberger trial many of them came back to testify about what happened in the past."

"Yes, correct, they have told something. Tell is what you do with fairy tales, young man. No, no, they have all been bribed."

The discussion went on in this way for quite a while without any changes.

When I left I could not abstain from reducing the man's certainty. The following dialogue developed:

"I'm fascinated by your certainty."

"Why?"

"Well, I don't know what the sources of your knowledge are, but anyhow they seem to be above any suspicion."

"Right. I don't believe in the nonsense that has been told to us for more than forty years. I have regained my independence. If more people would think like me, Germany would be better off."

"You are certain in a very remarkable way."

"What do you mean?"

"You say that not enough people think like you do. This means that the information you have about the persecution of Jews being fake has not reached large parts of the population."

"But everyone can read it up if he or she wants to."

"You said some time ago that one could write a lot. Maybe it's not that easy to distinguish between correct and incorrect information."

"In that you are right."

"But for you this generally doesn't seem to be a problem."

"Well, I don't want to say it that way, I have been wrong at times, too. But this taught me to be even more careful."

"Now I'm surprised. With someone careful I had imagined someone who is always in search for new information. And especially with this theme there have recently been some breathtaking discoveries made."

"Why? What news? Go on, tell me!"

"I have learned from you that one tells only fairy tales. And I have none of these to tell. I have paid already and am bound to leave. I'm sure you will find the new information on your own."

I was glad to be able to leave right then, since I had no new facts at all and had bluffed.

How much this short dialogue had unsettled the other guest was reported to me by the landlady on my next visit. He tried to wriggle out from her, what my profession was, if she knew which new facts I had meant etc. To the astonishment of the landlady and the two young men my dialogue partner did not say anything about the Holocaust any more for the whole evening.

It is very common to try to make the other uncertain by voicing doubts with him and with his statements. The other way is much more promising: You name what is understood for the other, i. e. his certainty. This way an unconscious, automatic behaviour gets attention. And it loses its spontaneity. A fable may illustrate that:

A centipede met a toad and said disrespectfully: "What an ugly and plump creature you are, incapable of moving with grace." The toad looked at the centipede and answered: "I marvel at your many legs and your abilities. In every single moment you know which of your many legs you have to move." The centipede thought about the turn of which it was, and fell. The toad hopped away with grace.

Instead of offending the other with our doubts like e. g.:

"Don't be so sure."
"How do you come to that conclusion?"
"Nobody will believe that."

His attention is directed towards his own certainty

"I just realise how absolutely sure you are about it."
"I'm impressed by the certainty with which you state that."
"You are extraordinarily convinced of it."
"The way you put it, you seem to be above any doubt."

The other will start thinking about it at once and will become uncertain, which is expressed typically with the question: "Yes, why?"

Sometimes it is enough to reduce the other's certainty by expressing your astonishment, like:

"I'm surprised."
"This is astonishing."
"This makes me perplexed."

You can also begin with stating your reaction to the statement voiced with so much certainty:

"Your certainty makes me wonder."
"You say that with a certainty that leaves me speechless."
"I'm just considering if I should envy you for being without any doubt."

So acknowledging these statements may be at first sight, at the end they contribute to emerging uncertainty. Based on his experience, the other counts on objections and resistance. Instead, his certainty is affirmed without any doubts, and this paradoxically leads to **having doubts**.

You can test it yourself: Think of something you believe in with a high degree of certainty, something that is true for you without any doubts. As soon as you ask yourself what is it that makes you so sure and where you get your certainty, you will start musing about it, and promptly doubts will arise.

The previous remarks lead to a conclusion that is essential for professional conversation leadership:

People develop their own view on many questions and have a strong desire to see these visions met. If you help to fulfil this latent desire, you will not only show the other that you strive to understand him, but you also make him say "yes", to agree to your statements.

> Descriptive listening fulfils your dialogue partner's need for acknowledgement.

In chapter 3, in the paragraph about descriptive listening, you have already learned to know phrases that make the dialogue partner say "yes" spontaneously and to feel understood. I want to add the following phrases to the list.

- "For you it is important that..."
- "You value..."
- "For you the main point is..."
- "You would like..."
- "You want..."
- "You have an interest in..."
- "In your opinion we should..."
- "It's close to your heart that..."

Participants of follow-up training courses told me how helpful it is to have these phrases always available and that they have a cheat sheet next to their telephone, just in case.

To make the dialogue partner understand that he does not have sufficient information, we ask him questions until he finds out by himself that he has no answer readily available and becomes less sure of his beliefs. Yet, to avoid the questions having an unsettling effect on his self-esteem, the questions are added with an explanation. Otherwise, there is a certain danger that the question causes fear or awkward feelings in the dialogue partner since he does not know how to react. In chapter 8 about conversation killers, I had explained that in detail.

> Convincing in conversations consists of three steps: acknowledgement, question, and explanation:

(1) The acknowledgement is bound to meet the dialogue partner where he is standing at the moment.
(2) The question leads him into the desired direction.
(3) The explanation makes him feel all right.

In the example at the beginning of this chapter, an assistant tried to persuade her supervisor to buy a new scanner. As it turned out, without success. I had the chance to practice the "triple jump" of acknowledgement, question, and explanation with the assistant. Three months later, the result sounded like this:

Assistant: "For you it is important that I deal with the paperwork in a way that secretarial tasks are not effected."
Supervisor: "That's right. The office has a higher priority than the other tasks."
Assistant: "How much time do you think I should plan to use for paperwork? I am asking because in the last weeks some things had to wait due to collecting the papers for some contracts."
Supervisor: "Oh, this shouldn't happen at all. If the office does not run smoothly, we are doomed."
Assistant: "The secretarial work has predominance over all other tasks – (confirming "yes") – But what do I do in such cases? I'm not sure when something is so urgent that it cannot wait."
Supervisor: "When you ask this way, in fact nothing can wait. Of course there will always be exceptions. For example I have drafted a contract, which I will hand you later. I would like to correct it during the weekend. So I need all required papers. It's not that much, around 30 documents. And it's not urgent, tomorrow afternoon will be alright."
Assistant: "You would prefer that these tasks are done so efficiently that the office remains running without any interruptions."
Supervisor: "Well, I mean, this must be possible somehow."
Assistant: "I don't know if you have an idea how many hour I spent last week with collecting papers or stowing them away. I only ask because I have noted it down during the last two weeks and was very surprised myself."
Supervisor: "As far as I know there were merely some letters."
Assistant: "Right. And then two contracts of your colleagues, a project

report, and a closing report. I could hardly believe it but it added up to 24 hours. The week before it was less, I counted 18 hours."

Supervisor: (clearing his throat) "That's quite a lot. But there is nothing we can do about it at the moment. I don't see a chance to engage another typist. Absolutely impossible!"

Assistant: "A solution that requires additional headcount is out of the question for you. – (Approving nodding) – How expensive might a solution be that would solve the problem once and for all? I'm asking because when investing eighteen hundred Euros we could deal with most of the documents in a way they would not affect the office."

Supervisor: "Don't mention temporary personnel."

Assistant: "No, you wanted a solution that needs no headcount and that does not produce consequential costs. – ("Exactly!") – What would you think when I could concentrate on the secretarial work and even so the documents are always ready on time? There is equipment available that is hardly to be beaten by a typist."

Supervisor: "What kind of equipment?"

Assistant: "Most of the texts are given to me as files anyway. Then there are the originals and newspaper clippings, but also older texts that have been written on a typewriter or exist as a printout only. A modern scanner can transform these into files ready for data storage and even text processing."

Supervisor: "That's very interesting. Where could I take a look at that? And how much would that cost?"

Assistant: "A scanner that meets our needs would be around eighteen hundred Euros. And you would like to test that first."

Supervisor: "That would be best. Try and find a company who will give us a demonstration. Maybe we can put it through its paces for two weeks. Then we can find out if it keeps its promises."

You can imagine that the scanner has been bought.

I have to admit that this way of leading a conversation seems to be very, very long winded in the beginning. How many summersaults one has to turn to finally get to the point. Yet, if we realise which goal the assistant did pursue, this second conversation was indeed successful. In contrast to her first try she managed to meet her supervisor where he stood mentally. She adopted his idea of a frictionless running office with efficient document management simultaneously and started her argumentation at that point. He did not need to give up his idea, but was only given some additional information. Thus the idea of a possible solution emerged which was turned down immediately and vehemently. Additional headcount and temporary personnel were out of question. Only when equipment was mentioned that is hardly to be beaten by a typist he did not have a clear idea and promptly asked what that might be. This is the point at which he gets the required information, but as a service he asked for. And on the basis of this information the supervisor develops a new idea. An image in which he visualises himself as someone who tests equipment. The assistant lead this conversation so successfully because the supervisor got to like this solution and could in a way turn it into an order to her.

This is for sure not the only possible solution. I can imagine that the assistant had gotten to the point much quicker when she had stated her first 'triple jump' more directly:

"You value a quick and frictionless settlement of the necessary paperwork. (**Acknowledgement**)
To what extent would it be helpful for you if I had more time for the secretariat work? (**Question**)
I am asking because a big part of the document management could be automated." (**Information**)

Most probably this introduction had made the supervisor curious and had made him ask what she had in mind.

One participant in a training course retorted that this was all very well but if something really mattered one had to use pressure. As an example he used the regulations for the prevention of industrial accidents, especially the ones concerning wearing a hard hat. Another participant volunteered immediately to test triple jump convincing in a role-play. This lead to the following dialogue:

Supervisor: "I see that you are not wearing your hard hat. I assume it's a bit inconvenient while working."
Shift foreman: "You can say that."
Supervisor: "Under which conditions would a you wear a hard hat

then? I'm only asking because I assume that you do not thoughtlessly risk your health."

Shift foreman: "Boss, don't worry. If things get dangerous, I'll put it on. I'm not weary of life. But just now, with normal work, it's just a handicap."

Supervisor: "With the hardhead on you cannot move that freely. How can you foresee when it will become dangerous? I think for example about accidents that hit from behind."

Shift foreman: "I take care of that. I know how things work here like the back of my hand."

Supervisor: "You say with the hard hat on you feel handicapped. I'm not sure I understand how you are being constrained. Since when it becomes dangerous you put it on. And I don't hope you feel handicapped in a dangerous situation in any way."

Shift foreman: "That's something different. And anyway, how does this look. I'm the oldest here and have done the job for a while. Really, I don't need any safety garments."

Supervisor: "You experience these safety regulations as a kind of paternalism. With the hard hat on one could mistake you for a beginner."

Shift foreman: "I don't want to say it that way. But there have to be certain differences between the newcomers, who really make dangerous mistakes and the old stagers who know their job."

Supervisor: "This means that with the youngsters you take care that nobody runs around without a hard hat."

Shift foreman: "I even take care that no one runs around without safety shoes. Really, I feel responsible."

Supervisor: "You take care conscientiously for everybody minding the safety regulations. To what extent do you tempt the younger colleagues? I can imagine that one or the other wants to emulate you and leaves off the hard hat when he believes it to be safe enough."

Shift foreman: "They cannot judge this. It takes years to get really familiar with the machines. I cannot take a joke there."

Supervisor: "On one hand you mind the safety of every single employee, on the other hand you have problems setting a good example. How would your colleagues react if you as a role model would use the safety garments even if it does not seem to be that dangerous? I don't know how far the younger colleagues go by you."

Shift foreman: "Well, most probably nobody would run around without a hard hat. No matter what the task is. And if, I would flay them!"

Supervisor: "In other words: You would increase your ability to assert yourself and could make yourself heard more credibly. This is at any time better than fannying around with the workers' comp regulation."

Shift foreman: "I mean, if we all do what's prescribed, we wouldn't manage our work."

Supervisor: "This is why I prefer you being a role model anyway. If you as an experienced colleague demonstrate cautious handling of everyday hazards we have the best prerequisites for a smooth and hopefully accident-free work flow."

Shift foreman: "I more or less view it the same way."

After this conversation the listeners in the room groaned. Some people said things like:

"If I would do this with every employee."

"No, for me this is too cumbersome. If the man doesn't comply he'll have to leave."

"Where would this get us, if one is not allowed to use pressure when regulations are concerned."

"If I lead such conversations, I wouldn't manage anything else."

"That's the last thing I need, that the supervisor needs to wear a hard hat, too."

A lot of thoughtfulness emerged when the participant who had played the shift foreman had his turn:

"Before the role play I had said the very same. But I must confess that I didn't take a shift foreman's point of view for quite a while. It's true, the conversation lasted long. I had most probably struck my fist on the table much earlier and said, either you mind the regulations or it goes into your files. But after this talk I view it differently. Since now I would start wearing the hard hat, and voluntarily, because I want to be a role model. I entered the role-play with the firm intention to remain in opposition. But as it turned out I didn't have any chance for any defiance reactions. Maybe you don't believe me, but the example dialogue convinced me."

When still having the idea of wearing no hard hat, every discussion will end up being persuasive from the employee's point of view, and be it the convincing via threats. To add to this image and make him visualise himself wearing a hard hat it is required that the supervisor understands and accepts the existing image.

When analysing the video tape recording of the role-play, the participant who had played the supervisor could recognise how he had hurried ahead in his thoughts and thus missed a chance by inaccurate listening:

Shift foreman: "There have to be certain differences between the newcomers, who really make dangerous mistakes and the old stagers who know their job."

Subsequently he had an idea how he could have even better responded to the employee if he had agreed to the fact that by the uniform safety garments differences are levelled. He constructed the following answer:

"For you it is important that the difference between those who know their job and those who still have to learn a lot is made visible.
How could a solution look that would be acceptable for you?
I'm asking so directly because I am certain that you will find something that marks the differences and makes it easier for you to wear the hard hat."

In the training course, a hard hat with rank insignia was promptly invented.

Even if the triple jump proceeding may seem cumbersome and time-consuming, it is in the defined sense **effective**. Effectiveness in the sense of goal orientation means to motivate the employee without further measures in such a way that he will be engaged for common goals. If this requires an unusually long conversation, but the employee is committed to the goals afterwards, the time needed is short in comparison to ongoing control and 'motivation' measures of the common kind.

At this point I would like to quote *Henry Ford* again:

> "If there is a secret of success, it is to understand the other's point and to see things with his eyes."

Understanding does not mean approval. We can very well understand something and at the same time dislike it, as we are able to approve or disapprove of things we do absolutely not understand. Accept means here, to view a statement or an idea of your dialogue partner as given. When the other senses that we view things with his eyes his tendency to defend his idea will be markedly reduced. When we acknowledge his point of view, this has nothing to do with approval or assessment. We only let him know that we try to get his point. Everything else is subject to further discussion.

But who already knows how the solution has to look like, is well advised to continue trying his luck with persuasion and pressure. The results of this authoritarian conversation style in contrast to partnership style will be discussed again in the next chapter.

Triple Jump

Your dialogue partner needs to understand that he is in no way in possession of all required pieces of information. Every time you make him understand that he does not know enough about something to rate its benefits, you will increase his uncertainty. This will make him curious, and he will tend to ask you. When informing him now, you only provide him with what he has asked for. One and the same piece of information can have the opposite result, when you present it before or after being asked for it by your dialogue partner.

> Convincing in conversations consists of three steps: acknowledgement, question, and explanation.

- The acknowledgement is bound to meet the dialogue partner where he is standing at the moment.
- The question leads him into the desired direction.
- The explanation makes him feel all right.

To make the dialogue partner understand that he does not have sufficient information, we ask him questions until he finds out by himself that he has no answer readily available and becomes less sure of his beliefs. Yet, to avoid that the questions have an unsettling effect on his self-esteem, the questions are added with an explanation. Otherwise, the danger exists that a question causes fear or awkward feelings in the dialogue partner since he does not know how to react.

By descriptive listening (s. a.) you make the other say "yes" and feel understood. The following phrases may add to your vocabulary:

- "For you it is important that…"
- "You value…"
- "For you the main point is…"
- "You would like…"
- "You want…"
- "You have an interest in…"
- "In your opinion we should…"
- "It's close to your heart that…"

Tip: It helps to have these phrases readily available. Try out how easy it is to have a "cheat sheet" next to your telephone.

When preparing for a conversation you can prepare some triple jumps, like for example:

(1) For you it is important that …
(2) In how far would it be helpful if …?
(3) I am asking because …

(1) You want us to …
(2) What would be the consequences if …?
(3) I am touching this point, because …

(1) You value that …
(2) Under which circumstances would you …?
(3) I imagine that …

15. Delivering Unpleasant Messages

The previous chapters dealt mostly with appropriate communication manners, a better understanding for our dialogue partners, and how to balance their and our ideas of goal achievement. Some conversations however have a more unpleasant cause, their content being more or less negative for the other. Often people have problems to criticise, to convey objections and complaints, or to deliver cancellations or disappointing decisions. In professional conversation you will not experience these situations as awkward at all and do not feel the urge to use excuses.

Please imagine the following situation: You are fully concentrated on a certain task when suddenly a colleague approaches you to ask for your assistance. What in the beginning sounds like a minor question, turns into a longer conversation, and your colleague talks the hind legs off a donkey. How can you make him clear that he is disturbing you, that you have no desire to chat with him at the moment and that he is asked to – please –leave you alone?

The following reactions may seem familiar to you:

Secretly peeping at one's watch.
Being demonstratively monosyllabic, even looking away.
Continue work or start sorting files.
"I'm sorry, but I have another meeting in some minutes…"
"Excuse me, but if I don't get this ready on time I got a hell of a problem, you know…"
"Oh dear, it's already three o'clock. Time is running, man."
"See, I'd like to talk further, but with this workload I can't afford."
"Can we continue this another time? I have a visitor coming."
Get up and leave the room: "I need to see Mr. …"

This list might be continued for a while. What makes it so difficult to tell the colleague the truth in this situation and to explain to him that he is disturbing you? The typical answer reads: I do not want to offend him, hurt his feelings, or alienate him.

This answer discloses a wild assumption. Do we know for sure how the other will react? Yes, why do we suspect that he cannot cope with the truth and that therefore we have to wrap it nicely? When we are in doubt if our dialogue partner can live with a rebuff, we seemingly do not have a very positive image of him.

And here I am again with the keyword: images.

As I explained again and again in the previous chapters we continuously create images in our mind and imagine how possible reactions of others. In this context the quote from the stoic *Epictetus* may be repeated:

> "Men are disturbed, not by things, but by the principles and notions which they form concerning things."

The classification of a message as pleasant or unpleasant contains already a subjective assessment, which is not without consequences. One has to be rather cold-blooded to inform someone about something of which one assumes that it will be horrible for the other. Someone, who has to transmit something nasty will tend to arm himself beforehand against possible reactions; be it that one talks especially carefully or calmly, be it that one punches one's weight. With this it is disregarded that this behaviour can provoke exactly the feared reaction as the following example may show:

After having waited for quite a while the guest is served his lunch. Unfortunately, it is only lukewarm, the sauce has already coagulated. The guest wants to complain but fears that he might not be successful with his wish and in the worst case will be verbally attacked. Even though, he addresses the waiter, who rushes past, faint-heartedly:
"Excuse me, but in fact I had ordered a warm lunch."
Without stopping, the waiter answers:
"Oh, I'm sorry. But you see how busy we are. Be glad that you have gotten anything at all."
The guest thinks: "I'd better not said anything."

As long as we do not realise that our behaviour is influenced by our visions we will overlook that unpleasant messages and the excuses accompanying them are nothing but a reaction to our "scary fantasies".

Let us assume that the guest who has been served with a lukewarm lunch is able to concentrate on his goal and can imagine that the waiter takes back the plate to reappear after a short while with an apology and a fresh dish. He would stop the waiter in a friendly manner and maybe say something like the following:

"I can see very well that you are especially busy today and may be deaf on one ear when it comes to special requests. You will do me a favour when you even though replace my cold dish against a hot one."

I come back to the example mentioned above with the colleague whom we try to move out of our office with an excuse. With these excuses we raise the suspicion that we ourselves might not be strong enough to cope with a possible rebuff. With our well-meant excuses we really do not cast a positive light on ourselves.

Some may argue that he himself would prefer an honest ending of the conversation, but that other people might react very sensitively and vengefully. In other words: The excuses are used to save us from unwanted reactions of our dialogue partner, according to the motto: I know to whom I am talking. Yet, I want to broach the subject again: Where? What is our assumption based on that the other might feel offended, be touchy, or feel hurt? Of course we will try to avoid negative experiences as far as possible. You will also be able to find these excuses in cases where no experiences have been made before and where it is acted based on assumptions. Our ability to draw conclusions from one single event to every other and this way to generalise bears the threat to lump all people together.

In order not to arouse suspicion of being the upholder of moral standards I want to turn towards the positive side of this assumption. If you, instead of generalising, imagine concretely what your dialogue partner will feel after your statement and how he may react, you will sympathise with the other. This intuition, also named empathy, becomes a key to the other. Which special importance belongs to empathy, I have discussed in chapter 3 in the paragraph on "active listening".

> When you state what you assume to cause in the other, you demonstrate understanding for your dialogue partner.

In the example above we imagine that the colleague may feel offended or be disappointed. When we tell him about our assumption we show empathy:

"Maybe I'm alienating you now when I return to my task. I would like to finish this." Or:

"I don't know to what extent I'm disappointing you now. I would like to stop here and continue with my work."

Some may say now: "You cannot say this to anybody so openly and directly." Well, and why not? Are the excuses listed above less offensive or disappointing? Do we really think that the other believes in one of them? On the contrary. Every one of us has at one time or the other been the victim of such a pretext. Have you always been thankful that you had been spared the truth? Or did the stale taste remain which one feels when sensing disingenuousness?

When you try to empathise with your dialogue partner and talk about what you will cause anyway, you may be surprised about the reaction. The other will most likely say:

"No, you don't offend me, I didn't mean to interrupt you any longer anyway..."

"O no, you don't disappoint me. I didn't intend to stay that long anyway..."

But one may fear worse, imagine the dialogue partner being huffy or feeling mortally offended. Well, and what is against that our voicing this apprehension exactly the way it is in our mind. Since when we understand the other well enough to expect a huffy reaction we better let the other take part in our worries.

"I fear you may feel offended when I interrupt our conversation at this point. I would like to continue with my work." Or:
"I'm not certain if you will leave in a huff when I ask you to leave me to my work again. At the moment this is just a bit too much, and I don't make any progress with my work."

Especially with these examples I have never met a dialogue partner who answered:

"Well, this really offends me." Or:
"No, now I'm huffed. You want to alienate me."

Here, the partner will appease, too, and explain, that it were not that bad. And even if you have made prior experiences with this colleague and want to end the conversation anyhow I is always more honest to let him know that you know you are taking a risk.

"Even if you may be huffy..."
"Even when I risk that you won't talk to me for a week..."
"Maybe I'll tread on your toes and you will think I'm uncooperative and would rather never deal with me again. At the moment it is important for me to interrupt at this point and to return to my work."

Openness and the willingness to show empathy make this strategy almost unbeatable. Honesty has something disarming. Exactly by allowing your dialogue partner to be huffy, feel offended or alienated you give him the opportunity to choose another behaviour. Yes, to avoid behaving the way you took almost for granted he will try to resolve all doubt rather than agreeing with you.

When someone hears in the statement "The numbers seem rather high to me" the message: "I don't trust you", he is nevertheless not obliged to react stroppily: "Do you think I can't calculate." He can also address the hidden doubts in a calm manner and talk about the relationship, like:

"You are sceptical about the numbers." Or:
"At the moment you don't trust me." Or:
"You don't believe my explanations to be trustworthy."

To address the subliminal relationship statement in each message directly does not only aid clarification but leads also to an emotional distance which keeps from reacting over-emotionally. In the example the answer to the statement "You don't trust me at the moment" might read:

"Oh excuse me, I didn't mean it that way, but it would help me if you could briefly name your sources."

And so this would be settled. Yet, you could also get the reaction:

"If you really want to know it, yes, in my eyes your explanations are biased and sugar-coated."

Maybe such an answer will now alienate you. But now we know where we stand. Instead of reaction in an offended manner we are also allowed to express our astonishment:

"In this case I'm surprised that you still continue our negotiations."

I have chosen the feeling of doubt on purpose for the example. Most people are not very skilled in voicing their doubts. And in every conversation we deal with the question how far one can trust the other or if one tends to be careful about the given arguments. This uncertainty is hidden behind a "matter-of-fact" facade, according to the motto: "I beat the sack and mean the donkey." Since emotions can hardly be influenced on a factual basis, the following rule applies: Doubts do not cease when one is told that these doubts are unnecessary. On the contrary!

Remember your experiences with this matter: How reliable is someone who swears to tell the truth? Where is your scepticism when you are told you can look it up "in cold print"?

Clarifying the relationship aspect also means here: to respect the dialogue partner and his emotions and to acknowledge his right to have doubts and reservations. It is paradoxical that emotions vanish the quickest when they are accepted.

We can take one further step: in many situations we can guess which arguments may be difficult to accept by the audience and may raise significant doubt. Yet, before your dialogue partners can declare them, you will beforehand give them a kind of allowance to have doubts on the relationship level:

"Maybe this sounds unbelievable in your ears." Or:

"I can well imagine that these numbers may seem totally exaggerated to you and that you'll have doubts about the seriousness of this analysis." Or:

"Maybe you are very sceptical now and think about how trustworthy I am in your eyes."

> This technique can be called "to take the bull by the horns". The other is really taken seriously and does not have to disagree in a pseudo-factual way.

When you name what you may cause inside the other beforehand, you do not only prove understanding for your dialogue partner, but you also produce a kind of spontaneity paradox. What does this mean?

You deprive an involuntary reaction from its spontaneity when you explicitly allow its formation.

I received the following letter from a training course participant:

I have used your method "deliver unpleasant messages" very successfully with our department mimosa. For years we have let her tyrannise us. Everything that does not fit her concept she will shove to other colleagues, and anyone who does not jump and run will be treated so icily that the rest of the department is happy when peace has been, at least partially, restored. Recently she tried to sneak out of preparing the charts and documents for a presentation and asked me to take the task over since this would be all too much for her. Luckily, I had practiced silently before so that I did not have to think about my answer:

"Even at the risk that you think I'm totally uncooperative, I cannot fulfil your wish. I have so much on my plate which would have to wait then that I run the risk of you avoiding me like the plague for a week"

"Why do you think that I might avoid you?"

I had not expected that question but tried to answer honestly anyway: "This was more meant as a worry. On the contrary, I do prefer getting along well and working in harmony."

I would never have expected that our over-sensitive colleague might answer:

"I totally agree. About the charts, I will manage that. I didn't know that you have so much to do or of course, I would not have asked you in the first place. But since you said it so openly, I'm really not angry."

In the meantime I get along with our "prima donna" as we sometimes

have called her rather well. She is very friendly to me. She has a totally unusually cooperative side and shows first signs of helpfulness, so that I feel obliged to meet her halfway.
To my great astonishment she treats the other colleagues like before. I am curious to see when the others will copy my behaviour.

Mind you, this way to deliver unpleasant messages is not a fad or a trick. It is the expression of personal and honest empathy. Whoever prefers to learn the phrases listed here by heart instead of trying to sense the momentary emotions of the other person will be seen through more easily than he would like.

I can remember how annoyed I was by a colleague who usually began delays or short notice cancellations with the words:
"Maybe you are angry, but I will not be able to make the meeting at 2 pm." Or:
"You may be pissed off because I haven't come until now. I'm really sorry but earlier was impossible."
With these stereotyped, sketched phrases I did not feel understood at all. After having thought about it for a while I realised with which formulations he had really expressed understanding and with which it would have been difficult for me to vent my anger. With the following statement he could have expressed real empathy:
"I cannot really make the meeting at 2 pm. Maybe you get the impression that I don't take agreements with you seriously, and I am risking to offend you." Or:

"I can understand if it alienates you when I'm late. I seem to show you that everything else is more important than the meeting with you."

This example may show that authenticity and credibility are strongly related to an open behaviour. Because after this start dates and minutes would not be talked about but the actual emotions and the assumptions related to them. A constructive dialogue might for example be continued like this:

"That's not entirely wrong. The meeting with you was very important for me and I had especially rescheduled other things, and from you I get the impression that I'm an also-ran. Especially since this has happened before."

What happens afterwards is a clarification of the relationship. The colleague would have the chance to explain how he sets his priorities and how important or unimportant I am for him, how he experiences my expectations and how he tries to meet them. And the other way around I had the chance to find out what the goals were which I need the colleague to achieve.

In this context I want to mention again that our right brain hemisphere is unable to imagine negative orders. In training course exercises I often notice that participants understand that empathy allows access to the dialogue partner, but they want to avoid negative statements if possible, which leads to some typical phrases:

"Please don't be disappointed, but..."
"I do hope you won't get angry if..."
"Please, don't get upset, but..."
These formulations offer an emotional image (e.g. disappointment), which one is to not able to imagine. Who will be surprised that the reaction sounds accordingly:
"I am not angry, just to make that clear, right?!!!"

Our natural behaviour loses its spontaneity promptly as soon as it enters conscience, or said in another way: **There is no conscience spontaneity.**

You can verify this any time by asking someone to get to his feet spontaneously and to stand relaxed. Who tries to follow this request will usually get up stiffly and tries to force an inner poise when standing, which looks anything but natural and at ease.

The same will happen to you when you, while doing something you are expert in, become aware of how well you are doing it. At once, the pianist will make mistakes, the tennis crack misses a ball, and the typist get mixed up whilst typing letters. The natural flow of an action is interrupted as soon as it enters our conscience. Even falling asleep will not work when we try to concentrate on it.

We can use this phenomenon to manage unwanted spontaneous behaviour. For example, think of a hiccup. As long as it remains involuntary, a hiccup is not or hardly to be influenced. Very different with the request: “If you can hiccup ten times in the next two minutes, you will get five Euros.” When you hiccup at will, a new situation arises. The concentration on the reward leads to muscle tension in the midriff that stands against a “natural” hiccup. Other spontaneous reactions can be influences according to the same pattern. Laughter will die after the request: “Please, go on laughing!” Maybe you have already noticed that some people prevent success when telling a joke by beginning with the words: “With the next one you'll die of laughter...”

It is a dirty trick to trip people by drawing attention to the natural course of action, which suddenly becomes so conscious that one clenches. One may be immune to the typical cry “this one fails” when bowling, but the best bowling champion will in the truest sense stumble over remarks like “That's really amazing to see, that you start with this leg, how you kick off, and at what angle you let go.” The grace of a well-practiced movement does not go along with observation and conscience.

In chapter 3, I had explained for **active listening,** how important it is to address the other's emotions so that the other will feel understood. Now another advantage of addressing emotions directly appears:

When you actively listen to your dialogue partner's emotions by naming them you will at the same time hinder the spontaneous expression of these emotions.

> Name behaviour you want to prevent. Make spontaneous behaviour conscious.

I admit that some inexperienced readers may have problems with telling a fuming opponent that one understands his anger and is well able to imagine it.

A customer complains in a loud voice: "It's a real drag. We had made it crystal clear that we need the delivery this very week. Now it is Friday, and we don't have any raw material for the weekend shifts. This will cost you something, I can tell you."

Whoever wants to come to the facts right away according to the motto: "Don't add fuel to fire" will only listen to the objective side of the furious customer, who is too deeply involved in his own emotions to be able to switch, and this is why such a dialogue usually escalates all too easily:

Is the customer blamed for something or has it really been his fault, an explosion might be initiated:

"Let me please take a look at the order. Yes, indeed, you have ordered 2000 pieces of xyz, but the delivery date is missing."
"Do I hear correctly? What did I phone you for to explain how important this delivery is? Or are you deaf on this ear."

Even if it was our fault and a fact-based excuse follows suit, this will hardly help:

"Yes, we are really sorry. We had problems with a supplier, so that we ran out of stock. It's not our fault, though."
"Do you want to bring tears to my eyes? I'm not interested in where you get your material. Our production is on hold for the weekend, because you did not deliver. This will have consequences for sure!"

Even an immediate solution for the problem does not take care of the anger and will provoke further attacks:

"Of course we will deliver on time. I'll take care at once, that you get an express delivery today."
"Is that really true? You only send the delivery because I've taken care of it myself now. I can't believe it!"

Some try to calm down the angry caller, which almost in every case goes wrong:

"Now please do calm down first..."
"I *am* calm, but you won't be in a minute, now listen..."

When we realise that we can best show the other with **sympathy** and **respect**, that we try to understand him, the following formulation may be helpful:

"You are outraged because we have left you in the lurch with this delivery. I can understand how worried you are about the weekend shifts. If we don't find a solution at once you are in a bad position."

Active listening answers the primary need: "I want to be respected and understood."

In addition you guide the self-perception of the other person by making his emotions conscious.

It is a difference if you, for example, feel you are angry or if you think: "This makes me angry". Or out of a slightly greater distance: "I react to XY with anger". When we are conscious of our momentary feelings we are not at their mercy any longer.

Being **conscious** about something allows us to gain **distance**.

We can use this knowledge not only for self-control purposes, but also in leading conversations for **aimed behavioural changes**. Each time you describe what the other is doing you prevent **spontaneous** continuation of this behaviour. If it is continued this can only be at will, i. e. conscious.

Since this proceeding is not very common, I want to add some examples to show the range of possible applications:

One dialogue partner gets so excited about his own view that you can hardly get a word in edgewise.

"You want to explain your ideas without any interruption." Or more directly:
"You want to convince me in any case." Or:
"You can hardly accept that I take another view." Or:
"You are very intolerant when someone does not agree." Or:
"You want me solely to listen (or: agree)."

Sometimes, dialogue partners will interrupt us and common phrases like "May I finish" or "I haven't finished yet" do not help. Next time you may try one of the following formulations:

"You are interrupting me." Or:
"Your thought seems to be so important for you that you want me to shut up." Or a bit more moderately:
"I shall stop explaining my idea now." Or:
"I'm not sure if you are interested in what I wanted to say." Or very directly:
"You would like to talk now."

In another situation your dialogue partner does not show any willingness to take you seriously. You can state exactly that fact:

"You have problems respecting me." Or:
"At the moment you don't want to take me seriously." Or:
"You don't want to deal with my desire now."

I received the following letter from a participant:

I was able to test the spontaneity paradox at my entrance door, when two members of a sect tried to force a conversation about religion on me. As an answer to my statement: "You would like me to join your belief." I first got a "No, that's not the point... on the other hand... see..." After I had broached the subject again they admitted what their goal was. On this I could only say: "You have problems with accepting other religious beliefs." Since both could not make up their mind for an open "Yes", they tried to evade: "No, not really, but..." This gave me the chance to tell them how I felt: "Since you have problems to accept my religious beliefs I don't feel respected. This is why I want to end this conversation right now. Have a nice day."

> Describe to your dialogue partner what you perceive or assume of him. This way you can interrupt a spontaneous course of action.

The first dialogue from chapter 1 might have developed in a totally different way if the supervisor, Mr. Quick, had considered this point:

Quick: (*Takes the receiver and dials*) "Good morning, Mr. Black, here's Quick. Could you just come to my office now? You may be surprised: I want to talk about a job change, which I can offer you. I'd like to talk to you about it. – – – Yes, you are right, it's a bit on short notice. – – – No, there are no immediate decisions required. I'd like to know your ideas about it. Do you have time now? I have another meeting at 10 am. – – – OK, see you.
(*Knock at the door.*) Come in! – Please, take a seat, Mr. Black. Thank you for having time now. Maybe I will unsettle you with the offer to go to Chile for two years. You may have heard that we will open a new subsidiary in Santiago de Chile in January."

Black: "I have though of a lot, but not that! Indeed! – – – This is very unexpected."

Quick: "I think I have unsettled you pretty much."

Black: "Yes, well . . . – It's more the thought about the Newton project. We'll need at least four months for that. You are aware how big the initial problems are. I really have to take pain. And now to drop it just like that– no, not really."

Quick: "I believe I can understand how much it annoys you that you have done all the spadework. And when it becomes interesting, others will harvest the fruits. Maybe you even have the impression we want to get you out of the way."

Black: "I don't want to say that– but my heart's blood is in the Newton project. Can't I close it first?"

Quick: "You would feel better if you could complete the project work."

Black: "Sure, – although it's not really necessary: When everything is up and running, others can take over as well."

Quick: "You can think about the offer to go to Chile more easily when you get a promise that you can set the Newton project running first."

Black: "Yes – – – No – – – Nonsense! I am just fooling myself. If I had an accident tomorrow it would also work out. And I'm not out of the world. I can keep contact with the colleagues via email and tell them about my ideas. –. –. –. At the end, what you say sounds rather promising."

Quick: "That sounds as if you are still hesitating."

Black: "True. Two years in Chile – this is not only work-related – it is also a question of how my wife reacts to it. Fortunately, our children are so young that I don't have concerns about that."

Quick: "I can understand your doubts. On the contrary, I think I would have been surprised if you did not hesitate. Such a decision needs to be thought over."

Black: "Thank you. --- My wife and I held forth about this a while ago, after all we have both learned Spanish because we can well imagine living in the South for a while. That it is so deep in the South that is what I have to break to her gently. If you tell me some more about the job and my tasks, it may be easier."

Maybe you have noticed that the positive example statements are lacking the word "but". **But** is a way to mark the beginning of an objection or a contradiction. Other conjunctions with a similar effect are "however", "though", or "only". As a common denominator we can memorise for professional conversation:

The words "but", "however", "though", and "only" always express a restriction and that something stands against what has been said before.

A sentence with "but" is a negation of the previous sentence.

You may often find that a "but" clause is preceded by a statement that has more or less a "wrapping" character. The well known "Yes, but..." technique uses this as a trick. The dialogue partner is lulled by an agreeing pre-statement, so that he does not feel the negation or restriction that deeply.

"Yes, you are totally right, but in this case it is entirely different..."
"I agree, but you have to consider the following..."
"Yes, of course, I view it the same way, but you have overlooked that..."

You will observe that "but" sentences follow a certain scheme:

In the first part the dialogue partner is addressed in a "nice" way, and in the "but" part one voices one's own position. Normally the most important content is expressed in the main clause, while the subordinate clauses are used to add something. With "but" this principle is inverted. What is really important is introduced with the added "but".

The effect of the word "but" is to contrast to aspects of something and to devalue one of these.

To verify this, you can turn a "but" statement around, i. e. you put your desire into the first clause and that of your dialogue partner into the "but" clause. This is done most easily with the natural reactions of children:

"I would like to sit here and read in peace, but you want me to play with you."
"I think inline skates are much too expensive, but you are longing for them."
"I am against that you are coming home at midnight, but it is very important for you."

In chapter 5 on "Guidance and Regard" and in chapter 11 "Behaviour is Goal-Oriented" I had explained that we make a possible agreement or concession dependent on whether we feel respected. In the three examples one's own position is named without any mitigation, but is weakened by the following "but" clause. The dialogue partner gets a chance to "sell" his wish in a better way. At the same time we deal with the opposing position in a more factual way than it would have been the case if the statements had been put the classical way. When we realise that **regard** is a prerequisite for successful communication, we will change the classical, **disregardful** pattern

- You want x, but I want y

Into a **respectful** one:

- I want x, but you want y.

Here I want to emphasise again that when showing esteem and respect for our dialogue partner we do not have to give up our own position at all. It proves that after a respectful beginning a conversation takes a turn so that the opposition of the two point of views is eliminated and suddenly one can talk about **the goals behind the goals**. Regarding the examples: What do the inline skates stand for? What is the meaning of coming home late? What makes playing together so attractive at the moment?

Some reader may even have eliminated "but" since he has already found out that a simple "and" is even better able to avoid possible controversies.

> When replacing "but" by "and" you can reduce conflicts. You demonstrate that two opinions can exist in parallel.

Many people use "but" statements and try to "hide" a possible conflict out of a certain disliking of confrontations. It is always impressive how well we can sense a "but", even if the first clause is extended in an eloquent way. I will always remember a participant who criticised the seminar with the words:

"This training course was really entertaining, not only due to the social events in the evening, but also because of the different contents and presentations. I have heard a lot of new things in these three days and I was surprised how many things you can detect in a video analysis. Much will become part of a changed behaviour, while I cannot say what this will be in detail. But when I ask myself what I have really learned, I have to say: nothing, or almost nothing."

After this devastating judgement he leant back in his seat, satisfied or even self-pleased, and handed over to his neighbour.

You may object and say that such an elaborate, but empty speech is hardly to be found in everyday communication. I have a different view. One recommendation to be found in many books, to create a positive atmosphere at the beginning of a conversation, is often misunderstood. Supervisors talk about the last vacation, inquire after relatives, or want to know in general if the employee is well, before they – sometimes rather abruptly – turn to the real issue: "..., but what I wanted to talk to you about..."

Especially with messages which one considers to be unpleasant, it is common practice to say some nice things before getting to the point.

A managing director has asked a salesman into his office:

"You know that I have always been very satisfied with your performance. There has never been a reason to complain. It is your engagement that makes you stand out from the rest of the department. When we get under pressure and can cope with the demand with extra engagement only, I know I can rely on you. We all value your sense of humour and the cooperative way with which you contribute to our team spirit, but what you have done in the case of Katz & Co., that's much more than a forgivable mistake, that's near to a deliberate act. I have here a letter of three pages. What you are accused of here should make me get rid of you or at least admonish you. But I won't be so. You go and visit Katz & Co. and take care that everything gets back into the right order and then let's forget it. But if I hear another complaint I'll put an end to it. I hope we have understood each other."

You will understand that after such a dressing down the employee will not remember any of the appreciative statements he heard from his supervisor at the beginning.

The inverse case can also be found sometimes. Particularly with criticism some supervisors tend to get directly to the point. And if the employee reacts shocked, everything said before is cut down with a "but".

A department head criticises a clerk with the following words:

"Say, what did you think, when you decided to sign this contract yourself and put it into the outbox. You know very well that we have a rule, which states as clear as daylight that such a transaction has to pass my desk. You can be glad that I have checked the outgoing mail yesterday evening. What you did comes close to insolence, and I am thinking about making an exempla."

(The totally shocked and paralysed employee takes out her handkerchief and starts crying silently. Her voice choked in tears she begins: "I only wanted to . . ." But her supervisor interrupts her and continues with a much milder voice:)

"You don't have to worry, we won't fire you because of this. And you know how much I value your work. On the contrary! Because of your great experience you cannot be missed in our department. I'm also often delighted by your helpfulness and loyalty. Some of your colleagues could learn a lesson from you. Well, now you know what I wanted. I hope that I can further rely on you in future."

In this case the employee will with a high degree of certainty repress the harsh words from the beginning of the conversation and reassemble herself with what the supervisor had said with benevolence and appreciation at the end.

The recommendation to create a positive atmosphere at the beginning of a conversation means, primarily when talking to employees, but also in sales or with customers, means to provide the other with the emotional certainty necessary to relax and prepare for the discussion. What may move an employee who has been called to see his supervisor? What thoughts may be in his head?

"What does he want from me?"
"Have I bungled something?"
"Is he looking for a culprit?"
"What does he want to get me to now?"
"How long will I have to sit here?"
"When will I be able to continue my work?"
Etc.

For professional conversation we can bear in mind that there are three points with which we can contribute greatly to our dialogue partner's emotional confidence.

> At the beginning of a conversation, explain the **time frame**, your **goals**, and your **expectations** to the dialogue partner.

- How many topics; and how long will the meeting most likely last?
- What is the meeting aiming at?
- What exactly is expected from the dialogue partner?

If you assume that fears may rise in your dialogue partner you can start with a corresponding empathic statement. This way you can meet the other where he stands, and it will take less effort to make him deal with your thoughts and expectations.

For the examples mentioned above this would lead to the following formulations:

The managing director asks a salesman for a meeting and tells him at once:

"Before you get worried about this meeting I just want to tell you upfront what it is all about. In the next ten minutes I would like to talk to you about a letter of Katz & Co., which contains five major reproaches to you. With this meeting I would like to achieve that our trustful relationship remains intact as a basis for future cooperation. In detail I would like you to give me your opinion on the different accusations, and then we can consider together what you and I can do to avoid customer reactions of this kind in future."

The department head asks the clerk for an interview and after the words "Please, take a seat" begins with:

"Maybe you are surprised or even worried since I have asked you for a meeting in this unusual way. In the next five minutes I want to talk to you about one topic in our work rules, which you obviously interpret differently from me. The purpose of this conversation is to clearly fix

your competencies so that neither I get annoyed about you nor will you get the impression that I interfere with your responsibilities. In particular, I would like to talk about the contract with Smith & Company where the final amount exceeds by far what you usually sign for."

These beginnings give the employee clear orientation and enable them to prepare for the coming dialogue. Orientation is mostly given by naming the **goal**, since the goal usually reaches far beyond the

single conversation. Especially criticism is often lacking a corresponding explanation of what the purpose of the conversation is. This is even more important, since employees tend to catastrophise and fear that they will be admonished or even fired because of a mistake. In this context it has to be mentioned that many supervisors, teacher, and even parents enjoy that the dialogue partner is at their mercy. You may have experienced something like the following example yourself.

"I expect you know why I have called you." (Pause)
"To be honest: no."
"Well, then think about it." (Pause)
"Well, to be frank, I cannot think of anything right now."
"So you would like me to help you. Well, just play up, what shot up in your mind spontaneously when you entered my office."
"Well, yes, I have somehow thought you may not be satisfied with me, that I have made a mistake or so."
"Aha. Not satisfied, made a mistake, ey."

Some readers may react with disbelief and say they cannot imagine that someone treats his subordinates in this manner. And maybe these readers will at once add that they would not dream of treating other people in this way. Yet, when in a training class I ask the participants to revisit their childhood, school and education time, they recall horrible memories. Suddenly one sees his late father in front of his eyes who began his dreaded philippics this very way. Another one recalls a teacher or an instructor who conducted their horrible grillings in this style. And when I ask people in this state of actual shock in which area they have the greatest problems with their current supervisors, I get answers like:

"I never know where I stand with him."
"I would feel much better if he told me what he really thinks about my performance."

"Once I have done something that does not meet his ideas I'll hear about it again and again until I feel really inferior. But how to do it better or right, I'll have to find that out on my own."

A department head told me: "I once said to the site director: 'Okay, I have understood that you don't like that, but please tell me how to do it differently in the future.' And I got in return: 'Well, then start to think about it. What do you think we are paying you for?'

"When my current boss is in a bad mood he can really knock the stuffing out of you. Then he's dwelling on the details until one does not know left from right. And when you think it's over he says 'Stop. That wasn't all . . .' and starts all over again."

When criticising, one is always in danger to start looking for causes and to turn towards the past. This is accompanied by latent reproach for not having behaved as desired. Who gets down to the level of fact analysis will all to easily get into a maelstrom of accusations and dogmatism.

Constructive criticism can have only one goal: How will the dialogue partner change his behaviour in the way we imagine? How can certain problems be avoided in the future? A lamentation about past transactions, which cannot be altered anyway, will have dissatisfying results, if you do not count the sadistic fun in slagging someone off. Nagging often looks like looking for a reason to deliver an "important speech".

> Whoever criticises in a constructive way will at first think about the desired target behaviour.

Take a look at your vision first and verify that the criticism is apt to lead to it. If this is not the case you can rather save the energy. In this case it may be useful to verify if the formulations used are better able to sustain the critical behaviour instead of stopping it. In chapter 6, "Resistance with the Dialogue Partner" I had explained how we cause reactance with the dialogue partner, even without being aware of it.

Now I have talked lengthily about how to criticise and you may have gotten the impression that supervisors only have unpleasant messages for their subordinates. The following example will show the wide range of areas of application for these conversation rules.

From lawyers, tax advisors, and consultants I often hear how difficult it is for them to assign a timeframe for a meeting. They shy away from open confrontation out of fear that their client could move to a competitor. They rather put up with the resulting time loss and distress than to skate on the ice in an open discussion. Now there are always people (clients, customers, patients,) who view lack of structure as an invitation to display their experiences and thoughts in great detail and to talk a leg off a donkey.

I just remind you of what your dialogue partner is interested in in the first place:

> How many topics do we have or how long will the meeting probably last?
> What is the meeting goal?
> What is expected of the dialogue partner?

For example you could welcome a visitor when accompanying him to the meeting room or while you lead him to your office with the following words:

"I've just taken another look into the files. I assume that in the next twenty minutes you expect me to address the following four topics in a way that afterwards you can make a decision with which you will be satisfied..."

A tax advisor told me on a follow-up training course that with new clients he used the following formulation:

"You are new in our office. So I assume that for you it is most important to find out if you want to cooperate with me at all. In the next fifteen minutes I want to carefully address your requirements, so that you can verify before going into the details how far your ideas will be met. I think that the following three questions will help you on this way..."

Sometimes I am reproached with the fact that giving a time frame means a dangerous limitation and may offend the dialogue partner since you announce in the beginning that you are going to chuck them out. On the contrary! First, this is a very suggestive formulation as talked about in chapter 6 "Resistance with the Dialogue Partner". The term "in the next twenty minutes" is not only a clear goal statement but is also apt to help the other to develop an idea of the **next** twenty minutes. And nothing has been said about how the conversation will go on afterwards. There are meetings that after completion of the topics continue in a more personal and effectual way.

Anyone who can make it within the estimated twenty minutes now has the chance to thank his dialogue partner for his active participation:

"Great! I just noticed that we made it within the timeframe. In order to give you an idea of what's necessary now I will...

- talk about the next steps, or
- schedule another meeting with you or
- send you the answer of the opposite party as soon as I get it, or
- introduce you to one of my colleagues who will take over your affairs."

Whoever against all expectation finishes earlier does not have to sit through the fixed time but can after a brief glance at his watch say for example:

"I have just seen that we have clarified these points much quicker than I had thought. I think this is mainly because of you, thank you."

If one gets to one's feet afterwards and ends the meeting also via body language or if one talks with the other about other things does not only depend on one's style but also on the further intentions regarding this dialogue partner.

And anyone who will, beyond his estimation, need more time can after another glance at the watch take the chance to involve the dialogue partner into further planning and say for example:

"I just see that we will need some more time. Do you mind if we add ten more minutes to really finish this point?"

This formal question gives the other the opportunity to allow you more time voluntarily. The most probable "Yes, of course" is also a "Yes, for ten minutes, but not more".

In this chapter I want to come back to the “Enchiridion” by *Epictetus* and quote the fifth paragraph which deals with mistaking one’s ideas for the real things:

> “Men are disturbed, not by things, but by the principles and notions which they form concerning things. Death, for instance, is not terrible, else it would have appeared so to Socrates. But the terror consists in our notion of death that it is terrible. When therefore we are hindered, or disturbed, or grieved, let us never attribute it to others, but to ourselves; that is, to our own principles. An uninstructed person will lay the fault of his own bad condition upon others. Someone just starting instruction will lay the fault on himself. Some who is perfectly instructed will place blame neither on others nor on himself.”

The title of this chapter, “Delivering Unpleasant Messages” needs to be restated as “Messages of which one assumes that they will be unpleasant”. You will agree that such a formulation sounds rather baroque and had to be replaced by a shorter title. *Epictetus* teaches us to consider that nothing is unpleasant on its own account. It is but our imagination that makes us react or carries us away.

Some may appease and object out of their everyday experience: “Well, but if this were the case, there wouldn’t be any problems in the world.” These critics I want to say:

That something is simple does not mean that it is easy.

Why we struggle with differentiating between something and our idea about it, is related to language. Since the main part of our thinking is language-bound there is a connection between the structures offered by language and what we “normally” think. I want to draw your attention on a small and unimpressive word in our language, the word “is”.

The use of “is” as an **auxiliary** does not produce any problems.

He is coming.
She is travelling.
It is happening.

Likewise, we will not be taken aback when reading “is” as a **main verb**, when we want to express the existence of something.

It is ready.
She is at home.
He is there.

But often we use "is" similarly to the equal sign in arithmetic. We put up an equation between a thing and a word. We create identity.

This is a house.
She is a mother.
He is a salesman.

And into this "is" for **identity** we all too easily integrate our personal opinions and judgements. You can test which idea you get spontaneously when reading the following example statements:

This is a homosexual.
He is a drug pusher.
She is a bitch.

You see how your emotions have been influenced. A neutral classification becomes "opinion making" underhand and can be used on purpose. You can test it yourself:

What do you associate with:
"This is a herb"?
And which impression do you get when you read:
"This is a pest plant"?

This becomes fatal when we get to the fourth use of the harmless-looking "is":

This painting is marvellous.
She is a good mother.
He is a bad presenter.

In contrast to the "is" for identity, this is an "is" expressing an **opinion**. Unfortunately, only very few people are aware of the difference between the various uses of "is". On the contrary, there is a widespread opinion that something that "is", is also "so". Yet, in contrast to "This is a stone" the statement "He is a bad presenter" has other consequences. Imagine a discussion with someone who says, no, this speaker is wonderful and can be compared to Cicero.

Shakespeare said, taking pattern from *Epictetus*:

> "Nothing is either good nor bad, but thinking makes it so."

Our very private projections creep into our neutral "this is" statements. That water is neither hot nor cold you may know from the physics experiment where you put one hand into a bowl of water with a temperature of 10 °C and the other into water with 30 °C. When you afterwards move your hands together into a bowl with water of 20 °C, one hand will transmit "very warm", while the other hand rates the same water as "rather cool". As I mentioned several times, we constantly compare reality to ideas and impressions. This complicated process of reception is not reflected in our language, we even neglect it with "This is the way it is" statements. Now we will not be able to alter our language, since for several millennia we have talked in subject-predicate-object sentences. Yet, we can be aware of the limitations of our language and especially of the simplifying "is" and form sentences, which really express the subjective character of a statement, like:

"I didn't like the presenter at all." Or:
"I found the rhetorical skills of the presenter rather mediocre."
And an answer could read:
"I've hardly ever heard such a wonderful presenter." Or:
"I can't believe that Cicero has been a better speaker than this one."

The difference to the previous statements is that in expressing clearly a personal statement the claim to "be right" is greatly reduced.

This detailed excursus into our language was to demonstrate that it is up to us if we assume messages to be unpleasant or if we see the chance for a change that is hidden in them. Everyone can try out for himself to what extent he is willing to take over responsibility for his visions, the opinions related to them, and the resulting reactions.

16. Chances in a Complaint

How often does it happen that something does not meet our expectations. Even if we are unaware of it: We are disappointed. Disappointed. In the truest sense of the word it expresses that a hope or expectation remains unfulfilled, that we do not get what has been "fixed" in our mind. In other words: the image we had in our head does not compare to what we get from reality; reality failed to keep the appointment we had in our mind. Maybe you are asking yourself what this has gotten to do with complaints. Some of the statements in this chapter may be easier to follow for you when you connect them to your personal experience. Since I assume that you have complained several times, be it in a restaurant or on a journey, in a workshop or to a craftsman, I am asking you now to close the book for a moment and try to remember cases when you had to complain about something.

You have an example in your mind now.

Now please spontaneously answer the following questions:

▸ **What exactly did happen and how did you feel about it?**

▸ **What emotional state were you in at the beginning, and how did the conversation start?**

▸ **How have you been treated, and how did you feel afterwards?**

Anyone who does not see his expectations met in a certain area, will spontaneously react with negative feelings, is discontented and upset. Depending on the intensity of the personal presumptions, indignation will arise or even the feeling of having been deceived. This negative and impairing emotional reaction stands at the beginning of each disappointment, no matter if we have the intention to criticise or prefer to let the matter rest.

But our feelings can be further influenced in a negative way,

- If we are in an awkward position, for example when we **have to answer** our superior why "our supplier" suddenly has quality problems or when we are **upbraided** by production because of a late delivery;

- When the brand-new dish-washer has flooded the kitchen or when we cannot record a thriller because the newly delivered video tape recorder does not work;
- When we feel a certain **helplessness** when finding out that we cannot solve a problem on our own account;
- When we are **angry about ourselves**, for example when we buy something without taking a closer look at it or forget to have a device tested or have the functions demonstrated to us;
- When we are spontaneously reminded of all the **circumstances** it takes to reinstall the desired state, be it that we have to return to the shop, be it that we have to state our complaint in a letter or on the phone, or that we need to look for another supplier;
- And when we imagine how we will be **treated** when we complain. For many people this imagination can be so frustrating that they rather abstain from complaining at all to spare themselves the humiliation in addition to the already existing anger.
- And last not least sometimes certain **remorse** arises. Our decision that seemed to be all right until now is questioned: Was it right to buy something here? Was the price fair? Should we have delayed the payment? Wouldn't it have been helpful to look for alternatives?

This list of unpleasant feelings could surely be added to. It can be said:

> Anytime you are confronted with a complaint, make sure to remember which negative mood your dialogue partner may be in.

Turned the other way, this detailed observation of our state of mind may show, which extraordinary amount of energy is required to be successful despite this negative starting point.

Anyone who complains feels that he is right. All too easily this results in an attitude, which wrongly blames the other from the start. This negative mood discussed before often results in stubborn fixation to one's own point of view. **In an emotionally unstable state, the ability to think is reduced**, creativity and flexibility get lost when dealing with problems. This overshadows the beginning of a complaint conversation. For fear of not being taken seriously, many peo-

ple chose the wrong tone in the beginning; they behave demandingly, are sometimes rude or arrogant. In addition, many customers go like a bull at a gate when complaining and expect immediate fulfilment of their request, special treatment and a quick solution. At the same time customers can radiate quite a portion of distrust, resulting from previous bad experiences, and so influence the conversation atmosphere from the start.

Anyone who complains tends to state his expectations in form of a claim, aiming at making the other feel responsible. All too easily, in the heat of the battle the required appreciation gets lost. The dialogue partner who deals with the complaint feels offended, since it is implied that he is not only responsible for the mistake but has even made it on purpose. All too often this becomes the basis of a struggle in which on the long run nobody will be winning. You may argue that the one who complains has the legitimate wish to get an adequate return on his investment (usually money). In addition, a complaint is always combined with a time loss, sometimes added by a loss of money.

But this chapter does not only address people who have to deal with complaints, but can also show which opportunities we lose in case of a complaint if we try to get what we deserve out of a position we assume to be more powerful.

> The wish for being taken seriously is equal on both sides.

Anyone who is destined to accept reproaches, to react in a friendly way to harsh demands or to being "crucified"? While dealing with the actual defect is the duty of the supplier, **the responsibility for the atmosphere lies at 50 % with us**. In the chapter "Behaviour is Goal-Oriented" I have discussed how largely our willingness to cooperate, to meet halfway, to give in, or to be generous is dependent from how well we feel in a given situation and if we feel taken seriously and respected. Whoever voices his justified request with appreciation does not only have the chance to be successful in the given case but builds a partnership style basis for future occasions.

At the end of a complaint conversation, one ends up with either a good or a bad feeling. This is independent of having achieved our goal or not. In the following, the four combinations resulting from this will be discussed:

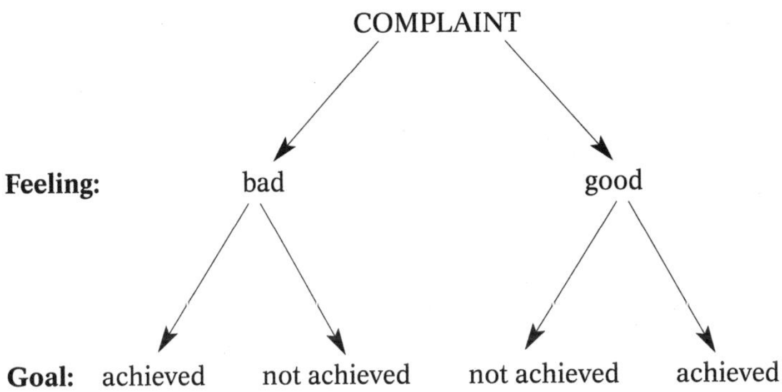

Lack of appreciation cannot be replaced by concessions. This means: Whoever gets what he asked for does not necessarily feel well.

At a neighbouring table in a pizzeria the following scene took place: Two couples have ordered a variety of pizzas, which were all served at the same time. When cutting the first piece, one of the four people notices that his pizza is merely lukewarm, the cheese already being like rubber. The waiter who just then rushes past is addressed: “Hey, you! I ordered a hot pizza. This one’s stone cold.” With this he hands over his plate to the waiter, who accepts it without another word. The three others have mostly finished their dishes, when the freshly baked pizza is served. Yet, with the following remark the waiter nullifies the guest’s “success”: “Here you go. For people who believe that only a hot pizza is tasty.” The guest draws a deep breath, but does not give an answer. Most probably he is aware that he cannot win.

If a complaint is related to a lot of trouble and many circumstances, a quick handling may be helpful, but neither takes emotions (anger, embarrassment, exposure, helplessness) into account nor the time consumed (detours, waiting, repacking, carrying). Even if in the "pizza example" the waiter had left out his cocky remark, the excuseless replacement of a lukewarm pizza against a hot would hardly have been sufficient.

Something similar happened to a colleague who returned a book since during reading he discovered that pages 80 to 96 were missing. The bookseller took back the rejected book, turned to the shelf, took out another copy, checked the pages and handed it over with the words: "Take this one instead." The indignation with which the incident was reported, ("Dump!...know nothing...,... real impertinence...") was in no way related to the facts, especially since the colleague had immediately received a replacement without any trouble. Complaints do not normally relate to an objective view of the facts but on the **feeling of not having been treated well**. And who feels mistreated tends to be unfair and to dramatise related problems.

It can be stated: the stronger emotional concern the less successful a business-like, matter-of-factual solution.

Imagine you have picked up your car from the workshop and two miles later the engine suddenly stops. It is raining cats and dogs. No phone box to be seen. Willy-nilly, you make your way back. Regardless of how friendly or angrily you explain your accident, the master craftsman in charge says: "No problem. You'll get a replacement. Here are the keys, the car's outside, and we'll take care of yours." No sooner said than done. Abruptly, you find yourself in ownership of somebody else's car keys and are expected to be content. Only extremely generous people will forget that they are dripping wet, have muddy shoes, have missed an important date, and can hardly walk around in these clothes any longer.

With many complaints, the customer will get what he deserves only on second or third try. When the customer starts threatening with measures like calling his lawyer, bringing this problem to public attention by telling his colleagues or the media, or when he asks for the supervisor, then the other gives in. Yet, in the meantime the negative emotions mentioned before have been added by others. In his first try, the customer was not taken seriously, there were objections to his wishes or he was even blamed for the problem. In the chapter "Behaviour is Goal-Oriented" I have explained that escalation will follow lack of appreciation. And often behind the customer's **threats** is hidden a merciless **struggle for power** that is out of all proportions to the goal behind it. Typical is the sentence "It's not the money, it's a matter of principle". And especially since in the next try it is only a matter of principle, any claim settlement that deals with the facts only, is bound to fail. There is hardly another way to explain why customers who have gotten what they asked for still remember the incident as unpleasant and tend to change suppliers and visit another restaurant, shop or workshop next time.

And who in spite of several attempts is not able to enforce his request leaves the workshop as a loser and will have related bad feelings. These feelings will stay so alive that even after years the whole rage will wake up again when one is reminded of the incident.

You can verify this when asking friends or colleagues to tell about a complaint, claim or reclamation. While talking, most people return to the very state they where in before. The voice changes, one can hear anger and frustration about the adversity one has gone through. Facial expression and body language show tension, and the incident is described so vividly that others might think it did not happen years but just a short while ago.

When you have listened to some of these stories you will soon find, that the material damage has usually been minor. What touches the storyteller emotionally is the memory of his helplessness. While anger, indignation, and rage are rather intense negative feelings, this will even be aggravated when we have to realise that all our effort will be without effect; we experience ourselves as **clueless, helpless**, and **weak**. In the truest sense of the word we have to realise that we are powerless. This is also expressed by: feel at someone's mercy. Not exactly a feeling that is bound to improve our mood. The material damage of an unsuccessful complaint is bad enough, but the related **humiliation** is almost unbearable. To seek revenge now is the most natural of things. In the least complicated case this act of self-protection consists of changing the shop, the supplier, or the workshop. In addition, it could be found that on average 11 other potential customers will learn about a complaint that left negative feelings behind. In a trade office I once read the aphorism: "There has never been a business who won a battle against its customers."

After having read in detail about the inability of a factual solution to replace appreciation, we will deal with the opposite case in the following:

> With aimed appreciation you can keep concessions small or replace them entirely. This means: anyone who does not get what he wants does **not** necessarily have **to feel bad about** it.

One participant told me about the following incident:
She had just bought a freehold flat. Friday after work she met with the construction manager for handing it over. While walking through the different rooms it was checked if everything had been carried out as requested. In the bathroom it turned out that it had been tiled in light pink instead of light beige. The complaint was added to the minutes including the hint to call the tiler at once. Up to this point the apartment owner of a few hours felt fine. To her astonishment, the tiler called the very evening. She noted down the contents of the phone call afterwards, so that it can be used in this context:
"Mr. Dudgeon has told me that we have used the wrong tiles in your bathroom. You had ordered beige, and we used light pink by mistake. If

it is important for you, we will of course change that. We can come on Monday and knock off the light pink tiles, on Tuesday the wall and the floor will be newly plastered, which will need to dry on Wednesday, on Thursday we can come and tile the room, and on Friday we can do the grouting. (Silence)
On the other hand, if you make up your mind to keep the light pink tiles, I can reduce the price in order to meet you. I offer a reduction of 250 Euros. You don't have to decide that now. You can take your time to think it over. Let me know only if we need to come on Monday to knock off the tiles."
I do not know how you would have decided in this situation, the participant still has light pink colour tiles in her bathroom. She told me that she did not need a break to think it over at all, but answered right away: "Then we leave it as it is." And she added that she was very glad to have "earned" 250 Euros so quickly and that she had already started finding the colouring in her bathroom rather acceptable.

In the subsequent analysis it was found out that this woman felt accepted from the start, that the tiler did not try to persuade her to keep the light pink tiles or to blame others for the problem. On the contrary, the description of how he would deal with the mischief created a scenario of dirt and dust in the brand-new flat into which she had planned to move during the weekend. She stressed that a quick decision was so easy for her since it was emphasised that she had time to think it over.

This example should not lead to the impression that when dealing with a complaint aimed appreciation can make compensation unnecessary. Of course, the tiler was able to save a lot of money and effort ingeniously. Yet, even if his customer had insisted on the colour she had chosen, this way of leading a conversation would have been a good basis for the repair work. Since I was curious I asked the participant how things would have gone on if the light pink tiles had had to be replaced by beige ones. She could imagine spontaneously making coffee for the workers, generously overlooking dirt and noise and making sure to pay the invoice on time.

How much it can contribute to avoiding maximum loss when taking emotional aspects into consideration can also be proven in the example of the driver whose car broke down after two miles and who had to walk back to the workshop in pouring rain. In the real event, he stepped up to his salesman and complained loudly:

"This is the very last time I'll bring my car to you. Botch, nothing but botch. And Mr. Leighton said, 'Have a good trip', as if! I made it to the building centre only, and suddenly the jalopy stops and plays possum. You cannot earnestly believe that I'm ever going to buy another car from you."

The sales manager who told me about this case realised at once that he could not do anything for this customer on the fact side, since he would have had to have all the background information about the repair, which to ask for would have been totally inappropriate in that situation. It was not to be missed that the customer was furious, so he concentrated on addressing the customer's bad mood and to alter it to the better:

"Oh, Mr. Jenkins, please come to my office, you are dripping wet. When you say your car stopped at the building centre, you must have walked at least two miles in this god-awful weather, in this case I would be cross, too. Maybe you even had a meeting and we screwed up your schedule."

"I can tell you. I should have been at 'Farmer & Huntsman' at four. I can forget about that now. You cannot imagine what depends on that."

"Since this is so especially important for you I wonder how I can help you now. Of course we'll take care of your car, but at the moment you need to get to 'Farmer & Huntsman' as soon as possible. Would it help you if I take you there?"

"That's very kind, but in this suit I cut a poor figure, and only look at my shoes."

"You are right, you need to change. And a cup of tea or coffee might be good."

"Say, can I do some undisturbed phone calls from here? Luckily, I took my files from the car (searches through his briefcase). If I could fax these four pages to 'Farmer & Huntsman', it might save the day."

"It is understood that you can use my office. Tea or coffee? When you hand me the keys I can arrange that somebody takes care of your car at once."

When the customer re-emerged from the manager's office twenty minutes later, he was in a much better mood and spontaneously agreed to waiting twenty more minutes since his car was supposed to be ready then.

> When dealing with complaints you will often find yourself being used as a "lightning conductor", and in this function your task is not to deal with the concrete facts but with your dialogue partners hurt feelings.

From a customer's point of view the ideal case consists both of **factual and emotional success**; he wants to achieve his goal **and** feel good about it. Now it cannot be the purpose of complaint management to play to the customer in every situation and to give the devil his due without looking into the details. The more important it is to show the customer one's respect in these areas without making concessions.

You can **influence conversation atmosphere in a positive way** when you let the customer feel from the start that you can understand his anger, that he had problems and trouble, that he is disappointed, and that his trust in you has been diminished.

It will usually contribute to a good atmosphere when you concede a point to the customer,

- because he had trouble:

"I imagine that it must have been very embarrassing when you were blamed for our supply problems."

- because he has complained at once:

"At first I want to thank you that even in such a situation you have come directly to me."

- because he expects a solution from you:

"You are entitled to expect that I rack my brain over it."

- because he wants a quick solution for his problems:

"It is totally correct that you want well- functioning equipment as soon as possible."

- because he forces a long-lasting solution:

"Of course a provisory solution will not do for you."

- because he tries to advert further damage:

"Of course our delivery must not lead to image loss for your company."

How often have we abstained from listening carefully to a dialogue partner who was in a bad mood due to lack of time or patience. We often act according to the motto: "Knowing the problem means knowing the solution". However, from such a premature reaction

the impression might arise that we want to get rid of the complainer as soon as possible. Patience is necessary because, before he came to complain, the customer suffered for some time. When you patiently answer to your dialogue partner's state of mind you will in a way provide compensation for the disappointment he suffered.

Only when the one who complains feels that you really take him seriously, a positive conversation atmosphere can develop, in which the hurt trust can be regained.

Only afterwards will a willingness to cooperate and to agree to a compromise arise.

When you deal with a complaint on the emotional level first, you can shorten the progress of settling it by re-establishing your dialogue partner's thinking abilities, which were reduced by negative emotions, so that he can actively participate in solving the problem.

If you achieve good cooperation this way, an image loss by negative word of mouth will be almost excluded.

17. Positive Talking

In chapter 1, I had explained how we react to negations. The right brain hemisphere will imagine something disregarding the clearly stated negation. You may recall: “Don't think of bears . . .”

Convincing in conversations will consider this fact, which leads to “positive talking”. Now what does that mean? Imagine the following scene at the breakfast table. The glass of milk of a three-year-old boy stands only some inches away from the table edge, while he is fooling about with his younger brother. Our brain is trained by experience to image what can or will happen next. In order to prevent this vision from becoming reality, normally the following sentence is used: “Take care, that your glass does **not** drop”.

Keeping the ideas from chapter 1 on effectiveness and efficiency in mind, such a sentence can at best be efficient, which means that it makes a great impact based on its volume and dramatic gestures. In the context of this chapter we will deal with which effect this sentence will have on the dialogue partner, in this case on the child. “Take care, that your glass does not drop!” will induce in the child the same picture as before in the right hemisphere of the adult: a falling glass. This does not automatically lead to the glass actually dropping. However, it is always interesting for me to see where requests that contain a negation or even a ban will lead. It is not remarkable as far as the glass is concerned that the child reciprocates: “It won't.” And in that moment the glass does not fall, indeed. Why has the same glass of milk been spilled to the floor two minutes later?

The request “Take care, that your glass does not drop” is lacking a **goal** statement, it is ineffective. It has not said anything about where the glass should actually stand. And this is exactly what “positive talking” is aiming at.

The dialogue partner gets an idea of the goal. For example: “Could you please place your glass behind the plate?” Not only the child in the example will move his glass in the middle of the table without any comment, without having to interrupt acting the goat, also adults react to “positive images” as requested in most cases. The sign

"No smoking in this room" does not only reduce personal freedom (chapter 6), but also contains subliminally an invitation in form of an image. Very different with the formulation: "Out of respect for the smokers, I'll plan for a 10 minutes break every hour."

> Positive talking is effective since it is goal-oriented.

Into this context belongs also the often to be heard order: "Drop it!" How ineffective this order is can especially be observed with children. When they tease and nettle each other, an angry "Drop it!" leads more often to ongoing and fiercer attacks. As long as the **desired** behaviour has not been named, a **change of behaviour** can hardly be permanent. Rather similar, students are rebuked day by day for unsuitable remarks, pert questions, or cheeky behaviour. Since non-behaviour does not exist, another behaviour, often as undesirable as the other or even worse, replaces the omitted one.

> Positive talking gives the dialogue partner an idea of the conceivable or even desirable target behaviour.

It can be a very exciting exercise for you to systematically pay attention to how the behaviour of people is bound to be influenced with negations. I call it 'exercise' because this intermediate step of observation gives you the opportunity to restate negative requests in a positive way from a distance. You will discover how important it is to create images that immediately lead into the desired direction.

Criticism often fails because all attention is focussed on the damage, the mistake, the shambles. This begins when educating toddlers, when children again and again hear the word "No!" and an interdiction is voiced by "You must not...", it continues at school, where mistakes are marked out in red and what was wrong is shown to the student quite plainly; and higher education hardly differs from this common praxis. It is always stressed what has gone wrong.

This behaviour is so frequent because the one who criticises has met a **discrepancy between** his **imagination** and observed **reality**. The reaction will correspond to the importance of one's own, the right, idea. This reaches from a casual remark over open disapproval up to a sharp reprimand. The dressing down results from a negative mood of the one who criticises, since he has just been upset by a mistake, a deviation from the target. To get rid of this awkward, impairing feeling he criticises and in a way transfers his negative feelings to the other, which is informally named "to bawl someone out". This is why after such a "bollocking" usually only the one who criticised feels well, whereas the inculpated leaves anything but happily.

Some readers may be afraid that now it is sentimentalised and talked about "namby-pambies" and "handling someone with kid gloves" and may think: "If the cap fits, wear it". In a leadership training course, a department head stated the opinion: "Sometimes you have to scorch your people, so that they obey again!" Another participant agreed with the words: "When I have faced up to somebody, he will not know if he's male or female. But I tell you: It works really well. Afterwards everything goes like clockwork."

This type of etiquette is apt to eat up the employee's self-esteem, to reduce his self-confidence, and to hurt his dignity.

In another class, I asked the participants which phrases or sentences said by their supervisors would drive them into a corner at once. I have collected the answers and give a selection here:

"Why did you do that?"
"You should have asked me before!"
"You could have known that!"
"I knew it, one day it had to come to that."
"What do you lack: willpower or knowledge?"
"I could have told you before."
"What do you have your head for?"
"Didn't you notice anything?"
"Man alive, you could really have thought about it!"
"How could this happen?"
"Typical!"

I assume that much of the often-complained lack of motivation in children and teenagers as well as of grown-up employees has to be paid into the account of the common orientation towards the negative.

Whoever concentrates on mistakes brings the other automatically into a bad mood.

When we envision that we usually want to feel good, it is comprehensible why people when confronted with criticism at first try to state that they are not to blame, according to the motto: "It's been somebody else's fault." *Eugen Roth* has caricatured this in a poem:

Insight

One man can prove as daylight clear,
That he's been really nowhere near.
Another man will stress to thee:
Whoever else – it wasn't me!
A third will hand something to read
About he did not do the deed.
A fourth one asks indignantly:
How? Says he, what? You think 'twas me?
A fifth one is so innocent
That it's a fault, he can't be meant.
A sixth will play the gentleman,
Who really cannot be our man.
A seventh – well, we captured it:
There's nobody to blame for it.
In this case we can name the truth:
It's more or less been all of us!

Eugen Roth

Even if a mistake annoys us and we get into a bad mood it does not help us a single bit to get our dialogue partner into the same or even a worse mood. In the best case we feel satisfaction and superiority, but this is fruitless, since these emotions do not contribute to getting correct results in the future.

In chapter 10, I had explained that we prefer to view reality as a cause-effect-relationship. It is obvious that when criticising many people deal with questions that are related to the past:

"Why did it happen?"
"How could it be?"
"Why was this necessary?"
"Why did nobody avoid that?"
"How could it be overlooked?"

But if we really try to make our vision and reality congruent, our attention needs to focus on the goal and the question what needs to be done to achieve it.

In positive talking, instead of dealing with the past, the attention is entirely focussed on the future.

By the way, people are easily motivated when they are involved in designing the future.

The thousand fold "no" with which our children should be kept from doing something prohibited can be replaced by drawing attention on the things and activities that are desired. When you take away your expensive fountain pen from a toddler, which it just then was about to take apart with great interest, you are faced with a screaming fit. Yet, as soon as you give the child something else (best also something to take apart) it will turn to it and leave the fountain

pen to you. Also the damageable hi-fi system gets special attention only through the vehement "No!" with which the child shall be kept away from all these attractive buttons. Since the goal is: The child is to play with **its** toys, the parent's attention is best focussed on **how** the child can be interested in **its own** toys again. I admit that answering this question needs much more effort than a quick "no". Since with the "no" we have only limited success, otherwise we would not have to repeat it so often, we should consider to what extent a one-time time-consuming conversation saves our energy.

Of course drawers and cupboards are especially interesting for a toddler. But instead of forbidding them by locking them up, by smacking them, or by saying "no", one can try to offer them one drawer or part of a cupboard for playing. Pots and sieves will normally not get broken and you will find that the usual screaming will stop when the child is moved for example from the cupboard with the table-ware to the permitted area.

Remember the corrections in essays and dictations from your school days. The mistake was marked in red, and the word had now to be repeated three times. Maybe you had the same trouble with one or the other word I had: How often did I have to correct the word "weather". None of these corrections had saved me from writing "wheather" with an "h" again in the new test. Why? Because the "h" boldly circled in red was burned to my memory. And I can still remember that during writing the essay I had been asking myself if it was written with or without "h". And the answer was typical: for sure with "h", since the red marking weighed more than writing the three repetitions, and the mnemonic rhyme was just altered in an "h"-containing way: "Whether the wheather is fine, or whether the wheather is not: We wether the wheather whatever the wheather whether we like it or not". I am always impressed when students tell me about their experience with other corrective measures. There are teachers who did not mark the wrong word but wrote it at the side in correct spelling or teachers who make the students look out for the wrong spelling by just stating the number of mistakes to be searched for per line or page. Apart from the fact that this proceeding differs from a dull repetition it is challenging to find the correct spelling by reading and comparing. Admittedly a more exertive exercise, but which focusses the student's attention on the desired spelling. And who has with a lot of trouble looked up the correct spelling in Webster's may try to find by himself a way to reduce effort, for example by learning and practicing orthography.

Also in apprenticeship and work life a deviation from the target can be corrected the positive way. Let us take a look into a training workshop where a trainee is just told about his malpractice:

"You are filing away too much. If you don't take care you'll have to begin again."

By positive talking, the attention can be directed towards the goal:

"When you stop filing from time to time and test with the calliper rule, you'll know when you have to stop."

This positive phrase is still lacking involvement and integration of the other into goal definition. In this example the trainee can take over the offered solution without having to exert himself. At the same time it is often complained that today's trainees are unwilling to take over responsibility. How should they? When they are treated all too often as dependent addressees of orders, solutions, and assessments, who get rarely the chance to make an effort and to show personal responsibility. One could think about the triple jump out of acknowledgement – question – explanation from chapter 14:

"I see you are filing full of verve. How do you make sure that you stop when you have met the given dimensions? I'm only asking because I assume that you want to succeed at first go."

Now the trainee does not only have to interrupt his work but also to think about what will be his next steps. The motivation for the "personal contribution" comes besides others from the fact that the foreman is confident that the trainee will find a solution by himself.

Maybe after reading this you feel like trying out how easy it is for you to restate given negative formulations:

	Your proposal for an appropriate positive formulation
(1) "When you run the cables in the wrong way you don't have to wonder why it doesn't work."	
(2) "With the delivery to Sawmill Inc. you forgot the final inspection. No wonder they complained."	
(3) "No wonder that the machine's down if you don't do any maintenance."	
(4) "When another guest complains about too much salt in the soup we need to rethink the renewal of your contract."	
(5) "When you don't check stock receipt correctly we will book the difference to your account."	
(6) "You need to be more careful when varnishing. The customer will explode when he sees these dust inclusions and varnish runs."	
(7) "On this invoice you forgot the value added tax, now Somechurch Ltd. pays 2,300 Euro less and we can wrestle with the problem."	

The following alternatives came to my mind:

(1) "When you run the cables in the wrong way you don't have to wonder why it doesn't work."

I do not want to exclude that the mechanic thanks you spontaneously and runs the cables the correct way. According to my observations, the reaction is more often rather aggressive, for example demonstrated disregard by ostensive silence.

"It will only work when the cables run correctly."

With this formulation it was abstained from highlighting the mistake, but it still does not assure long-lasting success. This can only be guaranteed when the mechanic in consequence takes over responsibility for each of the process steps.

"Latterly, you do these jobs on your own. How can you test in-between if all the functions are working? You want to finish quickly."

(2) "With the delivery to Sawmill Inc. you forgot the final inspection. No wonder they complained."

"Consequence in doing final inspections spares us complaints."

But the word "complaint" still focussed attention on something to avoid. As already stated in chapter 1, avoidance of complaints would at maximum be efficient. Effective and goal-oriented would be customer satisfaction:

"Regular final inspections significantly contribute to our customers always being satisfied with our deliveries."

Positive talking can also be used to unmistakably fasten the responsibility to someone:

"Sawmill Inc. has complained about the last delivery. What will you do to assure customer satisfaction in the future? I'm asking you because final inspections falls under your responsibility."

(3) "No wonder that the machine's down if you don't do any maintenance."

With this formulation you are forcing the dialogue partner into defence; excuses, accusations, or counter attacks ("Couldn't you say that before...") are close-by.

"You can achieve equipment reliability by preventive maintenance."

One may assume that this statement gets more spontaneous approval.

"It is important for you that the machine runs properly. How much maintenance would you think is necessary? You can best judge the strains."

With this triple jump, the dialogue partner's attention is directed towards machine utilization. Maybe he will deduct from his own judgement, how often and how intensive maintenance is required. This is the best guarantee for consequent use of the solution found.

(4) "When another guest complains about too much salt in the soup we need to rethink the renewal of your contract."

After this statement, the light-hearted and ingenuous cooking is gone once and for all.

"Please, do taste every soup yourself. This will spare us possible complaints from our guests."

As reasonable as this solution may sound, it still lacks trust in the chief's problem solving abilities.

With the following formulation it can be shown that the triple jump is very well apt to hint at possible consequences:

"I can understand that you are very interested that we change your temporary contract into a permanent one. For this I would like to know from you how you will assure that our guests will only give good judgement about the dishes they order here. I assume that you care about the complaints because of the salty soups and have thought about it already."

Even if the employee has not thought about it until then, the positive assumption will contribute to her thinking about it at once to develop a solution that secures her employment.

(5) "When you don't check stock receipt correctly we will book the difference to your account."

Threats are a very common tool to bring somebody to terms in a quick way. At first sight they seem to work, but they are only efficient. In the example the employee will try to avoid everything that has personal consequences. Yet, I can hardly imagine that such a threat is apt to further motivate the employee to be careful in other parts of his job, too, which until now have not been under the sword of Damocles.

"We can only complain about goods with our suppliers which we checked on arrival. Please organise your work in a way that each delivery is inspected for defects at once."

A positive, but typical statement of a supervisor. By working out and explaining the solution, the supervisor takes over responsibility for the employee's area of activities. And the employee will most probably not resist since it is much more convenient to have been told what to do than to figure it out oneself.

"You know that we can only complain the day we received the goods. What will you do to make sure that in case of a short delivery we make use of our rights? I'm asking you because in Purchasing we plan so strictly that we need to insist on the supplier meeting the exact number of items.

(6) "You need to be more careful when varnishing. The customer will explode when he sees these dust inclusions and varnish runs."

You can ask yourself how great your readiness for self-criticism is when you are blamed for lack of accuracy. Maybe you have already experienced that one has been rather critical about one's own accomplishments until somebody criticises them reproachfully. All of a sudden one comes up with explanations or plays the problem down in a way that one can only be surprised about one's own quick-wittedness. When talking positively we can spare ourselves many justifications and excuses.

"Customers tend to check their new car by the square millimetre. When you inspect it yourself first, you can secure customer satisfaction for us."

But if an employee regards a task as completed with dust inclusions, runners and all, the supervisor has to ask himself to what extent the subordinate has taken over responsibility for his own work results and which idea he has of what is expected from him.

"For you this task is completed. I am uncertain how your quality standard looks like. I would like to learn from you to what extent you want to be continuously controlled by me or if the responsibility for your work shall remain with you."

(7) "On this invoice you forgot the value added tax, now Somechurch Ltd. pays 2,300 Euro less and we can wrestle with the problem."

May the supervisor be as grunty as he is, this statement will most probably get the employee to make a guilty or conscience-stricken face, but to leave everything as it is and to tick off the damage.

"Our customers have only to pay the sum on the invoice. When you check for VAT each time you make sure that we get the money we deserve."

But when a member of accounting "forgets" to add VAT, I hold it for negligent to positively name a solution for goal achievement only. Apart from how the employee plans to make up for the financial damage, it is necessary to assure that future invoices are complete and add to company interests. **As soon as** the employee has satisfyingly answered this question he will be allowed to further execute this task. Some readers may argue that this includes a hidden threat. I admit that the consequences are named, which in the eyes of the employee may be "two fisted". Yet, to threaten and to name consequences are as like as chalk and cheese:

> A threat follows the pattern "if not ... then" or vice versa "if ... then not", and the attention is focussed on the negative, on what is to avoid.
>
> A consequence includes a logical cause-effect relation according to the pattern "as soon as" or "when", and the energy is focussed on the desired goal.

Some reader may believe this to be splitting hairs. Maybe it is best when you test the different phrases occasionally and find out about how your dialogue partner will react. For clarification I will add another common example from family life:

"You are not allowed to watch TV if you don't clean up your room."

Normally the child's protest is directed against the ban. And some children can be so persistently defiant that the desired programme is over, but the room is still untidy.

"You are allowed to watch TV as soon as you have cleaned up your room."

In chapter 6, I explained how we can avoid possible resistance when granting the other the **freedom of choice**.

Using "as soon as you… you may…", you transfer responsibility to the other. It is his decision how quickly he will achieve his goal.

Show the dialogue partner his freedom of decision.

I would like to add something to the previous chapter and show that when we have a complaint we can achieve our goal much quicker when we talk about it. Instead of with the words:

"Last week you sold me this watch. It's not ok. It loses horribly, about two minutes per day."

we want the dialogue partner, in this case the watchmaker, to be addressed in a positive way and receive an idea, which he will spontaneously agree to, like:

"I'd like to be happy about the watch I bought here last week. Can you adjust it so that it shows the correct time? At the moment it loses two minutes per day."

The "pizzeria example" is also apt to hand over responsibility to the waiter:

"You would for sure like me to be satisfied. Can you either warm up this pizza or swap it for a freshly baked one?"

I must confess that this sentence sounds rather overblown. When using everyday language it will sound less “elaborate”. When I come back to the example with the soaked car driver I admit that it requires quite a portion of self-discipline not to jump out of one’s skin and to turn towards one’s goals instead. It depends on what is more important to you.

“You want me to rely on your workshop. Now what will you do to help me save the situation? My car stands at the building centre and plays possum, and I should be in an important meeting with Farmer & Huntsman that started ten minutes ago.”

I have often expressed in this book that **stating the goal defines success.** The interest of my dialogue partner has to be what is possible and not on what is impossible. Even tough, we are confronted with “no” and “not” every single day. What does it help you when you ask for a spare part and get the answer:

“We don’t have that”, or
“We don’t sell this brand.”

But which degree of customer retention can be induced by the following statements:

“I can order the spare part for you.”
Or:
“This brand is produced by Braun. Do you know where they are located? I’m sure that they have this part on stock.”

I have integrated another exercise in which you can practice finding positive formulations:

	Your proposal for an appropriate positive formulation
(1) "Mr. Adams is not in."	
(2) "I'm not responsible for that."	
(3) "We don't ship to new customers without prepayment."	
(4) "I don't know anything about that."	
(5) "No money – no goods."	
(6) "Today is absolutely impossible."	
(7) "We can't repair it for that price."	
(8) "If you don't send the additional payment, we cannot deliver the machine."	
(9) "I cannot put you through. The boss is in an important meeting."	
(10) "I'm new here and don't know a lot about it."	
(11) "Our data processing doesn't work at the moment, so I can't help you."	
(12) "We can't accept your ordor. Hell's let loose here due to vacation and some sick-leaves."	

Regard my answers as proposals:

(1) "Mr. Adams will be back at eleven. Do you want him to call you back then?"
(2) "My collcaguc, Mrs. Abbott is responsible for this. If you agree, I will talk to her, and she'll get back to you."
(3) "If you want to avoid cash-on-delivery, you can send a prepayment, and we'll deliver at once."
(4) "I need to gather some information about that."
(5) "Would you like to pay cash or by cheque? We also accept credit cards."
(6) "Would you like to fix a meeting for tomorrow morning?"
(7) "Of course we can do a partial repair for this price."

(8) "With the extras you ordered the additional payment is 15,000.– Euros. If you want to meet at 13,000.– Euros we can of course deliver the machine in a simpler configuration."
(9) "The meeting will be over in twenty minutes. Under which phone number can we reach you then?"
(10) "I would like to talk to my colleague (supervisor), so that you get a reliable answer."
(11) "I'll just note down your question. As soon as our data processing is working again, maybe in around an hour, I'll get back to you."
(12) "We want to process your order as soon as possible. From Monday on we are four people in our group again. I'll personally take care that you get the delivery at the latest next Wednesday."

When we bear in mind how often we have been confronted with a "no" as a child and consider that we have been in a state of dependence, it is understood that "no" and "not" are able to reawaken negative emotions and memories.

In chapter 12, "Behaviour is Goal-Oriented", you had formulated your answer to the statement "That's impossible. I have more than enough to do." The examples at the end of the chapter were to show how we could pursue our goals with appreciation, even if confronted with negative statements.

Objections can always be viewed as negations, i. e. under the given conditions you will not get approval.

> Positive talking takes the objection seriously and looks for opportunities.

If for example the dialogue partner says: "I don't like the plan", common answers look like:

"Why not?" After which the other will concentrate on the negation.
"On the contrary, the plan is very good." Open antithesis calls for a struggle for power.
"Do you have anything better?" This challenge only provokes a discussion about assessment criteria.
"You don't understand the plan, or you wouldn't say that." This arrogant assumption leads directly into a cockfight.
"But with this plan you can save the most money." Who wants to be persuaded?

In chapter 15, "Delivering Unpleasant Messages", I talked about the use of "but". Many people use "but" as a habit when dealing with objections, although "and" would be much more appropriate. Yet, as soon as we have let slip **but** our dialogue partner will merely notice that we object to his ideas and may react mulishly. People do not like to hear that they are wrong.

When pursuing our goals it can be much more promising to help our dialogue partner to take a positive view:

"Under which conditions could you agree to the plan?"
"How must the plan look to suit you?"
"Where does the plan differ from your ideas?"
"How would you design the plan so that it meets your needs?"
"You don't like the plan, and until now I was more anxious about the costs."

I am often surprised with how short a rebuff sales people have themselves fobbed off. The customer merely says:

"No demand."
"No interest."
"No time."
"No budget."
"No storage capacity."
"We are very satisfied with our current supplier."
"We don't want to change the brand."

Whoever is used to influence even his own pattern of thought by talking the positive way will use the **"what if" pattern** for objections like these:

"This means if you have a demand for it, we could come to an agreement."
"When you say you don't have any interest you show me that I haven't managed yet to demonstrate the uniqueness of this product."
"When do you have time?" or: "If you had time, you would ask me to give you a product presentation."
"Especially since your budget is limited, I assume that you might be interested in our new conditions."

"As soon as the question of storage is clarified you are interested in doing business with us."
"Since you so are satisfied with your supplier you have a good basis to verify in how far our conditions are different or even more favourable for you."
"Do you want to compare your familiar brand with the advantages of our product?"

Positive talking means the ongoing description of desirable goals. I talked about the negation with "no", "not", "none", or "without" in great detail. In addition, positive talking concentrates on words which we can easily connect to an image. At the beginning of this chapter I made the point that we tend to imagine the right rather than dealing with the wrong, the mistakes, the shards.

"It annoys me when we are late."
"I would like to be on time."

Many composed words need only to be freed from the prefixes and suffixes to sound positive at once. It strikes me how often we define our goals with stating the absence of the negative, for example:

- trouble-free, in-fallible, un-assailable, flaw-less, fault-less, un-objectionable, seam-less, non-stop
- phrases containing "without", "no" or "not";
- negating verbs, such as: to hinder, to stop, to avoid, to prevent, to ban, to cease.

Concentrating on the negative does not lead to a positive vision.

"Could you please prevent your people agreeing to deadlines that have not been aligned with production."
"I would like your minutes much better if you had not used these many subjunctives and had avoided indirect speech."
"I forbid you to use my tools."
"Stop that noise!"

Even a well-meant **praise** can unawares be diminished or turned into the contrary, since the absence of mistakes, even if emphasised, does not equal masterly achievement.

"Not bad." But not good either.
"Thank you for the immaculate arrangement." In other words: a flawed or incomplete arrangement suggested itself or was even presumed.

"My compliments! You played the sonata without any mistakes." How many mistakes were expected?
"I'm very pleased by your final report. It can be handed to the board of management without any changes." Does this mean that changes are standard?

If you want to acknowledge something by positive talking, you will concentrate on what seems to be a desirable goal for you. I have to confess that in the beginning it requires a high level of concentration. Yet, it can be very interesting to pay attention to ones own man-

ner-of-speaking and if need be to clear out the familiar, but negative vocabulary. It does not only sound positive but has a more motivating effect when praise is stated in a goal oriented way. In this case it reads:

"Great"
"Ideal arrangement"
"That was absolutely according to the notes" or more gushingly "The way you played it is most probably the way *Mozart* had imagined his sonata."
"As precisely as you have formulated the final report it will pass to the board meeting at first go."

At the end of this chapter I want to address a language subtlety, which at a closer look reveals how positively or negatively the speaker is thinking.

An indirect question begins with the word “if” which expresses **uncertainty** and **doubt** about a certain question. With this way of talking you express subconsciously **if** you trust your dialogue partner.

“I’m curious if it will work.”
“You can try if you can manage it.”
“I need to know if you have time for me.”
“As the author I would like to know if you have done the exercises.”

“If” can be replaced by “**how**”, in which way we can ask indirectly **in how far** something is given. And “how” presumes a positive situation in general.

“I’m curious how it will work.”
“You can try how far you will make it.”
“I need to know how much time you have for me today.”
“As the author I would like to know how you have done the exercises.”

Positive assumptions usually lead to spontaneous acceptance with the dialogue partner. So, in a subtle way, an image of the desired state will be created.

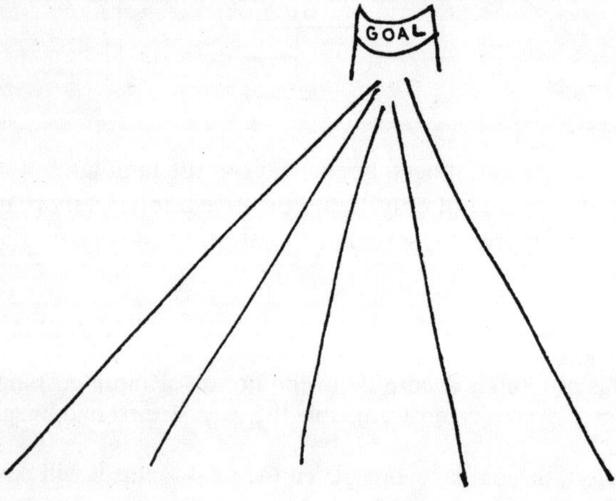

18. Talking from the Other's Angle

The **triple jump** discussed in chapter 14 is a tried and tested way to win others over. The first step, the acknowledgement, however will pose a bigger problem than could be expected. Some who have dealt with esteeming communication superficially only, may believe that the point were only to jibe and to say some nice things, and then one could get to the bottom of the matter. In this case, acknowledgement is mistaken for a kind of "niceness".

In the chapter "From Persuasion to Conviction" it read: Acknowledgement meets the dialogue partner where he stands. So whoever wants to acknowledge something needs to deal with the other's interests and to understand, which mental and emotional state the dialogue partner is in. This is by nature the easier, the more we can build on a variety of pre-experiences. It is always astonishing with which ease children adopt the moral concepts of their parents like a duck takes to water, when they want to achieve something. Since children know from prior experience what their parents value they cannot only take it into account but address it directly.

The question for a raise in pocket money for example will be timed skilfully with the parents' generosity; with a well-filled purse this can be addressed much easier than after a visit of the bailiff. At the same time every child knows what the parents value. They consciously chose a time when the parents are busy, being well aware that the parents want to get them off their back, others pick a relaxed Sunday afternoon and prepare for displaying their momentary school performance.

When we lead conversations with other people, we always want to get a reaction, we want to achieve something, if not we can as well remain silent (see also chapter 10, the appellative ear). Now it is easy to take over responsibility for a conversation when the reaction is the one we hoped for.

Dialogue situation party small talk: You tell about an exceptional event during your vacation.
Listeners' reaction: Everyone listens carefully and signals with nodding and eye contact that you are asked to go on.
Own estimation: "I'm a good story-teller and can entertain others."

But when the dialogue partners show a reaction that counts against us we reject responsibility.

Same situation as before.
Listeners' reaction: Low attention, side talks, and interruptions.
Own estimation: "Buggers. Why do I tell my great stories to these people..."

But blaming others is worthless, since it does not alter the further course of the conversation. Since whoever blames the other for a lack of accordance does not only assume that his own point of view is right, but is also convinced of having explained it in a comprehensible way. In consequence, neither will the own view be reconsidered, nor will the presentation be thought over. Instead, what has not been successful before will be repeated again and again. Sometimes with other words, sometimes only louder.

It is always inviting to call the other a hopeless fool who refuses to take plausible arguments into account. Since anyone who believes others to be stupid and pigheaded is safe from being called into question himself. Yet, this attitude expresses only that the focus is, to be always right. The question is only what any justification will help us when the other does not do what we want him to do. I always recite the macabre example of the car driver who forced his right of way and now enjoys it in the churchyard.

> A basic principle of professional conversation is to always understand the dialogue partner's reaction as a feedback.

Our attention does not focus on the disappointment or on the failed conversation, but on looking for opportunities to give the conversation a new direction. Instead of repeating arguments that did not reach the dialogue partner until now we find new ways how to get through to him. With this attitude we take over responsibility for our goals.

All previous chapters have shown that we will fail sooner or later when we do not show regard for our dialogue partner. I hold it for an expression of **respect** when we deal with the other so intensively that we not only address him with our statement, but also formulate it in a way that the other will feel really responsive. And the acknowledgement mentioned before is an excellent way to do so. **Professional acknowledgement** exceeds addressing the momentarily emotional situation by far.

We can express with our first acknowledgement that we do not only take the momentary situation of our dialogue partner into account, but consider also his general state of mind, his preferences and aversions.

If we, like the title of this chapter names it, want to talk from the other's angle we can do something in addition:

> We can realise according to which patterns our dialogue partner normally deals with information and adapt to these patterns.

Some readers may furrow their brow about "to adapt" and I am assuming the question: "What about spontaneity?" – "Is this still authentic?" – "Doesn't this lead directly to manipulating others?"

Admittedly, our spontaneity gets lost to a great deal. And maybe this is just fine, because "being spontaneous" is not an end in itself. A "proper licking" does not become good just because it has been given spontaneously. And I can very well do without other people's authenticity when it is at the cost of my interests, which is always the case when I do not feel respected.

In professional conversation we act on the assumption that our dialogue partner will only be interested in our thoughts when he expects some kind of benefit. The word "benefit" may sound too materialistic; it also covers everything that satisfies our curiosity, every question that startles us, but also every new joke which makes us laugh happily.

In every conversation the question is how to get access to the other's universe, since he will not necessarily focus on what is important for us. Anyone who in consequence deals with the other's view of the world will soon find out that there is no common formula for success. Like a joke that makes one laugh while somebody else can only smile weakly about it, and like the same idea can inspire one and make the other yawn.

For me as a university lecturer it was fascinating to find out that it is not my well-founded and well-prepared knowledge that makes the difference for my students' progress but my anxiety to address each individual participant with his personal background, his preferences, abilities, and desires with my lessons. It has been a momentous realisation, since I had to bid farewell to so-called "success trainings", which at the end are nothing but a scam.

As much as people differ from each other, so similarly do we stay ourselves. The way we focus our attention, gather information, and remember and organise experiences will always be done the same or at least a rather similar way. Since these patterns are processes, which can be described, there is a chance to familiarise with the specific thought patterns of our dialogue partner in a way that we can adapt to them. Even if you have learned foreign languages at school and are able to communicate in them when you are abroad, you will still find it very pleasant when a conversation is held in your mother tongue unasked. And your dialogue partners will experience it as pleasant when you adapt to their patterns of information processing.

In the following, I will explain four patterns and how they influence our behaviour.

Introspective or extrospective

With decisions or when we want to be sure of something, many people fall back to their natural pattern. For a demonstration, let us look at buying a sweater:

- **Extrospective decisions** follow the scheme: Do I get acceptance? What do others say? How does my mate think I look in it? Is it fashionable? Overstated it can read: "I like the sweater because the shop girl/my mate says it suits me."
- **Introspective decisions** will be made by intuition. The inner coherence comes to the fore. The analogous formulation reads here: "I like the sweater because I feel fine in it." If external approval

meets one's own judgement, this is of course welcome. Yet, in the inverse case approval by others will if in contradiction to one's own judgement change hardly anything. Since judgement is based on sense, external agreement will hardly ever alter it.

> When preparing your arguments you can take the opportunity to consider the other's preferred way of decision-making.

It will be of little help to try and get an **introspective** person interested in something by hinting at whoever else liked it and what others might do or say about it. They can only be convinced when something is addressed that they themselves know or will be able to verify.

Conversely it comes close to asking too much when asking an **extrospective** person for a decision without telling him how others might think and act in the given situation.

In the sweater example, experienced sales people will talk from the other's angle. For an extrospective customer this may sound for example likc:

"You are looking at me so inquiringly. I just want to tell you directly: The sweater suits you. This is the new colour of the fall season, so it's very trendy. And as a side remark, this sweater is designed by 'April', a fashion designer who has had a very good reputation for years, concerning style, quality, and durability of the knitwear."

The same sales person might address an introspective customer with the following words:

"When you walk over to the other mirror you can best see if the sweater meets your needs. When you just think about which other clothes you want to combine it with – it is most important that you feel well.
Maybe you want to walk over to the window and take a look at the colour in daylight."

Imagine you want to see a certain motion picture tonight. So as not to have to go alone you want to call a friend and make him or her come with you. The result of the conversation can be very much influenced by your preparation.

Please, take some notes on how you want to pursue your goal:

Common is a **spontaneous** call according to the pattern:

A: "Today they show XYZ, would you like to come with me?"

Success is uncertain. If the dialogue partner cannot or will not make up his or her mind so quickly it usually sounds like:

B: "I don't know..."
A: "Look, it is really good. Come on, brace your heart!"
B: "I don't feel well today, have had a headache the whole afternoon and don't feel fit."
A: "But the a movie will be just the right thing, you will forget about the headache then, get new thoughts and feel really fresh afterwards, you will see."

But anyone who has made the experience that the friend is influenced **externally** will make use of it in the initial acknowledgement, like:

Acknowledgement: "Today they show the movie everyone in the canteen talked about.
Question: Do you want me to try and get two tickets?
Explanation: I would like to view it together with you."

Since this statement will hardly influence an **introspective** person, a totally different argumentation is needed:

Acknowledgement: "With movies you like to form your own ideas and hardly listen to what others say.
Question: What do you think about XYZ?
Explanation: I would like to view it together with you and afterwards hear your thoughts about it."

Now you may try to classify yourself and find that this cannot be clearly defined. This uncertainty is caused by the fact that under stress and pressure we return to proven patterns, which no longer have any effect in well-known situations with a certain ending. The longer you do a certain task the more you will trust your intuition if a certain decision is right or wrong.

To find out if you are more introspective or extrospective you can answer the following questions and compare your notes to the answers on the next page:

(1) You take over a new job. How do you know if you are doing well?

(2) You have a party. How do you know afterwards if it was a success?

(3) You apply for a job or pass an oral examination. How do you know retrospectively if you have presented yourself well?

I have listed some typical answers of training course participants. Maybe you will recognise some of your answers.

Introspective	**Extrospective**
(1) "I just feel it." "I know if I have solved the problem." "If it's going well and I make good progress."	**(1)** "When my boss taps me on the shoulder." "When my colleagues ac-knowledge my work." "When I get a pay rise."
(2) "If I feel well, my guests will also feel well." "When I hit the sack and am satisfied, it was worth the effort." "I know from my sixth sense."	**(2)** "When my guests thank me or call the next day." "When I find that people ate and drank a lot." "When I realise that my guests acknowledge my efforts."
(3) "When I feel confident." "I'd feel good, if I was able to say what I wanted to." "When I'm relaxed afterwards and satisfied with me."	**(3)** "When the examiner makes a suitable remark." "When I hear how other ap-plicants have done." "I can see how benevolent the examiner is."

Before you give your arguments you can ask yourself if the dialogue partner is introspective or extrospective. In one case you will offer the information in a way that the other can form an opinion and make his decision; in the other case you will state a comparison or ask him directly to talk to others and get their view on it.

"Forward to" or "Away from"

As far as it is in our power, we chose our behaviour in a way that we prefer well-being to pain.

- Under the code **"forward to"** I summarize all activities that are undertaken to assure or increase our **well-being**. Every action is bound **to achieve something**.
- With the code **"away from"** I mean all activities with which we try to avoid something **unpleasant**. Here every action results from the wish **to prevent something**.

But what is regarded as to be avoided can be very different. If you have the choice you would spontaneously vote for **avoidance** with states like pain, illness, accident or emotions like embarrassment, fear, or grief. Yet, how do you react to the following catchwords? Death, divorce, layoff? Is this as clear? One sometimes says "Death came as a release", a divorce can end a painful state, and losing one's job can be the chance for a new start. Even more different are the opinions about the following activities: reading, driving a car, washing the dishes, sports. Maybe you hesitate and ask yourself confoundedly, why I listed just these activities, which to you seem to be altogether pleasant and positive – maybe with the exemption of washing the dishes.

While you have fun reading a new novel and it is done out of a "forward to" view, there are others who read the same novel but to avoid something like seeming uneducated or being left out from the discussions among colleagues.

Similarly you may do sports with greatest pleasure, while others exert themselves in the same sport in order to avoid being viewed as unathletic or feeling excluded.

In the same way, some like to drive a car and connect it to the feeling of mobility and freedom, while others want to avoid being called inflexible or that someone says they could not afford a car.

At the end, even the example with washing the dishes reflects two behaviour patterns. Some like to wash the dishes because they like a clean kitchen or because they can be lost in thoughts, others wash the dishes as often, but to avoid having to look at the piles of dirty plates all the time.

In one and the same activity some may look for pleasure while the others want to save themselves from something.

- In the "forward to" attitude, perception is concentrated on the opportunities → **"make something happen"**.
- In the "away from" attitude, perception is focussed on risks and threats → **"make something not happen"**.

With this behaviour pattern you may have also thought about whether you are more the "forward to" or the "away from" type of person. Of course you do not always react in the same way and in your life there is a lot which you try to achieve and other things, which you want to avoid. To be able to do a self-assessment, I am again offering you a short test:

What do you associate with the following words?

	Note down your thoughts spontaneously
(1) Cooking	
(2) Clean up	
(3) Ride a bicycle	
(4) Write a letter	
(5) Go on a trip	
(6) Concert	
(7) Further education	
(8) Motorcycle race	
(9) Conference	
(10) Kitchen garden	

Maybe you will recognise some of the answers from my training course participants.

	Forward to	**Away from**
(1) Cooking	Try out new recipes, make everybody happy, good smells.	So that it has been done, nobody remains hungry, great effort – no praise.
(2) Clean up	Then I'll find everything, it looks clean, find things.	Reduce untidiness, avoid chaos, nothing left to do.
(3) Ride a bicycle	Active, always a parking place, contributes to good image.	Exhausting, flat tire, saves time and money, don't gain weight.
(4) Write a letter	Love letter, clarify something, pick the words, read again before sending.	Bloody orthography, avoid style mistakes, the other's reaction is missing.
(5) Go on a trip	See new things, visit exhibitions, holiday mood.	Heavy suitcase, forgotten toothbrush, noisy hotel, homesickness.

(6) Concert	Enjoy music, wear my new dress, a feast for the eyes, interesting talks during breaks.	Not again a place behind a pillar, must not be late, what do I wear?
(7) Further education	Job enrichment, experience exchange, latest scientific results.	Get away from it all, sit still for a long time, questions proven remedy.
(8) Motorcycle race	Thrilling, speed is fun, companions.	Life threatening, loud, big crowd, pollution.
(9) Confe-rence	Focus things, draw conclusions, fix goals.	Endless discussions, victory of the behinds over the brain, much ado about nothing.
(10) Kitchen garden	Self-efficacy, pure nature, independence.	A lot of work slugs munch away every-thing, does not pay off.

Some readers may find that their answers will mostly fit either the left or the right column, and that they show some kind of common pattern.

> When you try to find out if the other in a concrete situation is more focussed on "forward to" or on "away from" you can ask him: "What are you aiming at with xy?" or "What do you connect with xy?"

At the beginning of a sales conversation the customer can be asked directly, like for example:

"I'm not sure what you are especially interested in." Or:
"I'd like to consult you in the best possible way, but I'm not certain about what you value specifically."

Or as a triple jump:

Acknowledgement: You are interested in XY.
Question: Would you tell me what you associate with it?
Explanation: I can then find something that meets your expectations.

When you know according to which pattern your dialogue partner scans information you can either stress the **advantages** of a certain activity or talk about the **disadvantages** that can be avoided with the same activity. Even if from an objective point of view this can mean the same, some people view the glass as "half full", while others call it "half empty". Correspondingly, we can view the very same thing from the positive and from the negative side.

A sales manager who talks from the customer's angle will adapt to his information processing pattern, for example:

With a car dealer, a customer shows interest for a sports car:
Customer: "Well, I think I'm interested in everything, safety, reliability, etc. What about the gasoline consumption? Gas prices are going up constantly."
Salesman A: "Yes, that's very important, since the less you need the more you can save. This is also true for longer maintenance intervals, so that inspections are required less often, which also avoids costs. But maybe I'd better begin with safety aspects and show you how with this model possible risks of an accident have been avoided.

Salesman B: "Just look at the car from the front. You will see at once that this is a brand-new, rather aerodynamic line. Excellent air resistance values in combination with a high-speed engine will hurtle off at every traffic light. I just want to show you what is newly developed in this model and which absolutely great possibilities you will have."

When you compare the reactions of the two salesmen, you will see how people can talk at cross-purposes. In the second case – even if the customer intends to buy something – no agreement will be found, since the customer feels misunderstood.

Now the impression may arise that it is in the first place sales people who benefit from this way of leading a conversation. I believe that we should better care for the thinking patterns of our dialogue partners in every case, if we want to achieve something.

Whoever wants to make a child write its homework properly and neatly will for the "**forward to**" type use the following sentence:

"The more carefully you write it, the better will the whole page look afterwards. Maybe you will be praised by your teacher again."

This will hardly impress an "away from" type. Whoever is mainly motivated by avoiding embarrassment, will feel addressed by the following sentence:

"If you write properly at once, you won't have to do it a second time."

When from now on you pay attention to whether your fellows act more according to a "forward to" or a "away from" pattern, you can also perform the following test:

▸ **Ask the other which pros and cons a certain decision or a specific object may have.**
Or which positive character traits they like in others and which negative ones others should rather not have.

You may make the astonishing discovery that people with an "away from" pattern usually start with the negative side and that they come up with more negative points. Vice versa, people with a "forward to" pattern prefer talking about the advantages, which they also typically begin with.

A personnel manager told me that with the following question he is very well able to compare the company's expectations with those of the candidate:
"Now we have talked for quite a while about the job and your work history. To get to know you better, I'm now interested in how you estimate your strengths and weaknesses."
Candidates with an "away from" pattern would almost without exception talk about what they did not know or what they had problems with. The personnel manager added that this pattern could be very beneficial, like for example, in quality assurance where finding and avoiding defects has highest priority.

Although I am explaining the different types of pattern one after the other, they will all work together. Maybe you will be a bit overwhelmed when I combine the movie example from the previous paragraph with the "forward to"/"away from" pattern. The following combinations are possible:

Introspective and "forward to":	Own judgement – self-experience – happiness – be active
Introspective and "away from":	Own judgement – avoid, to be uninformed and not to have an own opinion
Extrospective and "forward to":	Stress what others say and name the movie an "event"
Extrospective and "away from":	Stress what others say and how to avoid to be excluded

Maybe this also explains why **deterrence** does not have an effect in general. With "away from" guided people this strategy may have good results. Yet, anyone who lives according to the "forward to" pattern wants to find something attractive and can much better be motivated when he is shown positive opportunities.

Even if this requires a totally new way to prepare for lessons, students can be motivated far better when addressed according to their personal behaviour patterns. Children who tend to move forward, in the best case turn off when they are talked at about dropping something. As soon as they are shown which possibilities are offered they become curious.

Also employees are too often treated only one way. Instead of trying to get an "away from" oriented person interested in a certain task by talking about the chances in it, it can be much more appreciative – and less overextending – to show him which risks he can avoid and which disadvantages it will save him.

Opportunity or necessity

For a change, I am offering you a short self test at the beginning of this paragraph. Please, state spontaneously a brief explanation to answer the following questions:

(1) Why did you decide to take your current job/position?

(2) What was the crucial factor in choosing your current residence?

(3) Why did you buy the car you drive today?

(4) What had an influence on where you went for your recent vacation?

(5) Why did you take up your hobby?

You may most probably have guessed it already. Decisions are made out of an idea of their necessity or in search for opportunities. This decision pattern is the thread in one's life. The following differences are especially remarkable:

- **Understanding necessities:** Something is done because it needs to be done.
  Attention is focussed on the well known and secure.
  Decisions aim at stability and continuity.
- **Looking for opportunities:** Action is triggered by what is possible.
  The interest is focussed on the unknown and on new opportunities.
  Decisions are determined by choices and opportunities for development.

Some typical answers may be helpful here, too. In addition, the answers to all short "tests" are a chance to practice and to sharpen one's perception.

	Opportunity	**Necessity**
Why did you decide to take your current job/position?	Good career opportunities, prospect of working abroad, new challenges to work with different people.	You have to live on something, as a civil servant you do not risk losing your job, meets my professional training.
What was the crucial factor in choosing your current residence?	Was what we had planned for, I was able to rebuild a lot, I only live there until I find a better place.	It was the only place available, rather cheap, good traffic connections.
Why did you buy the car you drive today?	I'm interested in the latest models, fit for both business and travelling, I like to drive fast.	Company car, with 4 children you need a van, I always drive an XY.
What had an influence on where you went for your recent vacation?	I wanted to see something new, they promised the most alternatives, I had never been on a sailing trip before.	Tip from friends who had been very satisfied, we always go there, they have always good weather.
Why did you take up your hobby?	Thrilling, I can express myself, I love taking risks!	Very relaxing, I need nobody else, I just like collecting things.

Minding this pattern can help when hiring people to make sure that employees get a job that meets their way of information processing.

Anyone who, for example, prefers to act out of **necessity** may be happy about the offer to build up a new department and proudly take over the new and maybe even better paid job. Yet, only after a short while the variety of opportunities, the unstable developments in combination with the pressure not to miss any chance may nearly paralyse him. I often experience how highly qualified and engaged employees suffer from a job promotion since they all of a sudden find themselves in a job area where they miss the usual security and the familiar structures they would need to perform well.

Kurt Tucholsky may have thought about the typical necessity-finder when he wrote the ironical comment:

They go to work

"It is for work that man is in the world, for earnest work, that which needs a man who stands his ground. If it has a meaning, if it does harm or is of use, if it gives pleasure: it is all the same. It has to be a work. And one has to be able to go there in the morning, or the whole life is without purpose."

Conversely, people with preference for **opportunities** will in the long run be dissatisfied when their job does not allow for development and enhancement. Their supervisors are usually completely surprised when they quit – seemingly without any reason, just because they have been given chances elsewhere which are missing in their current job. Normally it is found out too late how this employee could have been made newly engaged and loyal by additional challenges.

But even one and the same task can be explained specifically for the other's perception mode.

- While one is told about the untaken **opportunities** and learns to view the **number of possibilities** not only as a welcome **variation**, but also as a challenging **alternative** for his personal **development**,
- The other will get **insight** into the **necessities** of a task when he can understand that his work results will help to **secure his employment**, that it is required to show **constant engagement** to safeguard what he has **achieved** until now by his **loyalty**.

When you deal with these patterns you will find that people with a **"necessity pattern"** love to hear explanations. Cause-effect-relationships ease understanding of necessities. With this pattern you will much less often observe the resistance discussed in chapter 6, which is normally caused by words like: **must, shall, must not, necessary, imperative, or required**.

With dialogue partners with an **"opportunity pattern"** you will stress the goal, the purpose aspect of an activity. The point is to give the other an idea of the number of opportunities and the variety of chances.

Anyone who works in sales will as a consequence of these thoughts take care in the future not to bother customers who act out of necessities with additional information about the opportunities of the product; and vice versa a customer looking for opportunities will feel addressed the right way only when he is given unwanted hints about what the product offers in addition to his requirements. To make it more clear, I have chosen the following example:

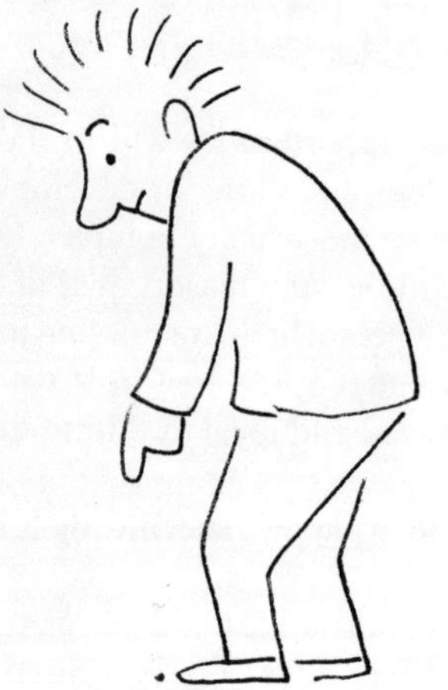

Customer: "I need a fax machine. Unfortunately one can't do without one nowadays."

Salesman A: "I will show you some of the latest models that will really fulfil all wishes. With this model you have the advantage that you can store 100 numbers, plus you have 10 quick dialling keys. In addition it has an automatic voice mail function, a remote control, and it can of course be used as a copier."

Customer: "Well, yes –, that is really great. Um. Do you have any folders so that I can think it over again?"

And again the highly motivated salesman A watches a customer leave and is disappointed...

Salesman B: "Now you have come to the decision to buy such a machine. What exactly do you expect from your new fax machine. I'm asking so directly in order to be able to show you exactly the equipment that meets your requirements best."

Congruence or difference

What is meant by this title you will understand best from looking at the following illustrations.

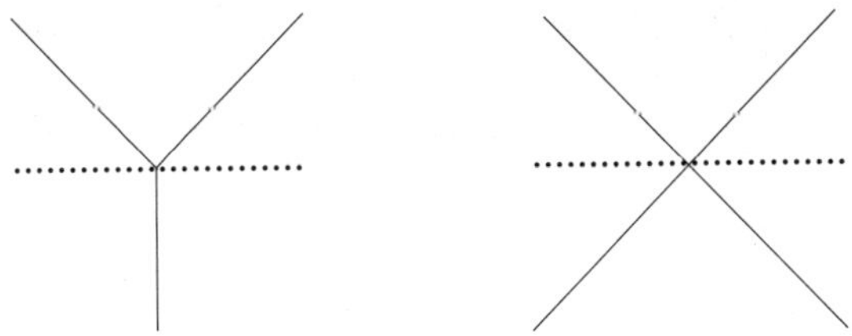

Please note down what strikes you when comparing the following two graphs.

Maybe you would like to compare your answers to the reactions of your mate, friends, or colleagues. You will find that some stress the differences, while others start with the similarities.

Here I have listed some typical answers of other readers:

Congruence	Differences
Both drawings look the same above the dotted line.	Two entirely different letters.
Both figures consist of the same structures	For the X one needs two lines, for the Y three lines.
Both are letters.	The left figure does not contain a 135° angle.
The upper left part is identical to the upper right part.	In the alphabet X comes before Y.
Both figures contain a 90° angle.	One represents a bifurcation, the other a crossing.
Both letters are the same size.	

When answering the following questions you may find how close in type your answers are or, in the sense of this chapter: how much the answers are influenced by the specific perception pattern.

(1) When you compare the tasks of this month to the ones of the previous month, what can you spontaneously say about them?
(2) What is the connection between the cities of Frankfurt, Munich, and Hamburg?
(3) What are your thoughts when comparing pizza to spaghetti?
(4) What do you associate when comparing cembalo, cello, and clarinet?
(5) In which relation do spring, summer, autumn, and winter stand to one another?

Even if the final result may be the same, the **congruence-finders** concentrate on similarities first before turning towards the differences, while on the other hand the **difference-seekers** begin with the separations before they admit that these things have also something in common. Even if the congruence-finders are the larger group – research has found a 2:1 ratio – this pattern is not rated higher.

One learns and understands information preferably according to the pattern:

- Where do I know this?
- How does this piece of information connect to other things I know?

- What is the common denominator?
- What is a good match?

The other will process the same piece of information by asking himself:

- What are the main differences?
- Where is this piece of information different from others?
- Are there discrepancies?
- What does not match or what cannot be right?

How differently people may react can be shown by the following table with typical answers to the questions on the previous page:

	Congruence	**Differences**
When you compare the tasks of this month to the ones of the previous month, what can you spontaneously say about them?	No changes. Same job like always. It was mainly based on the same decisions.	Can hardly be compared since now school holidays are over. Now it is the next quarter and we look out for new things.
What is the connection between the cities of Frankfurt, Munich, and Hamburg?	Major German cities. Important cities in Western Germany. Many historical things in common.	One "Mainhattan", one capital city, one city state. Different dialects are spoken there.
What are your thoughts when comparing pizza to spaghetti?	Typical Italian food. Both from wheat flour. Both feed me.	One is in a pot, the other in the stove. For the pizza you need fork and knife, for spaghettis fork and spoon.
What do you associate when comparing cembalo, cello, and clarinet?	Three musical instruments. All begin with a "c". All built from wood.	One woodwind, one bow instrument, one keyboard instrument. Totally different sound.
In which relation do spring, summer, autumn, and winter stand to one another?	Normal turn of the seasons. One year. One comes after the other.	Totally different weather. Great colours. In contrast to each other.

Knowing these patterns, the similarity-finder will no longer be annoyed when the difference–seeker corrects him and tells him about the discrepancies. This hint on differences and deviations is not meant to provoke the other but merely states one's own perception and information processing. Whoever looks out for similarities may feel annoyed when the other will force the following typical questions on him?

"Is this always true?"
"And what if…?"
"Really?"
"But this stands in contrast to…"
"This contradicts…"
"In my opinion this should read…"
Etc.

Even if these objections are sometimes stated at the wrong moment, they anyway help to sharpen one's view for differences and contradictions.

Like in the previous paragraph, this pattern may help to make personnel decisions in a way that tasks are assigned to employees in relation to their preferred pattern. Whoever looks for congruence will hardly be happy about an expatriate assignment that requires a lot of flexibility and constant change. And on the other hand a difference-seeker will feel unchallenged by routine tasks and will cease engagement when he finds out how seldom his analytical understanding is needed.

Beginning with task assignment the chosen formulation can make a difference in possible motivation.

Talking to a difference-seeker may sound like:

"I'd like to tell you to what extent this job is different from your previous one. When we talk about the changes you have the chance to verify if you rate the differences the same way I do and where you have another opinion…"

An employee who tends to look for similarities will be addressed differently like for example:

"In order to allow you to get an overview of your new job I want to work out together with you where you see similarities to your previous task.

We can then tick off the familiar topics, especially since I know that I can rely on you there. As soon as the similarities have been clarified you will be able to assess what is really new with the new job."

You can also use this pattern successfully in customer contacts. The following test question can be asked in this or in a modified form at any time:

- "When you compare this product to what you until now ..." Or:
- "I don't know if you compare this model to the previous one ..."

Whoever gives to understand that he is a congruence-finder does not want to be bothered with hints on additional differences, and vice versa the difference-seeker may feel brushed down when he is presented only with the mere minimum of information without hinting at deviations and contrasts.

Offer a difference-seeker the chance to view things differently.

Anyone who minds these patterns in his reactions will always make use of the following phrases for a **difference-seeker**:

"Maybe you have a totally different view on this."
"I have put it the easy way, but I can imagine that one can have an entirely different opinion."
"I'm very enthusiastic about my own proposal, but I would prefer to find out if I have overlooked important details."
"Even if we agree we'd better not forget the differences."
"You can best verify the differences when you ..."

Since a congruence-finder will not actively look for differences he may feel unnecessarily annoyed.

Tell the congruence-finder what is similar and how much known and familiar can be found in the new things or situation.

Here, words like "similar", "equal", "related", "same", "on par", "common" and others will help.

Summary

When you fail to convince your dialogue partner it is not necessarily the content, which makes him hesitate to agree. Maybe you did not arouse his interest because he has different perception patterns. Before taking back something from your statements you can try to reach him in another way.

When you want to prepare for a certain dialogue partner you can test upfront with which formulations you best meet the other's perception patterns.

In the following I have listed some practical phrases, which in the beginning may help you to prepare for different dialogue partners:

Introspective You on your own ... You can test verify, find out, Suiting you Meeting your feelings Make your decision You assess, judge, estimate ...	**Extrospective** Other(s) Stress, who else ... Compare with role models Agreed on by others In congruence with ... Others make the same decision Who assesses, rates it the same?
Forward to What else, in addition, plus Chose, select Curiosity, desire Convenience, enrichment Chance, possibility Opportunity Benefit	**Away from** Not, without, no Avoid Prevent Abstain Burden Inconvenient, unpleasant, straining Risk, threat, bad luck Change
Opportunity Take a chance Have alternatives Offer an opportunity Increase, Development For a change Can, will, may	**Necessity** Understand Needed, required, imperative Safety, security Continuity, over time, Stability Stay, keep, maintain Must, shall, must not

Congruence	Difference
Like . . .	Not, no, never, in no case
Same as	Different from . . . entirely different
Comparable to . . .	Not like . . .
Similar to . . .	In contrast to . . .
Matches . . .	Is different from . . .
Belongs to	Is separated by . . . to separate from . . .
Can be connected with	Difference

19. The Art of Causing Change

In chapter 6, I extensively dealt with the resistance people express when experiencing a limitation of their freedom. In this context I also stated that there is hardly anything we respond to as sensitively as to a restriction of our choice of behaviour.

This explains why the desire to change something with others in a sustainable way is very rarely crowned with success: our fellow men express reactance. Anyhow, the want to influence others and to move something on a long-lasting basis is still unbroken. Research studies find that 90 % of all change processes in the business area fail. When we observe that companies cannot achieve their goals in the market with the desired success, this is not due to lack of ideas. On the contrary: Entrepreneurial creativity is on a high level. Yet, the best strategy is bound to fail when implementation is a problem. And as it is often the case, the mind jumps ahead and is already developing new concepts, while the current projects are lacking acceptance or are even undermined.

For example a businessman explains to his employees which competitive advantage they will gain if customers can ask for maintenance work to be carried out during the weekend. The result: the emergency service is turned into regular weekend service. When the entrepreneur explains his future strategy he typically forgets his own thought development process. When he was presented with the same idea several weeks ago, he had many doubts and was anxious about cost development, yes, he even struggled with the fact that customer orientation should require so much effort and sacrifice. Yet, his own ups and downs, pros and cons belong to the past now, and now he has a goal which has to be realised. His employees do not seem to understand the use of his strategy in assuring the future of the business and their jobs. Therefore, he starts to explain the idea all over again, this time with a bit more effort...
You are asking yourself how the story ended. Well, the employees were able to "prove" that there was no need for this service from the customer side and that this strategy has many disadvantages on the operational side.

Elisabeth Kübler-Ross and Verena Kast have investigated what happens with important change processes like death, incurable illnesses, or divorce. The four phases to be observed in this area can very easily transferred to every process, during which we have to accept changes we have not been prepared for. Or more generally stated: we are confronted with information that does not fit into our current idea of reality. In this case we pass the phases:

- **Alarm**
- **Adherence**
- **Letting go**
- **Adaptation**

> Whoever wants to implement or sustain change and takes the four phases of change into consideration, is able to communicate accordingly.

Phase 1: Alarm

For each piece of information (and with everything they perceive), people distinguish between **pleasant** and **unpleasant**. Each perception that is unusual or is connected with danger or unpleasant memories will via the diencephalons and the sympathetic neural system cause direct stimulation of the adrenal glands. In a split second, the hormones adrenalin and nor adrenalin will be effused into the bloodstream. These substances, known as stress hormones, cause the immediate fight or flight reaction. For example, to be able to rescue oneself by running away, heartbeat is increased and the muscles become more intensively supplied with blood. At the same time all processes, which are required for neither fight nor flight, become reduced to minimum level. This includes next to digestion and sexuality also thinking, the activity of the neo cortex. So as not to slow down the rescuing jump away from the enemy by "thinking it over", nature has taken care that stress reaction includes **blocked thinking**. As long as this freeze lasts, a human being is so to say immune against new information, he cannot listen.

> In the Alarm phase all energy is focussed on retrieving lost security.

The resulting flight tendency reaches from inner sealing (including stony facial expression) via displacement activities (change to another theme) up to really leaving the setting.

Anyone who monitors his dialogue partner will find a retreat. With a dialogue in standing, this retreat will lead an advance backwards of at least one step, when sitting one can see how the dialogue partner moves backwards and literally presses himself against the backrest. Often the arms will be crossed in front of the breast. Typical for the alarm state is also to draw a short, deep breath that ends up in holding one's breath.

The face expresses all signs of astonishment: eyes wide open or with a surprised look, in combination with knitted brows. At the same time, the mouth is rather slightly open instead of firmly shut.

Try to do quite the opposite, like bending forward, but drawing breath at the same time, or moving backwards while pressing the lips together, or opening the eyes wide while trying to frown etc.

- As an exercise you can verify these rules by testing how your reaction looks when you are alarmed. Draw your attention to breathing, posture, facial expression, and body language. Also take care for how your voice changes.
- Look out in the next days for how you can recognise if other people are surprised, shocked, amazed, or even terrified. The closer you look the more details you will notice. It will help you to take note to become really certain in distinguishing different emotional expressions.
- Test in another step how little willingness to listen is expressed by people who have just been confronted with a displeasing message. Test out how much of your statement has been received after you have "shocked" your dialogue partner.

In this context you can understand, why some people react to an offer for reconciliation or to a present with repulsion. Anyone who is still dealing with shock is unable to be happy about advances.

> Anyone who knows that in the Alarm phase thinking is blocked will refrain from giving arguments. He is not listened to anyway. Instead, he will address the alarm state and gives the other person the emotional certainty that alarm is an appropriate reaction to the given information.

A customer brings his car for maintenance. The foreman of the workshop explains to him: "The exhaust pipe is broken."

The customer is shocked and looks at his exhaust in alarm.

"You can hear it yourself, how it rattles. There's nothing to be done about it."

The customer takes one step back.

"It's just a matter of time before you lose it. It has to be done."

The customer takes shelter: "Nay, you better leave it. I'll have it done another time."

To get away from "danger" the shocked customer turns to flight reaction and says "No". But this no is everything but a conscious negation, but is just an unreflected avoidance behaviour. If the customer would think calmly about his "exhaust problem", he would most probably decide to have the repair done, before he has a breakdown. Yet, it is doubtful if he will give another order to this workshop after his "No". This is how businesses fail every day.

An experienced foreman will notice the alarm in his customer's face and will address it directly: "I can see that I have shocked you."

"Yes, I mean, I didn't notice anything, until now one couldn't hear anything."

"Yes, that's right. It's still fixed. Now you are a bit surprised because I have said it's broken."

"True, it comes as a bit of surprise..."

To be able to react in an appropriate way I want to recommend the following list of words:

surprised	You are surprised.
surprised	You seem surprised.
perplexed	This makes you perplexed.
flabbergasted	Now you are flabbergasted.
speechless	You are speechless.
stunned	Maybe I have stunned you.
bewildered	You look rather bewildered.

shocked	I have shocked you.
alarmed	You are really alarmed.
terrified	This is terrifying for you.
alienated	Maybe I have alienated you.
puzzled	This puzzles you.
thunderstruck	You look thunderstruck.

> When showing respect for the other person's shock, you do not only show regard, but you will also shorten this phase.

In chapter 15 "Delivering Unpleasant Messages" I had explained that our natural behaviour loses its **spontaneity** as soon as it enters our conscience. There is no conscious spontaneity.

To better understand the alarm phase, I again offer an exercise:

	Your answer
(1) Due to job problems you have to explain to your family that instead of going on the planned biking tour you will have to work during the weekend. How do you prepare your family for this "change"?	
(2) Due to an unexpected quitting you have to convince one of your employees to move to another team. How do you confront this employee with this "change"?	
(3) How do you explain to a customer that due to human resource shortage you will not be able to deliver at the moment?	

My proposals:

(1) "I can imagine that I cause some trouble when I am changing our plans for the weekend..."

(2) "You may be bewildered when I move you from your familiar environment at such a short notice..."

(3) "Maybe I will shock you when I disappoint you regarding your order..."

You will experience that astonishment, shock, or anxiety on the part of your dialogue partner will vanish quickly when they are addressed and are regarded as a necessary intermediate step on the way to a change.

Phase 2: Adherence

When the shock fades off (depending on intensity the duration can lie between some minutes and many days) one will move forward into the phase of adherence. If the previous phase was dominated by confusion, we now enter the orientation on what is established. While shock was causing stress reaction that led to blocked thinking, we will find in this phase a kind of aftermaths of the stress reaction. Thinking is reenabled, but very one-sidedly. Thinking in this phase can be understood as insisting on the known and familiar. Orientation on the status quo turns backwards and does not yet allow for creative thoughts. Whoever wants to adhere is not interested in future opportunities but focusses attention on the question how to save the current state. This adherence is unfortunately also continued where there is nothing to gain from it at all. Just think of fighting couples who stay in the relationship with pertinacity even if nothing changes.

In this phase one can observe three steps:

- **Denial:** At first reality is denied with all available means. Typical reactions are: "This must be an error." – "That's impossible." – "I can't believe it." – "That can't be true." – A very impressing example is the sinking Titanic, where not only the captain but also many passengers have denied danger so perfectly that one stayed until the near end with one's normal activities. One has to understand that it is a kind of **self-protection**, to not accept reality.

> Whoever modifies threatening reality into something not regarding him can keep emotional balance.

This allows also neglecting parts of one's own personality, so that personal concernment is excluded.

For example an employee, who all of a sudden finds himself losing his job, might deny his own responsibility for it. And this is not the case because he lacks self- criticism, but because his organism is striving for stability.

- **Aggression:** After denial of reality will follow the typical forms of rage and anger. The other will be viewed as an assailant; he has attacked one's security, the status quo. This phase is often acted out intensively, but still contributes to the higher-ranking goal of adherence. One may remember in this context how often it is possible to make the other withdraw by venting one's anger.

Even if one does not spare the employee the cancellation of his contract, just because he reacts hotly, it can often be shown that openly demonstrated aggression leads to concessions. How often do subordinates experience that vehement refusal of change strengthens the status quo – and be it only that the planned change is delayed.

- **Negotiation:** When the phase of aggression fades out and allows rethinking the situation, an **adherence tactic** comes into place that aims at saving as much as possible. Whoever negotiates in this phase is not willing to deal with change and its goals and opportunities, here negotiating means adhering to the current state. According to the motto: "When I cannot keep everything as I am used to I will at least by tough negotiation try to save as much as possible."

In layoff discussions one can frequently observe how employees after the first shock and angry denial quickly move into the negotiation phase, to fathom under which conditions they may stay or how they can increase compensation.

The exhaust example from the last phase can be continued:

Although the customer can hear the facts (= rattling exhaust), he **denies** reality: "This cannot be. The car is just three years old."

"You can hear how it rattles when I knock at it a bit."

Now the customer switches from **denial** to **aggression**: "With my last car the exhaust lasted at least for five years. If I had only stayed with that make. What do you view as quality? This is all cheap scrap."

"An exhaust pipe is subject to thermal and mechanical wear and does not last for ever."

Now the customer tries out his luck in negotiation: "Nobody expects this, but three years, isn't that a case for some goodwill..."

But to hold on tight to the past does not automatically equal being against something new. It is just part of the natural change process. Opposition out of lost security is not real refusal.

Anyone who has learned to distinguish between real refusal and adherence can avoid unnecessary tension, misunderstandings, and problems.

Whoever perceives adherence just as an **interim phase**, will be able to fasten its passage by – in a way paradoxical – allowing room for it and by showing understanding for a persistence that is based on uncertainty.

An experienced foreman will show regard for the customer even when he says: "This cannot be. The car is just three years old."

"It doesn't suit you that the exhaust is broken after only three years."

"Well, it's really an expensive matter."

"I can understand your anger. I would be cheesed off, too, if I had to pay more, just like that."

"That's right, it really knocks me off my feet. Can you do it out of goodwill in this case?"

"The term of guarantee for your exhaust pipe ended two years ago, but you would be happy if the repair weren't so expensive, because it is so unexpected."

"Yes, well, I could have it done if I had to pay the invoice next month..."

I use the examples from the previous paragraph to practice how to treat people in the phase of adherence. Try to show respect for the other and his reaction of denial, aggression, and negotiation and abstain from stating justifications.

	Your answer
(1) "This can't be true. – You promised it. – You never have time. Your bloody job always comes first. Can't you join us later?"	
(2) "I can hardly believe that you want to take me out of the team. We are in the middle of the project. Couldn't I close that before?"	
(3) "That's a bad joke. You can't do that. – Say, are you mad? Do you know what that means?"	

My proposals for an answer:

(1) "I can understand that you are disappointed. It must alienate you that you can't rely on my promise. I think I would explode, too..."
(2) "Bother, I shock you like this and just realise how bitter it must be for you that I take you out of the ongoing project."
(3) "Maybe you would like to strangle me because I get you into a tight place..."

We tend to understand the "No" of this phase as an expression of **refusal**, which must be altered by arguments. Yet, even the best arguments are lost as long as the other does not listen to us. And he does not really listen because – as explained above – his thinking is turned backwards and on how to secure his ideas.

Phase 3: Letting go

Adherence is followed by **valediction**. In this phase one is sad about the lost past. The intellectual understanding accepts that the line is drawn and that it does not make sense to further resist change. After the active adherence phase now follows the more passive phase of **letting go**. The mood is melancholic and backwards oriented; it is what has been that is moaned about.

Out of the insight into necessities this phase **may** be followed by an orientation towards the future and on the forthcoming changes. However, it can often be observed that lack of open resistance is mistaken for agreement. According to the motto: Who does not say "no", agrees. This can have significant consequences: since in this phase agreement has not taken place, assuming it can lead to a regression to the previous phase.

It is also true here that hesitation loses its spontaneity when it becomes conscious. One cannot solve problems with a decision by the use of pressure or by adding further arguments.

> To calmly accept the other's **doubts** and to understand that this is a normal process will help the dialogue partner to become clear about his next steps.

Here an example may help: as long as the monkey holds on tight to the empty coconut shell, it cannot take the banana.

In body language a seesaw accompanies this phase. While we could observe a withdrawal in case of shock and bending forward in the aggression stage, we will now see someone moving from one side to the other. The other will careen, torn between one hand and the other. When you watch carefully you will find that during his argumentation he always takes the same positions. When stating the pros his weight will be for example, on the left leg, while he moves to the right leg when turning to the cons every time. You will observe the same with a seated person. One corner of the chair is reserved for agreement, while the opposite corner is connected to the negative view.

Let us in this context again use the three examples:

	Your answer
(1) "When we go on the biking tour without you, I have an entirely new role. I don't know if I like that."	
(2) "On one hand I'm interested in the new task, on the other hand it is hard to leave the project so suddenly."	
(3) "When you could make the other delivery earlier, we could at least keep running, although I really cannot understand that you can't deliver, or that you won't, who knows."	

My proposed answers:

(1) "You are uncertain if you want to agree to this experience."
(2) "This is all too quick for you. You feel really taken by surprise and don't have time to weigh the pros and cons."
(3) "You could imagine meeting me half way. But you have some substantial doubts."

Who does not simply leave the old, but helps to end it in dignity, wins energies for the new. Here one can see the special effect of **farewell rituals**, which are helpful for many people in turning to the new afterwards. So certain this is for us with important events like graduation, retirement, or death, so important is bidding farewell also for much less important changes. Many children take great care to collect their baby teeth, but also adults leave more easily when they have taken a last photo of the holiday resort or their old car. People vary in the time they need to pause and to take a look back. To grant this time will abbreviate this phase because pressure to move on quicker will all too easily be answered by returning to adherence.

It may sound technical when I suggest celebrating change. It can be shown that people accept new things much easier when the old has been closed. Although our life is full of rituals, in several countries people have problems to accept them – for example because they have been abused in their political history. Anyway, this does not change their general effect.

Phase 4: Adaptation

The new start can only follow after letting go. Expressed in an image: anyone who clutches the straw with both hands cannot catch the life belt. Starting with something new requires a farewell to what was before. The more successfully this is done the higher the probability that the new will work out well and the higher the probability that verbal agreement for the forthcoming change will turn into active participation in the implementation of new structures.

But even in this phase the other may **slide back**. If he, despite of best intentions, cannot cope with the effects of the changes and feels left alone, he will return to what he has been doing for years.

There is the clerk who with a heavy heart has agreed to do the salary accounting with the new computer software. Only after a short while it turns out that the programme does not work properly and that the representative of the software firm does not state clearly when the bugs will be eliminated. One morning we can see our clerk with her pocket calculator and pencil, writing the salaries into the form sheet as she has done in the past twenty years . . .

The adaptation phase is the most neglected one in change processes. The responsible people are already busy with the next project and believe it to be understood that everything is working. It is very similar for our customers, when they after endless discussions have made up their mind for a big investment. Now the equipment is here and we try to cope with it. Unfortunately, it does not work as it did in the shop. When the sales representative talks hot air now ("You have to call our service, I'm only responsible for sales"), we do not only regret that we bought it, we may also move several steps backwards and assert our right of return.

Anyone who understands that these phases can also be found in decision-making processes, will use this in every conversation with somebody.

Let us get back to the initial example and imagine that the businessman has made himself familiar with the four phases of change.
In this case he would have come to the conclusion that his idea of regular work during weekends will be a shock for his employees. Then the thunderstruck faces of his subordinates would not have surprised him. On the contrary, he would have been able to understand the threat of his plan and he could have expressly allowed his employees to feel alienated when hearing that their past engagement would be rewarded with additional workload.
In the next step he could solely have explained his vision of the future. In order to abbreviate the adherence phase the businessman has to take the expected refusal seriously. This can best be done privately. His activity is reduced to listening. His goal is to get to know as many reasons as possible that stand against introducing work at weekends.
The more honestly he shows his employees that he can understand their refusal of his idea, the less vehement will be possible acts of aggression. At the end of these dialogues he will verify the conditions under which the employees might open up to his idea. We are now in transition to the letting go phase. A paradigm change will take place away from backwards-oriented persistence on the familiar work hours: The employees turn towards the opportunities and check in how far they lead to a benefit that means also advantages for them.
Maybe our business man will make use of his knowledge on rituals by celebrating the implementation of the new shift system with a farewell party where on the last free Saturday everybody can formally and merrily say good-bye to the old times.
But our businessman is still not satisfied. He knows that the first times will reveal some obstacles. To prevent sliding back and yearning for the old times, he talks to the employees on a regular basis to ascertain that they are fine with working during the weekend and to check where amendments are required.

People move through the four phases with different speed and intensity. Yet, everyone will go through all four phases. Be aware what happens inside of people who are unexpectedly confronted with a change. When you want to lead change you can help your dialogue partners to let go of the old things and accept the new by making use of the phase model as a basic principle.

How to cause change

Dealing with alarm

When you confront the other with a message that is unexpected or unpleasant for him, you destroy his hitherto existing ideas, he loses security and is shocked. Physiologically viewed he feels stress.

The other will spontaneously react with withdrawal. His entire energy is focused on restoring the lost security.

You can observe that the other will move backwards, hold his breath and show the facial expression of astonishment.

The hormone adrenaline has partly or entirely blocked his thinking. He may say "no" or "I don't believe it", but you can abstain from giving any kind of explanation. He is far too occupied with himself to deal with you and your statements.

> Since you know that in the Alarm phase thinking is blocked you will refrain from giving arguments. Instead, you will address the alarm state and give the other person the emotional certainty that alarm is an appropriate reaction to the given information.

Whoever wants to cause change and is able to take into account which phases the other person is going through, can communicate according to the situation.

When you see that the other steps back or leans back in his chair, you may have shocked him. Stated in a less dramatic way: the dialogue partner shows all signs of surprise. You can often observe that he furrows his brow, the eyes widen and he holds his breath.

With the following phrases you can not only show that you sense the other's concern but also that you understand his confusion:

- "You are surprised."
- "You seem surprised."
- "This makes you perplexed."
- "Now you are flabbergasted."
- "You are speechless."
- "Maybe I have stunned you."
- "You look rather bewildered."

- "I have shocked you."
- "You are really alarmed."
- "This is terrifying for you."
- "Maybe I have alienated you."
- "This puzzles you."
- "You look thunderstruck."

Dealing with adherence

When shock and astonishment fade, one moves forward into the phase of adherence. Thinking will focus on the current state. On the speech level this is expressed by persisting on the known and familiar. Orientation turns backwards, and it is emphasised how things have been in the past.

Normally, people pass three stages: at first they **deny** the importance, the threatening information will be reinterpreted as not valid.

On denial follow the typical forms of **anger, rage, and fury**. One is viewed as an assailant, because one has attacked the other's safety.

As the last step follows the adherence tactic of **negotiation**, trying to rescue as much as possible.

> Whoever has learned to distinguish between real refusal and adherence can avoid unnecessary tension, misunderstandings, and problems.

As soon as you realise that the other overcomes his astonishment and shock, because he moves forward, sits up and raises his voice, you are in the **adherence** phase

Your dialogue partner may contradict you, but he does not listen to you. His thoughts are directed at rescuing his ideas, so arguments would have no effect.

Therefore you will not take a "No" in this phase as an expression of refusal, but just as an attempt to restore the lost safety.

With the following phrases you will not only show that you have noticed the dialogue partner's agitation but that you understand his anger:

- "You are angry about…"
- "You are annoyed when…"
- "It drives you crazy when…"

- "You are outraged about …"
- "This fills you with bitterness."
- "This makes you really furious."
- "You hate it when you…"
- "You are livid because…"
- "You could explode because…"
- "You are cheesed off when…"
- "You could freak out."
- "You breathe fire and brimstone."

Dealing with doubts

After adherence follows the phase of letting go. The view is still turned backwards and it is the past that is moaned about.

Whoever bids farewell to old ideas, has not agreed to the new one at the same time. This phase is indicated by **seesaw, hesitation, and doubts**.

In this phase you can observe how the other steps from one foot to the other and is torn between one hand and the other. He turns his head, moves from one leg to the other or moves from side to side on his chair.

In this phase it is crucial to avoid mistaking lack of resistance for agreement. Anyone who now – out of impatience – wants to come to a conclusion will find himself thrown back into the phase of adherence.

Difficulties in making a decision cannot be eliminated by pressure.

> To calmly accept the other's doubts and to understand that this is a normal process will help the dialogue partner to become clear about his next steps.

As soon as you realise that the other begins to deal with the changed situation, the **adaptation** phase begins. It will start with a hesitating inspection of the pros and cons.

Since hesitation loses its spontaneity when it becomes conscious you can abbreviate it by – seemingly paradoxical – allowing hesitation.

With the following phrases you cannot only demonstrate that you have noticed the dialogue partner's hesitation but you can also show that you are willing to patiently deal with his doubts.

- "You are hesitating."
- "You remain sceptical."
- "This puts you under pressure."
- "You are still in doubt."
- "You are still uncertain."
- "You have not made up your mind."
- "You still have objections."
- "You don't know what to do yet."
- "You feel a bit torn."
- "Somehow you have scruples."
- "This makes you feel uncertain."
- "You are still suspicious."

These entry phrases are usually answered with a "Yes, because . . ." You will experience that the other starts to explain in detail what he feels is missing to be able to agree without restrictions.

20. Deductive Communication

Chapter 13 dealt with postponing one's reaction in order to confront the dialogue partner with what he has just said. I had to admit that this behaviour might be taken amiss, since it is unusual for many dialogue partners to take over responsibility for what they say.

In this chapter, I will come back to this proceeding and enhance the clarifying approach by drawing conclusions in general. Instead of a reaction to what was heard, a loop can always follow in which it is mirrored to the dialogue partner which conclusions have just been drawn from his statement. This is so indispensable in important conversations because there is a principle that reads:

> Successful communication does not mean transfer of information, but to interpret information in a common way.
>
> Misunderstandings are always based on language problems.

Only when the other agrees can you be sure that you two talk about the same thing. For clarification: this does not mean agreement on the matter itself but on a consistent interpretation and that you also mean the same with the same word. Even if everybody uses the same language it is used and understood in an individual way. When using deductive communication you will find in many cases that the other does not agree to your conclusions at all.

A customer comments on an estimate: "I think this is too expensive. I'll leave the repair."
Service technician: "This means you leave it broken as it is and look for a new one."
"No, I only want to find out if I can get it done cheaper elsewhere."
A colleague complains: "I'm totally upset. The boss has invited me to his garden party."
"This means this doesn't suit you at all."
"O yes, yes. But I don't know how to dress."
A patient says to the dentist: "Since my wife has told me to brush my teeth more regularly I have a constant toothache."
"This means you blame her for your pain."

"No, I didn't mean it that way. But it bleeds when I brush my teeth, and everything feels a bit sore."

The more you vary between different phrases the less artificial this proceeding will seem to be. I have listed some possible expressions.

- This means...
- From this I conclude...
- I draw the conclusion...
- In this I find that...
- This leads to...
- This implies...
- In consequence this means...
- I understand that...
- In conclusion,...
- From this one could interpret that...
- This sounds as if...
- It looks as if...

As soon as someone opens his mouth to tell us something he has one or more intentions. When he does not utter them explicitly, the dialogue partner can only assume them. Many statements are hard to beat in their **lack of clarity**. And since we tend to turn an incomprehensible statement into a comprehensible one via interpretation, we are in danger of assuming wrongly. Sometimes this leads to difficult situations. Problems do always arise when people assume that others view, assess, feel, or value something the very way they do. In consequence, they expect that one acts accordingly; the way they think it is appropriate for the regarded situation. Yet, instead of verifying what really has been meant, one reacts directly to one's own interpretation.

"I'm in desperate search for a way to quit smoking. But I can't make it. I had stopped for three days, but today I had a fag again."
"I mean, one cigarette in four days that's hardly any. Not worth mentioning from a health care point of view."
"O yes, for you it' s easy. You don't have the problem."

The dialogue takes an entirely different turn when the dialogue partner reflects his conclusions:

"I'm in desperate search for a way to quit smoking. But I can't make it. I had stopped for three days, but today I had a fag again."
"This sounds as if you are worried about your health."
"No, smoking is not really the point. I am only annoyed that I'm not able to follow my own decisions."

We are used to interpret the incomplete statements of our fellows. We then believe we know what the other wanted to say. The statement: "Please, do this at once" sounds very simple and easy to understand. Whoever believes he knows his supervisor may interrupt another task to deal with the new one. Yet, by doing this he takes over responsibility for the unclear communication of the superior and has to be ready to accept reproaches when the postponed task is not completed on time. To avoid misunderstandings and to verify if one understands the priorities correctly I generally recommend to utter one's interpretation aloud. This is a chance for the other to agree to it.

"Please, do this at once."
"Alright. This means you want me to postpone the Board report."
"No, for Heaven's sake. I need that by twelve. But please, write this letter directly afterwards."

In chapter 14, "From Persuasion to Conviction", I had explained that many people tend to interpret the other's statement from their point of view. Instead of dealing with the other directly, one deals mainly with ones assumptions about him. One develops ideas about possible reasons for objections and then voices the counter-arguments against one's own interpretations.

A **customer** says: "I don't think the new machine is as good as what we have now."
The **salesman** answers: "Don't worry, this will open new areas of application for you."
Customer: "Maybe. But at first I'll have a lot of trouble with production, when they need to switch."
Salesman: "That's not a problem at all. Send me your head of production. Afterwards he will pester you with his wish to buy the machine."
Customer: "You seem to be very convinced. But to be honest, I have some doubts."
Salesman: "I don't want to offend you, but maybe that's because you

have not yet realised how this machine will enhance your productivity by twenty percent."

Customer: "Productivity increase by twenty percent, that seems totally unrealistic to me. Sounds fishy."

Salesman: "You see that much too one-sidedly. On the contrary. Since this machine is much faster, you don't only save time, but also money."

Customer: "Exactly! That's the very problem, that's much too complicated. It will confuse our people, and we'll have to invest much more time in training. This is no good for us."

Salesman: "No, you don't view this correctly. Of course this favourable offer does include a training course for your employees directly on the machine."

Customer: "O yeah. And we'll suddenly have quality problems, because our people are in training courses all the time. You make it sound too easy."

Salesman: "You are right, but when you look at it reasonably you should not miss this opportunity. What do your quality people say about it?" Etc.

We can understand that the customer will turn away being very annoyed after this conversation instead of giving up his resistance. I have described this dialogue in such a great detail because it reflects a piece of our everyday reality. Instead of listening one tries to break resistance with arguments. Said over-refinedly: When counter-acting arguments we counter-act the other as well – and by this turn him away.

But anyone who turns towards the other deductively does not deal with a clever arrangement of one's own arguments but with what the other says.

The **customer** said: "I don't think the new machine is as good as what we have now."

The **salesman**, having been trained in the meantime, answers: "This means, you will further count on the machine you are used to."

Customer: "Well, at least I know what I have. Admittedly, it has come of age and is very testy. But most of the time it runs without any problems."

Salesman: "I understand that you will go on running your production with the existing machine even if it has certain downtimes."

Customer: "Hm, one day it will break down completely. I guess it's as old as Methuselah. But somehow I do hope it will make it for another while."

Salesman: "This means you live with the risk that your production stops because your machine cannot cope any more."
Customer: "Right. Somehow it's madness! I decide based on hope and at the same time I'm responsible for the production results. But up to now it somehow worked out."
Salesman: "As a consequence this means that you really will start looking for a new machine, when production has stopped."
Customer: "That would be too late. It takes some time until the new machine will be running and the employees will be trained. We can't afford that in any case. No, no, in fact we'd need to order the successor right now."
Salesman: "This sounds as if you are still hesitating."
Customer: "That's right. There is also a financial problem. But I'd better be able to discuss this with the Board when we talk about some details now." Etc.

It requires a lot of self-control to react deductively even when the other says something that is hair-raising. Especially when we are emotionally involved, our **spontaneous reaction** leads all too easily to a **win-lose-situation** where at the end nobody gains anything. Since the loser is known to seek revenge, victory is overshadowed by the risk to be confronted with the other's revenge some day.

A classical area of examples is the parent-child-relationship. Anyone who has children will very well know the feeling of impotence when the children act against advice and admonition. Even if one may be able to carry one's point as a parent, in the long run the impression arises that the children choose their own ways and safeguard their threatened freedom by making different decisions and acting in other ways than their parents. Yet, we can also look at these examples from the other side: every one of us will be able to recall the feeling of inferiority that has been the thread of our childhood and youth. How often have we been overloaded with unwanted advice, how often have we been told it would be better to learn, decide, or act in another way. Yet, if we take the buzzword

of **learning responsibility** seriously it asks for letting children experience in the process of growing up that they are also responsible for what they utter without much thinking.

▸ **A pupil comments another bad mark in a French language test with the words: "As long as I'm with Mrs. Brown, I don't have a chance anyway."**

What will be your answer?

We do not need to go into the details of how this problem is usually handled. Yet, anyone who gives deductive communication a try will in a way set out on a journey the duration and destination of which are still unknown.

Maybe you will have trouble when reading the following dialogue since you will think several times that now a clear piece of advice or at least a recommendation would be advisable. The example dialogue is meant to show where deductive communication will lead to in consequence.

Child: "As long as I'm with Mrs. Brown, I don't have a chance anyway."
Parent: "This means you have already agreed to getting an E."
C: "No, I can't afford that. I want to get my move. And there's also the E in maths."
P: "Sounds as if the E in maths is unavoidable."
C: "I mean, before I deal with that I'd rather bone up French."
P: "In other words: you will get started right away."
C: "Doesn't need to be now. There are at least five to six weeks until the next test. I have to recover from this one first."

P: "This means you wait until the next test is announced, and then you take off."
C: "Yeah, about so. The new words stick in my memory much better when freshly learned."
P: "This means you have a concrete plan how you can successfully pass the test next time."
C: "What do you mean by 'concrete'? It mustn't go wrong, or otherwise I'm doomed. That's for sure."
P: "And I assume that you want to avoid that by all means."
C: "Yes, sure. I'm not a dull-head. When I master two C's, everything will work out nicely."
P: "I conclude that you have summed up already what you need to do for it. Since you say you won't take a risk."
K: "Well, first old Mrs. Brown needs to see that I know my vocabulary. And I shouldn't make mistakes in what we have just learned in grammar lessons."
P: "This sounds as if you have taken a close look at your French curriculum."
C: "Not that close exactly. But I think I can manage it if I start early enough."
P: "So you have already made up your mind about when to start practising."
C: "No, not really. But fifty words per week, that's not the world."
P: "In consequence this means: fifty words times six weeks, that's around 250 to 300 words."
C: "Gracious God! I can't make that! I'd have to start right away. Especially since I don't know the previous ones, either."
P: "This means, you'd rather give up."
C: "Bother! I have to start now. – But not more than twenty minutes per day."
P: "In other words: You have decided to practice French for twenty minutes per day from now on, to pass the next test."
C: "I think there's no other way. – Say, can you examine me later?"

I cannot exclude that one or the other reader may have winced during reading because so much freedom of choice is given to a teenager and because every influence, interference, or "clear instruction" from the adult's side was missing. Yet, I have to ask in return: What would have been the use of it? Are our well-meant reactions not often only expressions of our impatience and lack of trust into the other's ability to solve his own problems?

> Whoever operates with conclusions will help the other to become aware of the meaning of his statements and thus of the significance of his own responsibility.

Our patience will be put through a tough test when the other with one of his statements touches our own freedom and in a way offends our integrity.

As a training example let's use the experience one participant in one of my courses made when her son returned home from the supermarket with too little change. The mother had to deal with a cheeky shop-girl who instead of apologising merely said:

"We were so busy, so this may happen at times."

Before looking at possible conclusions, you may try to note down your reaction:

To confront the shop-girl with the consequences of her statement may sound like this:

"This means, any time you are busy one should not send children to buy something."

"I understand that I'm to check upfront if you are busy before I send my son to buy something."

"In other words, any time you are busy the risk is high that the change is not correct."

This way to communicate has also one downside: It may look like demonstrated **superiority**.

Most people will not be angry about their own stupidity but blame the others for being 'mean'. I will admit that it is emotionally strenuous to meet someone who demonstrates how to look at a situation from a distance and who is able to analyse it and to confront oneself with the results. To be confronted with one's own attitude without having asked for it can be awkward. This way the dark sides of one's self are revealed and unmasked. It proves that one has weaknesses and that others can reveal them.

In business life anyone who makes using the deductive loop before giving his arguments a habit will avoid being ripped by others without being asked. In the following I will explain some usual conversation structures with which others try to veil a purpose and to make people interested in them in an indirect way. My example reactions may alienate some readers at first. This may be caused on the one hand by this style being unusual, on the other by an irritating effect of so much reserved clarity.

You will be able to observe that many dialogue partners make use of questions as a means of conversation style. Even if the grammar structure of a question is clear and even if a sentence may clearly be started as a question, the meaning can be very ambiguous.

The starting phase "I have a question..." seems to ask for an answer. The simple question is often used to hide something entirely different. It is necessary to understand the underlying structure and to reveal the actual meaning.

Proposal, camouflaged as a question

Often ideas, suggestions, proposals, and recommendations are hidden behind a seemingly harmless question.

"I have one question regarding this. Can't we proceed in a way that we wait for a board decision?"

Deductive answer: "I understand that you want me to agree to your proposal."

Or: "This leads to the question whether we shouldn't move to plan X."

Deductive answer: "This means we should follow plan X."

Reproach, dressed as a question

Anyone who voices a reproach in form of a question tries to become invulnerable according to the principle: "What's the matter? It was just a question."

"I have one question: Why did Mr. White not tell us about it until now?"
Deductive answer: "This sounds as if you want to blame Mr. White for it."

Or the seemingly harmless question "Why not?". With this question an explanation is asked for something that cannot be altered any more anyway.

"Why didn't you call me earlier?"
Deductive answer: "This means you want to talk about who is to blame for it now."

Judgement, in form of a question

Whoever states his opinion directly takes the risk of being confronted with an opposing view. An indirect statement in form of a question seems to be less provoking.

"I have one question: Wouldn't it be reasonable if we follow Mrs. Browns idea?
Deductive answer: "This means that you want us to share your opinion on Mrs. Brown's proposal."
Or: "You want to pose the question whether it might be unreasonable to pursue this further."
Deductive answer: "This means you are against this proceeding and would like to know if I share this view."

Assertion, hidden in a question

To state an assertion without any proof can lead to vehement reactions. Therefore, some dialogue partners tend to hide it in a question, usually formulated in a suggestive way.

"I have one question. Is it not clear to everyone that we'll never get this approved?"
Deductive answer: "I conclude from your statement that you don't give this project any chance."

Or: "I'd like to ask directly if there's really anyone in doubt the effort required stands in crass contrast to the result."
Deductive answer: "This sounds as if our opinion is very fixed and you are not interested in another view."

Question to call something in question

When an agreement has been fixed, it is difficult for some dialogue partners to stick to it. A common form of disregarding decisions is to restart the discussion by asking a question.

"I have one question. Did we really take all possibilities into account?"
Deductive answer: "This means that you want to revise the current decision again."
Or: "I'm thinking all the time about the question if we have other alternatives to the current proceeding."
Deductive answer: "This sounds as if you don't want to put the current decision into action but would like to restart the discussion about possible measures."

With this kind of clarifying communication behaviour you may alienate your dialogue partner, since you force a clarity that is not desired. It may help you to be aware that the purpose of deductive communication is not to make oneself popular but to gain a common interpretation of the available information.

To be able to capture the implied message in a statement you will need some practice. You can add to your learnings when taking the trouble to note down your reaction to each of the following exercises before comparing them to my ideas.

	Your conclusion
(1) "I could agree with Mr. Roth. For sure we will disagree in one or the other point but I would think we could clarify that. I would only like to know how I have to imagine the related timetable."	
(2) "It is obvious that in the coming three months we should at first take a look at the existing results. We may take over one or the other without many changes."	

(3) "Please, don't misunderstand me, but for me the question is coming up if Mrs. Blacks proposal might be a bit out of the ordinary because of the uncontrollable scheduling."

(4) "Wait, wait! If possible I'd like to say something, too. For me the thought is obvious that we should put the most far-reaching proposal at the start. Mr. White, would you mind giving us the background of your idea?"

(5) "The mistakes in project management can't be ignored. Obviously no one is willing to answer to our criticism. Even if there is no doubt about the stated problems."

My proposals:

(1) "This means you will agree as soon as you know the exact timetable."
Or: "I understand that the differences in opinion are not big enough to disagree in general."

(2) "I conclude that you have an idea how to save effort."
Or: "This means that you expect that it might result in workload reduction."

(3) "I conclude that you disagree with Mrs. Black's proposal."
Or: "This means you want us to know your reservations against Mrs. Black's idea."

(4) "From this I understand that you want to move Mr. White's proposal to the beginning."
Or: "This means you want to begin with the most far-reaching proposal."

(5) "This means there is no doubt about the criticism and according to your view project management is not willing to deal with it."
Or: "I understand your statement in a way that you hold project management responsible for the mistakes that have been made. You assume that not reacting to your criticism has been done on purpose."

Successful communicators have trained their listening skills in a way that with each statement of the other they ask themselves: What does he say about himself? What do I hear about him? Anyone who is so concentrated on the other is immune to hasty answers even if facing an unexpectedly negative reaction.

Anyone who is aware that every statement reveals something about the speaker can deal with the other's interests and address what the dialogue partner has said about himself.

I get back to the five examples from chapter 17 which include a refusal. This time the task is to deduct a conclusion and to mirror it back to the dialogue partner.

	Your conclusion
(1) "We don't have a demand for this."	
(2) "This is not in my interest."	
(3) "We don't have time for something like this."	
(4) "We don't have it in our budget."	
(5) "We don't want to change the brand we use."	

Please, regard my answers as proposals.

(1) "I conclude from that, that you already have a very satisfying solution to cover your demand."
(2) "In other words: your interests lie in a totally different area."
(3) "I understand that if you had time you would ask me to give you a product presentation."
(4) "This means that your decision latitude is limited by your budget."
(5) "This means this is your final decision."

Whoever concentrates on the self-disclosure of his negotiating partner avoids the risk of ending up in side discussions just due to misinterpretations.

At the end of this chapter I will deal with a typical problem participants bring up in my courses as an example. You can test how far you have become familiar with deductive communication already.

▸ **How do you react when your dialogue partner reacts to an offer you are about to make shortly: "Thanks, I got all I need."**

Whoever wants to raise interest best shows interest himself:

"Then you are in the very happy situation to have found amidst all offers available the best one for yourself."
"Oh, how good. Can't have been easy to find someone who can meet your needs 100 %."
"Your success has my respect. I can imagine one envies you for it" – ("Why?") – "Since it is extraordinarily challenging to separate the wheat from the chaff in today's economy with all the competition."

The dialogue partner is taken seriously regarding his statement "all I need". He is played back that one concludes from his statement that he is responsible for his success and that his future will be as successful, when he actively deals with the market.

Whoever has read the entire book may have tried other ways to react. When you for example try to show understanding for the other's emotions it may be advisable to address the lack of interest openly:

"At the moment you feel hassled by me."
"I have the impression that you feel importuned by my offer (my call)."
"Maybe with my visit (my call) I am keeping you off an important task."

The other will feel understood and say, "yes" spontaneously. Normally, the other will add some more information to this "yes", which may become a link.

But nothing stands against using the negative answer for self-criticism:

"When you say you are not interested you show me that I did not manage to point out what is out of the ordinary with my offer."

"Thank you for your frankness. I've just realised how inexpertly I have presented my offer."
"I should take your 'no' as a hint to think about how to present the three major advantages of my offer to you."

The dialogue partner does not expect that his statement will lead to a self-critical remark from your side. This entirely new dialogue situation will often result in the other opening up. A conversation can begin.

When you get the impression that the negative answer sounds like lack of time, the following respectful opening may be useful:

"I assume that you cannot afford from a time aspect to monitor market development."
"Your workload may not allow you to compare all offers available."
"Then I have guessed correctly." – ("Why?") – "Because in your situation you do not have the time to have every offer explained in detail."

The dialogue partner's "amour propre" will be addressed, which he will usually like and makes him talk about his "difficult situation". And again you may find a link.

But maybe you will also use deductive communication to confront the other with his decision:

"It's because you are so satisfied that you don't want to see anything new at the moment."
"In other words: I have called too early" – ("Why?") – "Because I can only arouse your interest when you had bad experiences with your current provider."
"You are very determined because you know already that your current supplier is unrivalled in price for you."

The dialogue partner is taken seriously and at the same time brought into the paradoxical situation that sticking to what he has cannot be a long-term solution.

A very offensive way is to address the "no" in a provoking way:

"I assume that one can only cut the ice with you when one gets directly to the point."
"Anyone who is unable to indicate the use, stands no chance."
"Your answer makes clear what is relevant for you." – (Why?") – "Your interest has to be aroused." Or: "Your time has to be used the optimal way."

This provoking proceeding is unusual and can make the uninterested dialogue partner curious.

Since every statement offers the chance for many different interpretations, it is very conducive to gaining a common understanding to disclose which meaning you find in the message. It is not the speaker but the listener who gives a message its meaning. Whoever wants to avoid being held responsible for his "misinterpretation" according to the motto: "You should have known what I meant" will leave responsibility where it belongs when using deductive communication: with the dialogue partner.

At the end of this book I want to come back to Mr. Quick. Even if the dialogue in chapter 16 turned out rather ideal I want to mention a downside of his communicative success. Even if the supervisor has been oriented towards his employee, orientation towards the managing director did not take place. This may – as often the case – lead to wasted effort. Let us make him use what he has learned by now:

Phone call of the managing director: "Mr. Quick, in your department you have a Mr. Black who speaks Spanish so well. For our new subsidiary in Santiago de Chile we need someone with these qualities. Please find out whether Mr. Black will be available for this job for about two years. And let me know by Wednesday, it's urgent."

Quick: "For you it is important that I get an ok from Mr. Black as soon as possible."

MD: "Yes, we'll have a board meeting next Friday. We'll probably talk about names then. It would be good to prepare some proposals."

Quick: "This means you are in need of additional candidates."

MD: "Not really. Mr. Short from Research & Development has signalled his agreement already. He is in line with the board and will most probably make it. But as I said, for such a decision you don't give only one name if you know what I mean."

Quick: "Yes, okay. You want to be able to present a real choice. If you want I could also talk to Mr. Brown. In his department is Mr. Lamberto, who is from Spain."

MD: "Great. Then I could name three candidates. That sounds good. Okay, you get back to me then."

Under this prerequisite the conversation with Mr. Black will be entirely different again …

Epilogue

Many statements and examples in this book might raise the impression that I was aiming solely at improving communication **techniques**. Yet, there is a common idea behind all chapters: appreciation and empathy. Whoever tries to use the idea explained here to his advantage and is lacking the **necessary regard** for the other person will only make the same experiences as before. Yet, whoever has changed his **attitude** and makes the other feel respected in each situation, will find richness and depth in his relationships.

I take the liberty of quoting *Epictetus* again:

> "Nature hath given men one tongue but two ears, that we may hear from others twice as much as we speak."

Behind the title "Leadership in Professional Conversation" – promising competence – this book holds several inconvenient truths. You were confronted with an understanding of professional conversation that decidedly calls for personal responsibility. I will admit that this is not everyone's cup of tea.

The background of this book is the view of life influenced by the philosophy of Stoicism, and the Roman word "temperantia" or self-control is one of its main concepts. It requires balance rather than suppression of emotions. Today's psychological research knows not only the IQ, the intelligence quotient, but also the EQ for emotional intelligence. In the meantime it has become common knowledge that the "winners of life" have strategies, which allow them to deal with emotions (other's and their own) without losing themselves out of sight. What makes the difference is to take over responsibility for one's (communicative) actions and thinking. The best way to put it – in my opinion –was found by *Marc Aurel* in his Stoic maxim:

> "Our life is what our thinking makes it."

Buchanzeigen

Schaub/Künzl

Arbeitsgerichtsverfahren

Rechte · Pflichten · Verfahren · Instanzen. Klagearten, Klageerhebung, Güteverhandlung, Vertretung durch Anwalt, Rechtsmittel, Vollstreckung, Einstweilige Verfügung, Beschlussverfahren, Kosten.

7.A. 2004. 475 S.
€ 14,–. dtv 5205 §

Schulz

Alles über Arbeitszeugnisse

Zeugnissprache, Haftung, Rechtsschutz.
Arbeitszeugnisse beeinflussen maßgeblich die Entscheidung über Erfolg oder Misserfolg einer Bewerbung. Der Ratgeber behandelt nicht nur Rechtsfragen, sondern gibt auch Einblick in die „Geheimsprachen" und die Möglichkeiten zu ihrer Entschlüsselung. Mit Zeugnismustern und Beispielen.

7.A. 2003. 189 S.
€ 9,50. dtv 5280 §

Schmidt

Freie Mitarbeit - Ehrenamt - Minijob von A–Z

Rechtslexikon zu den arbeits-, steuer- und sozialversicherungsrechtlichen Fragen bei der Ausübung eines Ehrenamtes, einer Nebentätigkeit, einer Tätigkeit als freier Mitarbeiter oder Ein-Personen-Unternehmer.

2.A. 2005. Rd. 390 S.
Ca. € 13,50. dtv 5678 §

In Vorbereitung für Herbst 2005

Rittweger

Altersteilzeit

Mit Beispielen, Faustformeln und Vertragsmustern.

1.A. 2001. 233 S.
€ 11,50. dtv 5636 §

Hansen/Kanstinger

Zeitarbeit von A–Z

Fachbegriffe, Zusammenhänge, Checklisten.
Die übersichtliche und handliche Informationsquelle zur Zeitarbeit in Deutschland, die das breite inhaltliche Spektrum sachlich, kurz, prägnant und verständlich wiedergibt.

1.A. 2001. 152 S.
€ 8,50. dtv 50850 §

Gröner/Fuchs-Brüninghoff

Lexikon der Berufsausbildung

Über 1500 Begriffe für Führungskräfte, Ausbilder und Personalentwickler. Didaktik und Methodik, Rechtsgrundlagen, jugendpsychologische Fragen, Grundfragen der Berufsbildung.

1.A. 2004. 486 S.
€ 15,–. dtv 50835 €

BeamtR · Beamtenrecht

BundesbeamtenG, BeamtenrechtsrahmenG, BundesbesoldungsG, BeamtenversorgungsG, BundesdisziplinarG, Beihilfevorschriften und weitere Vorschriften des Beamtenrechts.

Textausgabe.
21.A. 2005. 514 S.
€ 8,50. dtv 5529

Neu im Juni 2005

BAT · Bundes-Angestelltentarifvertrag

mit Vergütungstarifverträgen, Versorgungs-Tarifverträgen und anderen Tarifverträgen, BundespersonalvertretungsG mit Wahlordnung, Beihilfevorschriften.

Textausgabe.
15.A. 2003. 318 S.
€ 6,50. dtv 5553

BAT-O · Bundes-Angestelltentarifvertrag – Ost

Tarifverträge für Angestellte und Auszubildende.

Textausgabe.
10.A. 2003. 252 S.
€ 8,–. dtv 5565

Der Start in den Beruf

Hugo-Becker
Der Test zur Berufswahl

Meine Motive, Vorlieben und Stärken.
Der Test zeigt, wo Stärken, Schwächen und Vorlieben liegen. Die Ergebnisse helfen, den passenden Beruf zu finden und Fehler bei der Berufswahl zu vermeiden.

1.A. 2005. 250 S.
€ 9,50. dtv 50884 €

Nasemann
Richtig bewerben

Praktische Hinweise für die Stellensuche, Inhalt und Form der Bewerbung, alle Rechtsfragen zu Vorstellungsgespräch und Einstellungstest.

5.A. 2002. 129 S.
€ 7,–. dtv 50608 §

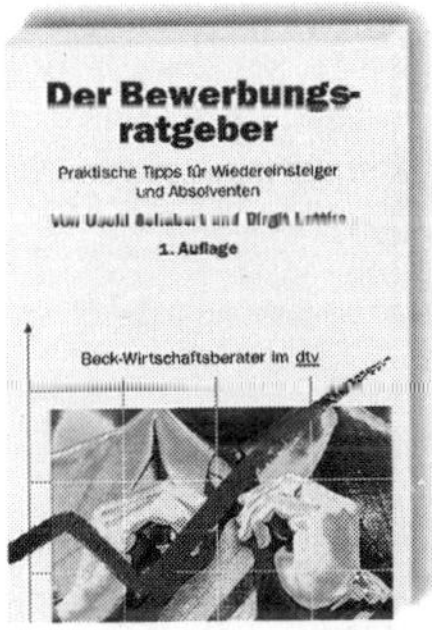

Schabert/Lattke
Der Bewerbungsratgeber

Praktische Tipps für Wiedereinsteiger und Absolventen.

1.A. 2001. 145 S.
€ 8,50. dtv 50856 €

Der Start in den Beruf

Mensch und Beruf

Göpfert
Argumentative Bewerbung

Tipps für die Stellensuche, Bewerbung und Vorstellung. Anschauliche Beschreibungen und Beispiele, Formulierungsvorschläge und praxisnahe Tipps helfen, ein individuelles Bewerbungskonzept zu entwickeln und in allen Phasen der Bewerbung überzeugend zu argumentieren.

5.A.2002. 190 S.
€ 9,–. dtv 5818

Lee
Jobsuche weltweit

Global Job-Seeking Strategies in English. Bewerben in englischer Sprache. Mit Informationen zu Arbeitsmärkten, Branchen, Gehältern, Einreisebestimmungen, Arbeitserlaubnis, Förderprogrammen, Arbeitsverträgen, Sozialabgaben, Recherchemöglichkeiten u.v.m.

1.A. 2005. Rd. 200 S.
Ca. € 10,–. dtv 50867

In Vorbereitung

Reinker
Das Job-Lexikon

Erste Hilfe für den Berufsstart.
Eine Fülle von Informationen, praktischen Tipps und Denkanstößen, garniert mit witzigen Beispielen aus dem Berufsalltag.

1.A. 2004. 768 S.
€ 19,50. dtv 50878

Pressestimme:
„Die wichtigsten Finten und fiesesten Fettnäpfchen für Berufseinsteiger."
SPIEGEL online

Cassens
Work-Life-Balance

Wie Sie Ihr Berufs- und Privatleben in Einklang bringen.
Möglichkeiten für ein System zur erfolgreichen Bewältigung Ihrer individuellen Aufgaben und zur Vermeidung von Zivilisationskrankheiten.

1.A. 2003. 214 S.
€ 9,50. dtv 50872

Knieß
Kreatives Arbeiten

Methoden und Übungen zur Kreativitätssteigerung.

1.A.1995. 228 S.
€ 8,64. dtv 5873

Hugo-Becker/Becker
Motivation

Neue Wege zum Erfolg.

1.A.1997. 419 S.
€ 10,17. dtv 5896

P137716-S24

Mensch und Beruf

Haug
Erfolgreich im Team

Praxisnahe Anregungen für effiziente Team- und Projektarbeit.
Mit Diagnose von Erfolgsfaktoren und konkreten Hilfestellungen.

3.A. 2003. 187 S.
€ 9,–. dtv 5842

Bender
Teamentwicklung

Der effektive Weg zum „Wir".
Systematische Führung durch die Phasen der Teamentwicklung mit Anleitung für effiziente Teamleitung.

1.A. 2002. 284 S.
€ 12,50. dtv 50858

Fuchs-Brüninghoff/Gröner
Zusammenarbeit erfolgreich gestalten

Eine Anleitung mit Praxisbeispielen.

1.A.1999. 203 S.
€ 9,15. dtv 50834

Zander/Femppel
Praxis der Personalführung

Was Sie tun und lassen sollten. Das Was und Wie der Personalführung,
99 Tipps, Fallbeispiele, Führungsgrundsätze.

1.A. 2001. 129 S.
€ 8,50. dtv 50841

Lobscheid
Mitarbeiter einvernehmlich führen

Dieser Wirtschaftsberater zeigt, wie durch positives Führungsverhalten Zufriedenheit und Erfolgsorientierung entstehen und auch Verantwortungsbereitschaft.

2.A.1998. 253 S.
€ 8,64. dtv 5848

Hugo-Becker/Becker
Psychologisches Konfliktmanagement

Menschenkenntnis – Konfliktfähigkeit – Kooperation.

4.A. 2004. 418 S.
€ 13,–. dtv 5829

Lang
Schlüsselqualifikationen

Handlungs- und Methodenkompetenz, personale und soziale Kompetenz.
Wie mehr Menschlichkeit am Arbeitsplatz zu mehr Wirtschaftlichkeit führt.

1.A. 2000. 600 S.
€ 15,08. dtv 50842

Mentzel
Personalentwicklung

Erfolgreich motivieren, fördern und weiterbilden.
Bedarfsfeststellung, Planung und Durchführung der Förder- und Bildungsmaßnahmen, Kosten- und Erfolgskontrolle.

2.A. 2005. 318 S.
€ 10,–. dtv 50854

Drzyzga
Personalgespräche richtig führen

Ein Kommunikationsleitfaden.
Der rasche Überblick über die fachlichen und psychologischen Faktoren des Gesprächs mit Mitarbeitern.

1.A. 2000. 148 S.
€ 8,64. dtv 50840

Nückles/Gurlitt/Pabst/
Renkl

Mind Maps und Concept Maps

Visualisieren, Organisieren, Kommunizieren.
Mit Lern- und Arbeitstechniken das individuelle und kooperative Wissensmanagement auf einfache wie effektive Weise unterstützen.

1.A. 2004. 162 S.
€ 9,50. dtv 50877 €

Klotzki

Wie halte ich eine gute Rede?

In 7 Schritten zum Publikumserfolg.
Perfektes Reden kann jeder lernen. Das Buch zeigt die richtige Technik und liefert das nötige Handwerkszeug für die schnelle Anwendung in der Praxis.

1.A. 2004. 116 S.
€ 8,–. dtv 50873 €

Barth

Telefonieren mit Erfolg

Die Kunst des richtigen Telefonmarketing.
Dieser Berater betrachtet Telefonmarketing als Wirtschaftsfaktor und Marketing-Instrument und führt in die Grundlagen der Kommunikation ein.
Bewährte Methoden und Tricks werden ebenso vorgestellt wie kluge Fragetechniken.

2.A. 2005. 137 S.
€ 7,50. dtv 50846 €

Neu im Mai 2005

Breger/Grob

Präsentieren und Visualisieren

... mit und ohne Multimedia.
Detaillierte Schilderung unterschiedlicher Präsentationsmöglichkeiten bis hin zur aufwendigen Multimediapräsentation.

1.A. 2003. 265 S.
€ 11,–. dtv 50855 €

Briese-Neumann

Optimale Sekretariatsarbeit

Büroorganisation und Arbeitserfolg.
Ein Leitfaden für Chefs und Sekretariatsmitarbeiter.
Mit Checklisten, Tipps und Beispielen.

1.A.1998. 308 S.
€ 10,17. dtv 50804 €

Zeichenerklärung: § Rechtsberater € Wirtschaftsberater

P137716-S27.3